Quarantine of the Mind

Obedience Training for Adult Humans:
Preventative Imprisonment for Crimes Not Yet Committed

GUERNICA WORLD EDITIONS 38

W. STRAWN DOUGLAS

QUARANTINE OF THE MIND

Obedience Training for Adult Humans:
Preventative Imprisonment for Crimes Not Yet Committed

Additional text and editing by Larry A. Etkin

TORONTO—CHICAGO—BUFFALO—LANCASTER (U.K.)
2021

Michael Mirolla, general editor
Larry Etkin, editor
Cover and interior design: Errol F. Richardson
Cover art: Larry A. Etkin, includes elements
from royalty free images in the public domain.

Guernica Editions Inc.
287 Templemead Drive, Hamilton (ON), Canada L8W 2W4
2250 Military Road, Tonawanda, N.Y. 14150-6000 U.S.A.
www.guernicaeditions.com

Distributors:
Independent Publishers Group (IPG)
600 North Pulaski Road, Chicago IL 60624
University of Toronto Press Distribution (UTP)
5201 Dufferin Street, Toronto (ON), Canada M3H 5T8
Gazelle Book Services, White Cross Mills
High Town, Lancaster LA1 4XS U.K.

Expanded and Revised Second edition (2021).
Printed in Canada.

Legal Deposit—First Quarter
Library of Congress Catalog Card Number: 2020952277
Library and Archives Canada Cataloguing in Publication
Title: Quarantine of the mind : obedience training for adult humans : preventative impris-
onment for crimes not yet committed / W. Strawn Douglas ; additional text and editing by
Larry A. Etkin.
Other titles: Obedience training for adult humans : preventative imprisonment for crimes
not yet   committed | Preventative imprisonment for crimes not yet committed
Names: Douglas, W. Strawn, author.
Series: Guernica world editions ; 38.
Description: 2nd edition. | Series statement: Guernica world editions ; 38
Identifiers: Canadiana (print) 2020041657X | Canadiana (ebook) 2020041660X | ISBN
9781771836715 (softcover) | ISBN 9781771836722 (EPUB) | ISBN 9781771836739
(Kindle)
Subjects: LCGFT: Essays.
Classification: LCC PS3604.O94 Q37 2021 | DDC 814/.6—dc23

Editorial Note

EXCEPT WHERE SPECIFICALLY noted as fiction, the material in this book is a nonfiction amalgam residing at an intersection between a personal memoir, a self-help book for people with mental health and addiction issues, and a journalistic exposé. Opinions expressed are strictly those of the author, couched within details of events that are accurate recollections to the best of the author's memory. Actual names, where used, are those that are either of publicly known individuals, or are of individuals whose identity could be readily determined by any diligent investigator. As memories of the events described in this book are the author's own, and memories are always less than totally perfect, they may differ from those of others involved with or who were witnesses to those events. As the author is neither a medical professional nor an ordained religious practitioner, any statements in those veins are obviously those of a person only generally knowledgeable in those arenas. Although the author and editor have made every effort to ensure that the information in this book is correct, they disclaim any liability to any party for any loss, damage, or disruption caused by errors or omissions, whether such errors or omissions result from negligence, accident, or any other cause.

A significant portion of this book was previously published by Chipmunkapublishing, United Kingdom, copyright 2014 by the author (ISBN 978-1-78382-094-8).

Contents

Preface to the 2021 Edition

THINGS HAVE BOTH changed and remained the same since the original edition of this book was issued in 2014. As I noted in the foreword to that volume, in February of 2012 our psychiatrists quit in protest over one of their colleagues getting fired. Many of us residents at Saint Peter State Hospital saw this as a blessed event: the council of dictators finally having a moment of justice. They had been torturing people here for decades. The only difference was that this time they got caught. The chief administrators were taken aback by what had transpired in the case of an inmate who was brutally imprisoned in 2010 for about thirty-five days in solitary confinement. When I met him he was in leather restraint straps, much like a strait jacket, and attired in a disposable paper dress.

This is the journal entry I later made on my memories of the events of that inmate's—Gary Cochrane's—torture:

I met with Dr. O today. He was stunned at the facts and figures of the 'exodus' as he called it. He hadn't heard the tale of the mass quitting of the psychiatrists in 2011 and 2012. He knew it existed but had no idea why.

I characterized it as a pack of oligarchs getting caught torturing patients and throwing a tantrum over having their illicit toys taken from them. I characterized it as bad children being subject to a spanking and reacting in the only way they knew how.

I covered the role of Gary Cochrane and his behavior of protesting his commitment after doing twenty-five years in Stillwater. He was a murderer and did not expect an additional eight years being added to his sentence without trial or legal defense. He died a year later of bone cancer.

He had been locked for over a month in solitary confinement. He smeared feces all over the inside of his cell and blocked the window to his cell with torn-up pieces of mattress. He flooded his cell by stopping up

1

his toilet with mattress pieces and flushing the toilet until it overflowed.

The staff took the view that 'if he is going to mess with us, we will mess with him.' It became an identity issue of who would assert themselves as the ultimate boss of the situation.

Instead of staying boss he became a legend in protest and ill-fated defiance.

Then his psychiatrist got fired. Then that doctor's professional brothers and sisters all quit 'en masse' to protest the end of an era where torture was daily operations behavior.

Dr. O was taken aback and left with some unique things to consider. I told him about my illness and the delusions it gave me. Only I and a close cadre of others had awareness of my personal demons, but hundreds of people witnessed the abuse and torture of Cochrane.

I feel the MSH system can operate well. It chooses to operate poorly.

I feel it is doing the best it thinks it can. It is a very authoritarian environment. It can do better.

I've seen staff body-slammed into brick walls, sustaining brain damage from concussion trauma.

With relations between the staff team and the inmate's team being so poor, such a medical event elicits silent applause from the inmates. That applause is bound in the voluminous lists of rules staff use to humiliate and torture patients.

There were rules about not using headphones in an area defined by the floor tile that was installed there.

There were rules about making your bed. This is not the army. Life will not stop if I fail a cosmetic effects inspection.

We were woken at 7 a.m. to go to two group therapy sessions to make sure we woke up at a hardworking Christian hour. I am not a morning person.

For a long time we were used as free labor for things like janitorial duties, until we were eventually replaced with paid staff.

Our daily activities were all bound to threats of losing privileges. They ruled with an iron fist in a rubber glove. We couldn't eat, shit or sleep without the staff's say-so. Any form of disrespect to the staff could result in the loss of freedom to shop at the canteen or to freely mingle with other residents.

It bears repeating: It was a very authoritarian environment.

I remember the union representative for the security counselors saying: "Not a day went by that I couldn't find a rule infraction on anyone I wanted to put on restriction." His background as a former Marine Corps drill instructor supported that assertion.

The division between patients and staff was great in those days. These days that gulf often seems just as wide, reinforced perhaps by the politics of our time. Painting with a broad brush, it seems to me that Republicans generally want the poor just to die off and quit filling out the welfare rolls, and adding costs to public services. The mentally ill are usually poor.

Democrats may be less vindictive to the poor but are afraid of appearing soft on crime. A lot of crime is committed by people who are mentally ill.

As I write this late in 2019, our Federal government is led by a person I just don't trust. That American president credits all gun violence to the failures of the mentally ill. Crazy people don't assemble arsenals of firearms. They put tin foil in their hats and stockpile gum balls.

Here at the epicenter of madness the staff and patients fought with a tremendous amount of animosity. They killed one patient "accidently" in a take-down exercise around 2000. His name was Jamal Ryce. Ten staff members piled on Ryce, who wasn't even resisting, and when they got up off of him one-by-one, they found he was dead at the bottom of the pile.

Then they realized they had killed him by smothering him to death. Oh how reminiscent of the callous institutional responses to police street violence against any person seen to be a member of an undervalued segment of society.

***

On a good day I'm able to use a credit card to buy a book. I'm also sometimes able to access privileges like being given access to a computer and the internet. For instance, I needed such a "good day" to be able to find the codes to download a copy of the original manuscript of the 2014 *Quarantine of the Mind* from the site of that edition's publisher so I could refer to it as I considered the revisions and additions for this volume. I could have just used a print copy, but to make any changes I'd have to scan that in one page at a time, and run it through character recognition to create an editable file, and spend time correcting any mistakes that process might introduce before I could even get down to any writing. That would not be much fun.

***

It should be noted before the reader gets into the body of this book that most of what constitutes the 2021 additions to the 2014 text involves discussions surrounding the role religious beliefs have in mental health treatment and drug recovery programs. While these elements were discussed in the previous edition, the major 2021 additions are chapters addressing how god (both the generic and specific), and church and faith intersect with additions that themselves intersect with mental health.

Foreword

THIS BOOK IS grounded in my personal battle with mental illness and my experiences with it at the mental institution where I've lived for almost three decades. Different portions of it were created in different times, with me in a variety of different mindsets, and it concerns itself mainly with the hoops that the government wants people who are mentally ill to jump through in all too often vain hopes of regaining their freedom. Some of the hoops are admittedly linked to reasonable goals and ideals. Unfortunately, too many others only serve the whims of our captors, serving the traditions of abuse in the oxymoron of "forced care."

By the time you finish reading this book, I will have used up about 80,000 words of your brain's tolerance and patience. I do hope you get something out of this book that justifies its cover price. The text deals with the impacts on people of the laws of mental health, but is more complex, more comparative, especially with respect to the too many people who are incarcerated full-time in hospitals, institutions and prisons when other better options could be employed. I hope to highlight the complexity of the issue with some in-depth evaluations of several popular treatment models.

Psychiatric predictions of a patient being "cured" are considerably less than reliable. Too many truly sick people are pronounced "cured" and let out. Too many people who could be safely making their way back into the world are kept under lock and key. I suppose if you honestly think someone *might* be dangerous, there's really no alternative. That's because, instead of funding well organized and supervised community-based programs, our society has chosen to fund a psychiatric system that errs way too far on the side of locking nearly everyone up and throwing away the keys. It's a system that results, in prison terms, in "indeterminate sentences," something that's illegal in prison sentencing, but common at institutions for the mentally ill.

Our system of indeterminate sentencing incarcerates people on very subjective criteria. You're made a permanent resident until you can prove to your care team that you are no longer insane beyond any shadow of doubt. Even perfectly sane and normal people have days of depression and relatively irrational activity. Historically, it's been an almost impossible standard to meet. That's why you can meet so many "perfectly normal" residents in places like the Minnesota Security Hospital, now known as the Saint Peter Regional Treatment Center, in Saint Peter, Minnesota, who have been there for decades, incarcerated and charged via "crimes" for which those not declared insane would have served only a year or two of jail time.

But then, if we took away the laws that permit this, what would we do about people who truly are dangerous to society? The need is obviously there. Unfortunately, once we create such a box, it becomes so much easier to just fill it up than not, until we have a diverse collection of incarcerated souls on display and reporting to the state.

I touch on many themes in this book. I consider the interactions of mental illness and substance abuse, the variety of alternative treatment approaches, undesirable alternatives, historical antecedents, forensic dual recovery models, the "spycraft" part of the street drug scene, rehabilitation torture and coercion, and quite a bit more. I cover the scene largely from my personal perspective.

I've also included some fictitious scenarios that shed light, I hope, on how the system operates, and what our future may be like if things continue the way they seem to be going.

I'll also note that there could be positive change in the future. Most of this text was written reflecting a history operating on what should be called a punitive health care model. In 2012, this model was overturned because of a case of excessive maltreatment of a patient at Saint Peter, a change that was heavily reinforced during the subsequent brief tenure of a mental health reformer in the position of director at the Saint Peter facility. Will those changes become the new positive norm, or will the system backslide to its old ways? I hope you tolerate clichés: Time will tell.

As I said, the old system was characterized by punitive and arbitrary care and treatment. Calling parts of it torture would not be an exaggeration. Fortunately, I find that most of the workers at the Minnesota Security Hospital do not torture their children, or small animals, and if they are free to choose, they also do not torture their charges at the locked box we call Saint Peter. I believe they have wholesome hobbies and interests of their own. But some of them seem to hang up their morals with their keys when they come into the building, because it is not uncommon for staff to fabricate charges or rules violations against inmates. This is called "bait and switch," where a staff person restricts somebody for a petty rule violation. If a patient should have the audacity to point out that the rule had not actually been broken, staff would get mad at the challenge to their authority, and in order to enforce the punishment would then either find a different rule that was broken, or would completely fabricate a rule violation. We had a staff member who once brazenly bragged that, on any given day, he could always find a rule violation on any patient.

As I noted above, many of the staff at Saint Peter have good families, degrees, outside interests, and satisfying hobbies. When it comes to changing a patient's behavior, they try to avoid the more onerous trappings that seem to naturally go with state-enforced behavior modification, and at least occasionally there are some unavoidable predicaments. Staff works with a list of rules that has many good ideas, but always there is an autocracy rule that reads, "anything not covered above," which always, of course, leaves situations subject to individual interpretation. Staff always has the final say.

This book in its entirety is meant to shed light onto a dark corner of forensic mental health treatment. "Forensic Mental Health" is the technical term for what this all is. We who live within the shadows of the circumstances of its application savor and enjoy things like our AA and NA meetings with delight and relish. If any psychiatrist threatens our moments in such lights of clear sanity, then we should all perhaps pray to whatever higher powers we each might believe in, that the next act of God will mollify how our psychiatrist might look upon such circumstances.

This book also means to cast a better light on the relationships religion and spirituality have with chemical dependency recovery, because such a recovery is almost as much a religious leap of faith as are leaps of faith into religion. The chemical dependency crowd often relies on the almost religious ritual of a leap of faith in their therapy process, as with the religious basis behind most twelve-step programs.

This new edition of the book starts with harsh criticism of the American mental health system. You may not perceive the presence of the "leap of faith" concept until after about the first third of the book has been read. From then on this text is about the intersection of mental health and chemical dependency. Start your research at chapter seven if you doubt me.

I particularly want to disseminate my view that mental health law in Minnesota, and by extension to the many American jurisdictions that operate with similar laws, rules and regulations, is punishment for crimes not yet committed. Furthermore, it is like chemotherapy, in that it is a potentially deadly therapy that is used to fight a virulent and very dangerous disease.

Also, it needs to be said that I love you all just for reading this book. Without you it has no meaning. The reader is most valued. And, before we get you into the body of this work, I'd like to take a few lines to thank several people: Lynn Hill and Ken Eichman of my care team for their time, patience, and support for my writing activities; my editor, Larry Etkin, for the valuable improvements he's made to this manuscript; friends like Lily Rothbart and Chris Bailey who take the time to visit with me and keep me connected to the world; and Pat Mahoney and Susan Draves, two others who also fill that role.

As for my last note here, I'd just like to remind you all that I created this manuscript with no training; from inside of a Minnesota prison hospital, in whatever free time I was allowed. I've tried to be blunt but not pretentious. Try and see the flaws as you would note scars and blemishes in fine leather, as indicators of uniqueness and character. Normally, I just write science fiction, and it is my firm belief that it is difficult to be pretentious when you are writing about bug-eyed aliens and flying saucers.

I wish you luck on whatever quest has led you to this book. My answers are not the only ones out there. If you have the inclination, when you finish reading this book, write one of your own, and send me a copy when you finish it. I would like to read it.

Chapter 1: Why This Book

THIS BOOK IS a personal commentary on how mental health law is being used to effect social changes through what I consider to be otherwise illegal means. Today, in jurisdictions like Minnesota, it only takes two doctors and a judge putting their signatures onto a court order to imprison somebody for life with limited parole and without trial rights.

The connection between withdrawal of basic freedoms and mental health law is caught up within the new label of *Behavioral Health*. Your right to vote is a behavioral freedom. Your freedom to control your own bank account is a behavioral freedom. Your vocation is a behavioral freedom. Your choice in a domestic partner is a behavioral freedom. These are all liberties that can be attacked in the name of behavioral health.

Amongst other things, this book catalogs various hoops that the government wants us, persons labeled mentally ill, to jump through. Some of these hoops are linked to reasonable goals and ideals, while others only serve the whim of our captors. Some make sense, while others only serve traditions of abuse in the oxymoron of "forced care."

I have written this book for all those types who might buy gold and guns, and books on black helicopters, UFOs, and all legends of Nazism and conspiracies going onward trying to stamp out all virtue in a greedy, glum world. In other words, one primary audience for this book is those individuals with tendencies toward paranoia, who see government or corporate conspiracies around every corner, and who tend to lean very heavily toward being libertarians politically.

But this book is also written for the large community of caring people of every political stripe who advocate for the protection and rights of the vulnerable adult community. The mentally ill—including residents of facilities such as Minnesota's Saint Peter Regional Treatment Center, a security facility for those deemed mentally ill and dangerous, or sometimes just sufficiently deviant—constitute a significant portion of that vulnerable adult population.

This book is also here to define boundaries for neurochemical freedom in a world bound by Scientologists and Bilderbergers, the former being a cult that abhors any use of pharmacological medicines to attack mental illnesses, the later being a club of the world's richest and most aristocratic movers and shakers. I hope my text will both educate and amuse you. I believe there are some real conspiracies for us all to acquaint and amuse ourselves with.

One of these "conspiracies" is that our present legal system virtually makes it a crime of possession to have a mental illness. There are many mentally ill people who go quite unnoticed by the government because they never create any public trouble. The law only concerns itself with that subset of the ill population that inconveniences others and makes trouble. If you have a dangerous mental illness, a thing sometimes defined overly broadly, you are deemed as much of a threat to society as if you were a "Typhoid Mary" or had Ebola, a machinegun, or poisonous drugs.

At that point you get arrested, committed, and tortured until you are deemed to no longer be a threat. This is how our coercive behavior modification systems and scenarios deal with anyone looking suspiciously like they have a dangerous mental illness. Torture the subject until he or she capitulates.

It's not pretty, but it is quite common.

People who repeatedly point out the facts and ways and means of coercive behavior modification often position themselves to be driven mad, even from a starting point of great sanity. When capitulation is deemed to be health, then the world denies itself the best spirits our human resources can provide.

During the Reagan administration, there were plans drawn up to create what conspiracy theorists called "concentration camps." These were to be used for imprisoning people that the Reagan administration defined to be "undesirables." It was said that these camps were to be devoted to political activists, anarchists, communists, and anyone who criticized our government or the president. It was also not beyond thinking that such camps would also be useful for warehousing people who were identified as the dregs of our society, including such people as the mentally ill.

When he was governor in California, to save money in the state's strained budget, Reagan chose to remove mentally ill people from the high-cost relationship of commitments to long-term residency in regional psychiatric treatment centers. Reagan wanted to balance the State of California's budget by cutting any programs that did not overtly serve the needs of the state's conservatives, especially programs that liberals might like. His cuts included significant parts of the budget allocated to care for the mentally ill. The dollars allocated to provide care for an average mentally ill person were reduced from the equivalent of the salary paid an airline pilot or general practitioner doctor, to the equivalent of about one-third of the pay for a kindergarten teacher, itself not a highly paid occupation.

A few key points are worth remembering. From the state's perspective, their primary duty in dealing with the mentally ill or chemically impaired is to subdue them, so the ill or inebriated can do no harm to themselves or others. The state seems to also feel itself obliged to disable the accused person as much as necessary to stop any behavior that it feels is a threat to somebody else, or to themselves, or to property, or to the state in general. We should not be surprised when people get their civil rights impounded as if they were cars parked illegally.

Members of state legislatures get elected by promising their varied supporters lots of things, all too often including that they will essentially ignore or imprison all who cannot be bought to vote for them. Laws are crafted for the benefit of those who can pay for an election campaign. If there are only homeless alcoholics and prison inmates in favor of a *legality*, then it will be beneficial for it to be redefined to be an *illegality* from the perspective of many elected officials.

In Minnesota the accused may undergo a Rule 20 (20.01 and 20.02) evaluation. These Rule 20 evaluations occur in criminal cases when the authorities believe the defendant may not be competent to proceed with the case, or that he or she was not responsible at the time of the offense because of mental illness or developmental disability. This Civil Commitment process is a legal standard that allows the State of Minnesota to legally order a proposed patient into treatment even if the person objects. Because the process strips away most of a person's civil rights, it is typically used only in narrowly defined circumstances.

Also of note are *Mens Rea* and *M'Naghten*. Those are the two standards of mental health law from the "old days." *Mens Rea* is a Latin phrase that literally means "guilty mind," and suggests that the accused has the mental capacity of a wild animal. It refers to criminal intent or consciousness of guilt. Such a person supposedly cannot be executed for his or her crime, even if that crime is murder, though we've seen some jurisdictions execute people who it can be questioned ought to have been spared under this standard. Under *Mens Rea* a person can, however, be detained for the rest of his or her natural life.

M'Naghten was the name of a Scotsman who experienced paranoid delusions about the prime minister of England in the year 1800. It seems that, because of his delusions, this M'Naghten fellow, first name Daniel, tried to shoot the prime minister. He failed at that mission, but succeeded in getting a new standard created for detaining the mentally ill. This is where we get the criteria, or test for mental illness being called the *M'Naghten Rule* (alternatively spelled variously as McNaghten or McNaugthon).

The M'Naghten Rule is a test for criminals using an insanity defense. The legal definition of the M'Naghten Rule is: "It must be clearly proved that at the time of committing the act … that the accused was laboring under such a defect of reasoning from disease of the mind, as to not know the nature and quality of the act he/she was doing or if he/she did know it, he/she did not know it was wrong." In Minnesota the accused pleading not guilty by reason of insanity has two trials, one to establish guilt and then another to determine if the defendant meets the standard for the M'Naghten Rule. If the M'Naghten Rule is met the defendant is found not guilty by reason of insanity, but may still end up incarcerated in a security hospital through a civil commitment.

In the state of California, Governor Ronald Reagan, who served in that capacity from 1967 through 1975, wanted to foot the bill to detain all communists and anarchists, but not pay a single dollar to help anyone mentally ill. There are laws now that essentially say the government reserves the right to indulge in preventative imprisonment for crimes not yet committed. That is the essence of the concept of therapeutic imprisonment. I beg your indulgence to point out the obvious, that this behavioral health idea is often not in the best interests of the accused.

The forensic mental health system is, technically, designed to provide civil attorneys and hearings appropriate to protect the rights of those accused of crimes who are believed to be mentally ill. This creates the impression that the process is fair, but unless a person has his or her own resources to hire competent and not overworked private lawyers, one's civil rights often seem trampled through a process with an outcome that is seldom fruitful for the accused. That court appointed attorneys often have too many clients to give each the attention which might be demanded is a function perhaps of callous disregard for funding that need by elected bodies of government.

With that all said and done, I will give you the rest of this book. Several sections have material in a fiction format, but I stress these incidents are terribly or potentially real. Because these incidents are so bloody, the state has been given the means, rights, and responsibility to imprison, for life, if deemed necessary. That is how indefinite mental health commitment is defined to the state legislature. It is life imprisonment for the safety of the community, an imprisonment with the too often only theoretical option of parole.

***

This book was created over several periods of time, with me in different mindsets from one writing session to another. A major portion, concerned with what I formerly called *Forensic Dual Recovery*, was written in winter of 2009. Other sections focus on what I have called *Spycraft*. As I noted in the *Foreword*, there are also several fictitious sections, clearly labeled as such, which I use to try and illustrate some of ways the mental illness treatment industry operates, and to express a bit of my frustrations with that system. There is another part that could be called the *David Proffitt Effect* section, because it focuses on some major changes to the routine ways lives were handled at the facility where I've resided for almost three decades, the Minnesota Security Hospital at Saint Peter. What I've label punitive health care came to an end in February of 2012, as many of the changes David Proffitt championed were put in place.

It's important to remember that, while the Forensic Dual Recovery portions were written before the punitive care system came crashing down, it's impossible to know whether those changes will be retained over the long term, or will be allowed to be subverted in a return to elements of the older system.

During the time before Proffitt, it was common for staff to fabricate charges or rules violations against inmates. We inmates called the process "bait and switch." It went like this: A staff person would restrict somebody for some petty rule violation; the patient would point out that the rule had not actually been broken; staff would get mad because their authority was being challenged; staff would then either find a different rule to punish the patient under, or would completely synthesize another, different rule violation. There was one staff person who once explicitly told a group of us that on any given day he could always find a rule violation on any patient. Bait and switch was only part of it.

There are two phrases that need noting early in this discussion. The first is "insight into treatment." This is a bona fide consideration with respect to whether or not you are willing to let the staff be your guide through the pitfalls and triumphs of the treatment experience. To this question, I can truly say I do see some legitimate benefits, such as sobriety and helpful medication. However, not all of the bright ideas connected to the concept bear fruit. I am aware of many flaws in the process, so a lot of what I have learned is merely to keep quiet when an issue comes up that would inspire the state to compose, and impose, a new fifty-page treatment plan just for me. Insight can also be defined as a staff asking a patient if the patient sees the benefit of the staff bullying the patient in the name of treatment.

The second phrase is "invested into treatment." This is actually a question as to whether you are going to pursue getting out of jail through a judge and your lawyer, or you are going to work with your warden, your guards and your therapists to secure your exit. Going through the state's health care professionals is called investing in treatment, while using a lawyer and the judicial process is obviously not making that investment.

My county case manager is terrified that I might one day win a case at a *Writ of Habeas Corpus* hearing. She does not like that and regards it as a loophole that is dangerous and undesirable. She says she wants transparency, but what she really wants, in my opinion, is "command and control."

I live in a de facto prison from which I am periodically up for de facto parole. I am sustaining a de facto fine called cost of care, and unlike people in criminal detention, through that cost of care I pay for my own incarceration. That is as much of a sense of torture as using one's own cell phone minutes to idle on hold for hours at a time waiting to talk with someone at the Department of Motor Vehicles about license plates that haven't arrived, preventing you from using a new car.

***

Conservatives and many libertarians, who seem to mostly identify themselves as Republicans, are a multi-faceted lot covering a range from those economically tightfisted, to people with extreme reactionary social agendas. Across the spectrum, however, the programs and positions they support tend to strongly assail any hope for the mentally ill to gain parity with the support provided for physical illness, or indeed any real form of state provided therapy. As a way to eliminate costly wasteful government activities, such people are often the first to want to use hospitals for the mentally ill to imprison them, or oppositely to throw the mentally ill out on the street with little support.

Unfortunately, with conservatives leading the way for false imprisonment, in today's economic and social climate all too many liberals, most often people identifying themselves as Democrats and independents, feel themselves forced to toe similar lines fearing the backlash of being labeled soft on crime, or as unnecessarily coddling people with expensive programs who should be picking themselves up and fending for themselves.

It's a type of social fraud from both camps, and it's something I point out with a clear conscience. The extremes from both camps are insane, and while as a person with a mental illness I use the word "insane" advisedly, I don't accept the insanity plea from either camp.

My view is that Republicans are worse with it than Democrats. Democrats often fight for a system that borders on socialized health care, while Republicans most often seem to fight for the elimination of health care completely for the poor.

I loathe such Republicans because, in my opinion, our current legal state of health care affairs is mostly their fault. Their lack of support for a proper medical system has brought us to the brink of having a failing system, leaving us with a system akin to that of a sinking ship. We spend an ever increasing portion of our national budget, and far more than any other developed country, for a system of health care that provides positive cost effective outcomes for only the wealthy or those covered by good health insurance options through their employers. That leaves an awful lot of people outside looking in. Catastrophic health care expenses are said to be far and away the largest reason for personal bankruptcies in our United States.

Our politics leads many congressmen and women to fight tooth and nail to avoid anything positive getting done. Even our vaunted Medicare programs have significant problems. They pay only about 60 percent of the real cost of caring for a patient, according to the hospital industry. Doctors and hospitals are theoretically expected to eat the real cost, but in reality they just past those loses on to privately insured and uninsured patients.

The Patient Protection and Affordable Care Act, currently more popularly known as "Obamacare," is our first real attempt at healthcare for all, and as I write this it has had a floundering rollout. And that's a generous description, from many peoples' perspectives. Perhaps the failures accompanying this first American attempt at healthcare for all will result in revisions that both parties will eventually endorse.

If conservative and libertarian types were interested in real reform they would build a system with an option for treating the poor at little cost, the middle class at a moderate cost, and price truly private care at another tier entirely.

My father, William Wallace Douglas, MD, a doctor at the famed Mayo clinic from 1960 through 2006, was a duck hunter conservationist, a shotgun naturalist, a Republican from the time when the party actually had a moderate wing. He was in favor of a woman's right to choose when to create a viable fetus. He was not very religious. He was a scientist.

If we could get more Republicans like him, people who are wildlife protectors, who defend women's reproductive rights, who are more like Unitarians than religious fundamentalists, then I think we would have a chance to create much better health care options. If the population could focus on saving 3,000 adult lives every day rather than 3,000 fetuses unwanted by their bearers, an unknown number of which would be otherwise born into socioeconomic-illiteracy-gang related poverty, then a lot more people among us would have a much better lot in life than just watching Republicans and Democrats verbally tear each other to pieces on our news and public affairs television and radio programs.

I could really use those long gone moderate Republicans in our current trying times. Our nation's mentally ill need the real opportunity to thrive that they are simply not getting. The extremist politics characterizing debate over health care in our nation appears to have positioned a great many white people as supporters of racist appearing options, opting for approaches that would not pay for the health care of Blacks and Hispanics, who are disproportionately represented amongst our nation's poor.

Former president Barak Obama had tried to be a *New Deal* type of Democrat with his signature passage in 2010 of the *Affordable Care Act/Obamacare*. As a political moderate, he infuriated reactionary white conservatives because, amongst the other things I've already pointed out, the extremist conservative viewpoint is basically in favor of using mental health issues to imprison people rather than fund recuperative health care for our nation's mentally ill.

There are broader problems associated with the conservative extremes, problems that include persecution. Once you claim that you have a mental health need, all too often you also bar yourself from future attempts to become employed, and until the *Affordable Care Act*, to obtain insurance coverage to help pay for hospitalizations and medications.

The mentally ill do not have time to wait for health care, and in the many states that have opted to not expand their Medicaid programs with the federal subsidies provided under the *Affordable Care Act*, too many such people continue to have scant access to care. The mentally ill need that access, need parity with those well insured, for coverage giving them needed access to treatment for their illnesses.

Parity lobbyists say a broken brain and a broken leg should get the same funding, the same hospital bed space. But that can also be a double edged sword. In jurisdictions where it is present, such parity can be used for imprisonment. We with mental illness who are current detainees of healthcare, can often feel that *defunding* the ability of the system to commit, to inter the mentally ill indefinitely, could be a preferred alternative. We'd say that eliminating funding for that option, for those commitments, is the only way to stop a ravenous machine that can't otherwise fail, but we'd also say that alternatives need to first be present.

Extreme conservatives are in favor of zero funding for health care. The mentally ill are deemed by definition to not have the capacity to mount a defense supporting their individual needs. The poor often lack the resources or the education to mount a defense. Observing us caught in the middle, extreme conservatives laugh all the way to the bank.

In the richest nation in the world it is deplorable to see children go without access to routine health care, to proper dental care. On the other hand, how can I in good conscience accept taxes at a rate of about 50 percent, which without resorting to cash dodges is about what my father would have paid in his final years at the Mayo Clinic?

My grandfather, Wallace Strawn Douglas, was also a physician. He practiced medicine for sixty years. He treated workers of the timber and paper mills in Lewiston, Idaho. His patients there were men who would lose fingers to saws and be out for six weeks, and then go back to work to lose even more flesh. They needed the work so they felt they had to go back to the mill and its saws.

Grandfather treated the survivors. He also treated war casualties at a 10,000-bed Army hospital he created on the island of New Caledonia, near Australia and New Zealand.

He used to say that all the crazies from Europe came west and stopped when they got to the Pacific Ocean. Then they all went south and stayed in Southern California. He was an honest man, and I can sympathize with his observations.

I believe that my father and grandfather would be both appalled by today's American state of mental illness medical affairs, and amazed at what potential there is for major reform. They'd be particularly appalled at the psychological ablation and chemical lobotomies that have until recent years been the norm.

I call myself both a conservative and a Democrat. I live in fear that the two major political parties will achieve the kind of understanding that will enable them to effectively initiate a regime that will actually seize my funds and bill me for my own involuntary incarceration. They are already trying to do that, just not legally effectively. I get a bill for about $600,000 every month; I send them $500 and go through life with a clear conscience.

All of these are the types of dilemmas that permeate this book.

Chapter 2: Cuckoo Reality

I MET WITH one of my doctors recently, someone who was a relatively new addition to the staff. As I recounted some of the more notorious past events at Saint Peter, that doctor was stunned to learn the details about the reasons behind the turnover of staff about a decade ago. He hadn't heard the tale of the mass quitting, the "exodus" as he called it, of the psychiatrists in 2011 and 2012.

I characterized the events of that period as a pack of oligarchs getting caught torturing patients, having their illicit toys taken from them. I characterized it as bad children being spanked and reacting in the only way they knew how: throwing a tantrum over it.

I recounted the role of inmate Gary Cochrane in instigating that change as he protested being committed to Saint Peter after doing twenty-five years in Stillwater State Prison for his original criminal conviction. Though a convicted murderer, he felt he had "done his time" and did not expect an additional eight years being added to his sentence without trial or legal defense. Fortunately for him or otherwise, he didn't have to serve all that extra time because he died a year later of bone cancer.

But before his death, Cochrane had been locked in solitary confinement for more than a month. His response to that was to smear feces all over the inside of his cell, and to block the window into his cell with torn-up pieces of mattress. He flooded his cell by stopping up his toilet with additional mattress pieces, flushing it until it overflowed.

"If he is going to mess with us, we will mess with him," was the staff response. It became a power and authority issue over who would assert themselves as the ultimate boss of the situation. Staff asserted their power and retained their authority, but Cochrane became a legend for his protest and ill-fated defiance.

Then his doctor got fired. Then the doctor's professional brothers and sisters all quit in solidarity to protest the end of an era where torture was permitted as daily operational behavior.

In his awareness of the details of my illness and the delusions it gave me, my new doctor could have simply discounted anything I'd told him, but with hundreds of people who had witnessed at least parts of the abuse and torture, he was left with some unique things to consider.

***

All our daily activities are bounded by the threat of losing privileges. Any form of disrespect to the staff could result in the loss of an amazing array of things "normal" people take for granted, from shopping (at the canteen) to watching television, from choosing your own bedtime or when to wake up, to the simple freedom to choose who and when to interact with others.

It was a very authoritarian environment. We couldn't even eat, shit or sleep without the staff's say-so. They ruled with an iron fist in a rubber glove.

One of the most important pieces of literature on the subject of mental health is Ken Kesey's *One Flew over the Cuckoo's Nest* (including the novel, play and movie versions). It tells the tale of Randle Patrick McMurphy, a petty offender who assumes, eventually severely mistakenly, that a short mental health residency would be more enjoyable than a long year of prison incarceration he would otherwise have been ordered to experience by a local judge.

McMurphy assumed his stay at the local mental health institution would be a cakewalk, but soon finds every part of his behavior being held as evidence of his need for yet more imprisonment. He also finds himself at loggerheads with the willful and domineering head lady, one Nurse Mildred Ratchet.

Ratchet plays classical music when the men are getting their medications. She lobbies the local psychiatrists to try to get McMurphy a longer sentence, which she claims would be in his best interests. And, as subsequent events demonstrate, at least in terms of some of his antisocial behaviors, maybe she was at least somewhat on the right track?

Ratchet asserts and tries to convince a psychiatrist that it would be best for McMurphy to become a temperance-touting Christian. She may be convinced that McMurphy needs help, but for the most part it's pretty clear that McMurphy is just an anti-authoritarian iconoclast to his core.

McMurphy breaks ten of his fellow inmates out of the hospital and takes them fishing in a stolen boat. The boat is returned, and as no harm is apparently done, all goes back to "normal." It is only after McMurphy breaks out again and then returns to his locked ward with whisky and a couple of prostitutes that things take a turn toward lethal.

Nurse Ratchet shows up in the morning after the party of booze and women and takes actions that today would be strictly forbidden in mental health law. She targets a mentally weak inmate who she finds out has slept with one of the prostitutes with the diminishing scold: "I will have to tell your mother about this." Such behaviors by mental health hospital staff today are strictly forbidden. The reason why is that such belittling can lead some on the mental edge to attempt suicide.

McMurphy attacks Ratchet and is removed. The next scene we see with him in it features a nearly brain dead McMurphy in the aftermath of his having been subjected to a lobotomy, a surgical procedure that severs connections in the brain's prefrontal lobe from other parts of the brain. It is a controversial procedure that was widely performed over several decades as a treatment for mental illnesses such as schizophrenia and bipolar disorder. "Lobotomy" was also used as somewhat of an umbrella term for a number of different procedures that purposely damaged parts of the brain tissue in order to treat mental illness diagnosis.

Finishing the synopsis, one of McMurphy's friends on the ward smothers the mentally dead McMurphy, tosses a sink through a window, and escapes.

I've actually talked with a chemical dependency counselor who sided with Nurse Ratchet. Perhaps that counselor's views on temperance found an ally in Ratchet's bland quiet moves on securing power. We inmates, however, pretty much all looked at Nurse Ratchet and saw a murderer.

In many respects, Nurse Ratchet really wasn't too far from some of the mainstream thoughts around recovery from mental illness, at least those manifestations associated with drugs use and alcohol abuse. With respect to her Christianity push, with drug and alcohol use therapies that include involvement with Alcoholics Anonymous and Narcotics Anonymous can be effective for some, and each of these communities uses a religious framework of Christian belief as a significant element of their approach.

I personally try to not share my religious convictions too assertively. I will say, if you encounter the twelve-step methodology for staying sober and choose to use it, you will have to make peace with your god concepts. The god relationship is a requirement in twelve-step programs. They are inherently religious no matter how much chemical dependency counselors try to point out that while "God" may be stressed, the variety of deity is up to you. They call it a generic appeal to higher power, but for 80 percent of America's population, that means a variety of Christianity.

One of my best friends said: "I can accept Christ only by accepting the fact Christ was Buddhist."

So since most of what the courts identify as twelve-step treatment is actually Christianity, the Nurse Ratchet connection really isn't too far off from how the legal system of mental health incarceration also sees it.

You have every right to reject the connections I see. I choose to accept large pieces of that religious diatribe because it works for me. I believe Christ's disciples worked well at creating a faith, and that they knew what they were doing. I don't have a lot of faith in the resurrection but I don't body-slam people who do have that faith.

It really does matter, as probably 80 percent of the nation's mentally ill have consumed too much alcohol and/or prescription or illegal drugs. The whole twelve-step scene being 80 percent Christian, only a small percentage of people in those communities avoid Christianity. I accept that a lot of religion will creep into my life without any part of me actively seeking it out.

***

There is a special issue with respect to minors within the considerations of mental health issues. Minors, after all, are already assumed to have limited rights to self-determination. Within that context of concerns for mental health, the fates of medical/psychiatric care for young people are dismal at best.

The status of minors differs from state to state. For instance, some states provide a lot of rights to young people that most of us across the country might even say are predatory. An example: Couples can marry, or be married off under pressure from a parent or guardian in some states at fourteen years of age. And I believe some states allow children as young as thirteen to control their own money in amounts sufficient to buy crack cocaine or other drugs on the street.

And, in too many states, parents have the right to use mental health commitments to place their children in what should only be described as Christian prison camps, where efforts are made to "re-educate" them for almost any reason, from "curing" their "gayness" to eliminating "disrespect" towards parents or particular family religious beliefs. Young people often have no avenues of relief from this until they reach a particular state's legal age of majority, typically at the age of eighteen, or if they can connect to resources to help them petition the courts for legal independence.

I don't like thirteen-year-old hitchhiker prostitutes or re-education camps. Perhaps we have it good in the parts of the Midwest I come from, where more reasonable strictures on minors are more the rule.

Here we also have the Mayo Clinic, Hazelden/Betty Ford clinics and resources at places like the University of Minnesota. I particularly value the Mayo Clinic, at least in part because of my family's history with being a part of it.

There's a Dr. David Senjem, who is an ex-Mayo doctor, and who is currently a Republican state senator to the Minnesota legislature. He once told me that he knew my father, who was at the time also a Mayo Clinic physician, and that he and my father got along quite well. I think he would value the concept of avoiding juvenile mental health commitments by parents, and would also point out how he has problems with teen prostitution and substance abuse. Most of the time drugs and alcohol are ill-advised for young people.

I need to note that, while I have not raised any teenagers myself, I've obviously been a teenager, and some of my experiences during that portion of life were in the vein of being a teen of the troubled type. That was in part my fault, but maybe not totally my fault. Not totally my own fault because the availability of street drugs exploded in the 1960s era of "tune-in, turn-on and drop-out."

And then by the late 1970s the drug treatment industry was in its first full financial bloom. Treatment facilities and programs seemed to be popping up everywhere and a part of this phenomenon was a great expansion of twelve-step religion. The real connection between mental illness and the courts was one consequence of this expansion. Only through drug court does government force citizens to become religious. Telling teens to pray their way into being viable financial members of society is not tenable. It makes no sense. Teens and their dwarfed ability to pay bills makes outfits like the military look viable, a route I took when I enlisted in the Marines.

***

Some might argue there is a rare set of people for whom drug use at a young age is not so bad. Creative people, for instance those interested in careers in music performance, people who depend on drugged fueled creativity over decades to give them an artistic edge, or maybe it could just be an outlet for someone who would drop out of a career as software engineer or accountant and spend a year or two creating and performing.

In any case, however it might be created, music enriches our lives. It can be therapeutic to people needing order or peace in their lives. It can be a lightning rod for discharging chaos. But the presence of drugs in the whole rock-and-roll music scene makes it a fertile ground for mental illness.

Of the musicians in the Eric Clapton band Derek and the Dominoes, eventually every one either turned up dead from drugs and alcohol, or ended up institutionalized. Most were dead. One had killed his own mother, the crime being described as a moment of mental illness gone especially wrong. He claimed: "She has tortured me for years." That statement warrants a special degree of caution from me. I am trying to put forward the case that in psychiatric care one commonly finds torture. I am trying to avoid moments where the mentally ill claim their behavior is a response to therapeutic workers trying to torture them.

I don't believe the staff of psychiatric hospitals go home and torture small animals or abuse their families. Most of them probably have relatively normal, productive and meaningful lives. I guess my only point here is that some occasionally leave their humanity at the institution's door when they come to work. Then they pick up keys for the interior of the psychiatric hospital, and their personas and how they see themselves begin to change.

There was a Cheech and Chong movie featuring a visit to a mental institution where Timothy Leary portrayed himself dispensing LSD, calling that elemental product "the key." If you've lived your life in a monastery, then perhaps you might not recognize the drug-oriented comedy duo Cheech and Chong. Trust me when I tell you that they are socially relevant.

Chapter 3: A Scenario

THE FOLLOWING STORY is a thinly veiled fictional pseudo-autobiographical composite, but it's an accurate reflection of an all too real episode of a person who experiences the type of mental illness that can land you in government-operated mental health incarceration. Consider, as you read, how you would react to the experience, the environment, were you one of the participants of ...

Medical Imprisonment

In the twelfth year of the second millennium, he looked out of the prison window, through the bars at the courtyard below. He was on the second floor so it was a sixteen-foot drop to the ground. From there he could climb up to the top of the fence. The barbed wire was there at the top.

He looked at the people around him. There was Matt and Paul and Shawn. Nobody was free of the black brush of captivity. They all came to it through different paths, from different sources. For all of them that was in the past, no longer mattered. It was the here and now that was of value. Here mattered. Here made a difference. Here was home, and here was a form of slow torture that they all shared.

Here was insecurity labeled as security. Here was the MSH, and that MSH was the Minnesota Security Hospital. This was no surreal abstraction. This was tangible and real. The prison was operating on a basis of torture as therapy.

Somebody had escaped. There was a general lockdown while the crew looked for an errant mental patient.

This time it was William who had departed. He was gone. He had escaped. We no longer needed to even think about the barbed wire.

Not much of a shock. Things like that happened not too uncommonly.

About once per year we would have somebody get 'happy feet' and take off.

The newer realities were that one could take off with only the need to cut off the monitoring bracelet and run wild. 'On the loose,' it was said.

He remembered that morning when light rain had fallen on the parking lot of the local Wal-Mart. There was something special and rural to the aroma of rain on blacktop. It only was notable when the rain came just as a light sprinkling, with the odor of it evaporating off the blacktop that was warm from the sun.

It was that deep breathing exercise that every kid from a farming town knows.

This was the agony and the ecstasy of the difficulties and promise of living with mental illness. Sure there were books, and therapists who knew all the same answers. The problem was that, for all the efforts put forward, there were few handholds on the outside of that seamless sleek machine. It would obey its masters, but it was designed to create no mercy for its prey. The machine moved forward, an eating machine, and it never fully rested or slept. Always it moved forward, devouring everyone in its path.

One learned to avoid the shark-like machine, or at least to avoid being the person directly in front of it. There had always been those odd questions to answer.

"I feel as if I have a tight band around my head," or "I wish I was a boy (or if I was a boy, I wished I was a girl)." Or personal but strange questions like: "Can you menstruate? Can you ejaculate? Can you menstruate and ejaculate at the same time?"

Those lists of questions from the MMPI, the Minnesota Multiphasic Personality Inventory, were lengthy. The same question would appear up to three times. It hoped to catch you in inconsistencies.

It felt like the whole process was designed just to catch people in traps. Such devices did not help paranoia. Like drugs and mental illness, there was only limited benefit. Such combinations rarely bore fruit.

To the state, though, merely asking the questions of sanity granted permission from the Federal government to imprison. Only as the result of a mental health court hearing could you be held for an endless period of time with no trial rights. All a state had to do was to ask the right question and the rights of the accused could be forfeited.

Given eight or ten years, the state could usually even induce a mental illness if there wasn't one actually there in the first place. Given time, anything was possible. Whenever somebody slipped away, however, the MSH system reacted as if it was shaken to its core.

Medicine can do that. He used to try to think about medicine from other perspectives. As a Native American thing? Maybe. Many of them believed that long hair was good medicine. And their witch doctory was in obvious opposition to Western medicine. Most of the time the Western medicine would win, but it felt better to at least investigate another path. Like the medicine wheel and the Great White Buffalo. It certainly wasn't a toss up to see which would prevail, but as an MSH inmate one could always hope.

Those were the raw materials of a thought. Those were the ideas that made sense to the inmates at MSH. These were men of great medicine and even a little power. Here was Prospero born. Here was a man of doubt who would dispense Christianity to all the seekers but who would trust nobody.

Here was William Dellarose and his fellow William, William Jensen, who had gone AWOL. Dellarose was on lockdown, as were all the inmates at MSH. But others had skipped out in the past without a lockdown, so why this time?

Soon, morning came and he found out the real reason for the lockdown had nothing to do with the other William. Another fellow inmate, released back on the world with a day-pass, had tried to kill his mother, again. He had tried to do this ten years earlier and failed to kill his mom on that occasion. He'd managed, however, to kill his sister with a hammer on that previous occasion.

This murderous inmate had been such a heartbreak character. Now he had virtually repeated his crime. That was truly bad news. He stabbed his mother repeatedly with a steak knife, putting her into a hospital. She was in critical condition, with damage to several organs and severe blood loss, and she was also blinded by having tongs plunged into her eyes.

Of course he would present a "not guilty by reason of mental illness" defense, or as it is more commonly known, an "insanity defense." And of course with his insanity so well known, proving that he had no idea it was a crime to stab his mom would not be a stretch for any lawyer to work with, especially because he was back under commitment to the MSH system. Now, more than ever, the system was working at an issue that is truly what it was designed to deal with.

A day in the life of people at MSH: On the very same day that the stabbing of the mother occurred, there was the escape of another inmate, and also a damaging fistfight in one of the buildings. Problems came in clusters for MSH; the stabbing, the AWOL inmate and the fistfight, all in one day.

Violent or not, William Jensen was absent without leave, a status label based on that old military phrase for abandoning your post to go to Paris and drink wine with Bohemian artists and sexy French women. That, of course, was the older World War I version of AWOL.

Nobody saw any of these things coming that day. Sure, we could have something like William getting 'happy feet' and taking off like that, but there was more to it than that with the stabbing. For instance, that inmate had been in therapy for ten years. People looked at him as a poster boy for success in psychiatric care. Nobody had a clue that he was still dangerous.

He proved everyone wrong.

The whole campus was on lockdown because of William's 'Happy Feet.' None of us had had a clue that any other Saint Peter denizen had been off stabbing his mother on a day pass into the community.

It just doesn't get any worse than that.

So thought William Dellarose.

***

William considered his addictions. How anyone could love "crack cocaine" was a mystery to him. He had tried it and noticed a great similarity to the "high" gotten from Nitrous Oxide. When any racecar driver could legally buy Nitrous in a hundred-pound bottle from a compressed gas company, he wondered why anyone would have a need to fill up on cocaine. Nonetheless, coca was king on the street. You did not see women prostituting themselves for a bottle of Nitrous.

William thought about his cars. The small Datsun and Volkswagen, the pickup truck, the Mustang, the Chevy Citation, the Ford LTD; they'd all served him for a while. They cost money, each, and every one, money he had back then. Now he was at the end of his financial rope. Mom and Dad were dead.

Two sisters were dead. All that remained was his alcoholic youngest sister. She was a piece of work all on her own. William thought it was kind of sad that she had taken that path in life. She had truly chosen it on her own. Both were attached to their parents. Dad had gone six years ago, that was after Mom had finally succumbed to the slow decline from the ALS discovered to be eating away at her nerves. ALS, Amyotrophic Lateral Sclerosis, Lou Gehrig's disease.

William had money from his inheritance, but how much time would he ever have as a free person to spend much of it? He was already approaching fifty years old.

At least Mom and Dad had had their time together to remember. They'd taken trips to Africa, New Zealand, and Australia. They spent time visiting friends who lived all over the United States.

The philosophy they'd lived their later years with was derived from observation and deduction. They'd too often seen another pattern among people they'd known. They'd noted how many of their friends had never gotten out before in their twilight years they'd gotten too frail to travel. So they'd traveled as much as they could. They'd each died relatively young, in their mid-seventies.

Dad was finally overcome by cancer, dying from lung disease and complications brought on by side effects of a drug called Oxalyplatin. It took his life after three months of chemotherapy, in a bit of an embarrassment for the great Mayo Clinic, because dad had been a senior physician there.

William considered his addictions. He could go out the way dad had done, with lung cancer from smoking, if liver disease didn't get him first, or he could seek sobriety and abstinence from all, including nicotine, alcohol, and marijuana. They all tugged at his sanity a little bit.

Sadness crept in when he realized the older social styles would not be repeatable. The marijuana, at least its hallucinogenic component, has become a harsh influence on his mental health. It was a sad fact that his old way of life, one that called for drugs, was no longer being friendly to him. He pondered whether even tobacco would ever be viable again?

***

Jensen was discovered the next day. The stabbing victim was mostly on the mend, or at least she wasn't apparently getting any worse. The hospital would only give reports out on her condition like a sports highlight embargoed until the end of a game.

William Dellarose contemplated his reality in this adverse environment. Here was the debris, the junkyard of humanity. Here were a few people who would never move on. Their death would be slow and prolonged. For some of them, at least, suicide might be a more humane option. In fact, about once a year, actions spoke louder than words as somebody carried out such a sentence on his or herself. But, then again, other times inmates tried to kill each other off. Was there really a difference?

***

Soon William would be before the "parole board." It wasn't actually called that, and all connection to calling MSH a prison had been scrupulously scrubbed from the law statutes, to the very names of the court hearings themselves. This hearing was technically called a Special Review Board, but in reality it was a parole board hearing. The board was comprised of one doctor, one lawyer, and one member of the community at large. Some people get out in five minutes and others stay for life. For William, trying a criminal law route had been a nineteen-year wait for a court hearing that he never got. That had largely been a waste of his time, but at least he was now medicated and sober, and considered to have "insight" and "investment" into his treatment.

As noted in the chapter introduction, the gist of this story is based on the reality of this author's assignment to, and incarceration and treatment at the Minnesota Security Hospital. There was nothing in the account that had to be made up out of whole cloth. All of the aspects of that account were thoroughly grounded in reality.

In 1993, this author committed a crime. He'd stabbed a girl in the leg. The two had disagreed over an issue pertaining to drugs being sold in the neighborhood, and in his schizophrenic perception of the situation he'd decided his only option for dealing with his disagreement with her had been to file his complaint with her leg.

Not being one to rest on his laurels, for two years he went on insisting on having a criminal trial. It took two years of torture before he gave up his right to trial.

In the year 2000, the girl's employer got raided for drugs.

William thought this was his big break, his vindication. Now that her business was raided, he could no longer be accused of being delusional about the drug connection to his crime.

The vindication never came. The lawyers refused to bring the case forward. The process was not meant to work. The system was designed to not work in the fashion he desired. Dysfunction for the accused was apparently deemed to be of higher value, and so it went for this author and for his fictitious stand-in.

We pick up the story:

Now, William was up for parole in two months. All he had to do was hold his breath for sixty days and he could become a semi-free partial citizen again.

He walked the campus as he had done a thousand times before. There was nothing unusual about it. The only odd thing was William himself. He had moved up in the system to such a point and degree that he could walk the campus without anyone else accompanying to supervise.

William spotted Matt at the other end of the sidewalk. Matt was walking with a backpack and a pocketful of electronic games. William waved. Matt waved back.

As they got closer, came within hearing, Matt said: "Hey there Will, how's it going?" It was actually an unusual conversational start by Matt, because he was the type of person who liked to use a lot of big words.

"Can't complain much," William replied. "It's just another day here in paradise. You heard about the stabbing, didn't you?"

More in his normal conversational mode Matt responded: "It's certainly the conversational focus of this vicinity, that and William Jensen's departure on the same day. Problems come in an assemblage. Statistically that is more the norm than a homogeneous osmosis."

"Yeah, whatever, I am so relieved his mom survived. I hope she pulls out of it," William said as he passed Matt and continued his walk toward the meditation garden maintained on the hospital's grounds.

Chapter 4: Alternative Approaches

WE NEED TO abandon the idea of the descriptions in this book being at all fictitious. The reality they are based on is too dark, too depressing.

We should talk about Bob confiscating Andrew's fun and his "D," an important letter in this world. My form of incarceration and punishment is based on being determined by the court to be "Mentally Ill and Dangerous." In discourse, it's usually just shortened to "MI and D." The "D" is the part that endorses the complete confiscation of civil rights. "D" stands for "Dangerous." Once that legal label is on you, you cannot live free in the State of Minnesota.

Contrast this system with the one I'm given to understand is used in Canada, where I believe they have much more stringent criteria for assigning such a label to anyone. In northern border states like Minnesota, we obviously have a closer relationship with Canada, and therefore we'd probably consider moving there to be a more viable option than would, say, someone who lives in Arizona. Canada, which has a socialized medicine system, covers psychiatric illness equal to its coverage of physical medical conditions, but because not all mental health problems are psychiatric, people with addictions, alcoholism, and a variety of behavior and adjustment problems undoubtedly fall through those many cracks in their coverage. On the other hand, that probably results in their being left alone to lead their lives as they see fit. Their system has its fans and detractors.

Satirically speaking, here in the U.S. all is good for us inmates.

The real person represented by the character who stabbed his mother in my earlier "fictitious" scenario did an act of true barbarity, and I don't think he would survive as a long-term consumer of mental health services. He burned out his last transistor. That stereo is gone. It's toast. Goodbye. I will visit you in hell. Honestly, I really will visit you in prison.

I actually wrote a much shorter version of this book once before, even shorter than the version originally published in 2014. It was quite a gloomy tract. What I offer now, especially in this expanded version with the assistance of my professional editor, is a much better thought out and constructed presentation.

It is certainly more than just an enhanced short story collection. It is, as you surely should already have recognized, a collection of stories and accounts enhanced by their largely being real-life references. I'll trust that these accounts and my associated commentaries will justify the time you are spending reading this book, hopefully attentively. Without an attentive reader, no book based on reality has any meaning and purpose.

This book could be read as, and in a broad sense really is, the memoir of an inmate at the Minnesota Security Hospital in Saint Peter. Saint Peter is, at its core, a prison hospital for two inmate populations, one the mentally ill and dangerous, and the other those deemed sexually deviant predators. The two groups are kept apart in separate sections of the facility, but I'm pretty certain that the public doesn't really understand that distinction. How would anyone who has no direct experience with anyone in either part of the facility have the opportunity to develop any real understanding of the difference? For too many people the mentally ill are thought to be dangerous, and predators are thought to be mentally ill, and predators are dangerous and, well, you get the idea. Our two separate populations are sort of all lumped together in too many, in most people's minds.

This might be an appropriate point to introduce you to Mary Ellen Copeland's WRAP, an acronym for the Wellness Recovery Action Plan. The organization established to promote her ideas has a website where they archive assistive resources, provide online support, and sell books and other materials to help people recover their mental health. Copeland is herself a psychiatric survivor who experienced a powerful mood disorder. In addition to having been a consumer of mental health services, she has a Ph.D. in Psychology.

Copeland was racked with the symptoms of severe depression. The advertising blurb promoting her video biography says "her journey" was one "from a life struggling with mental health challenges to a life of wellness and recovery."

Copeland and her team of cohorts and companions pioneered approaches to recovery. Her original WRAP book almost single-handedly invented the process I call crisis cocooning, where the patient or stressed individual is recommended to withdraw and heal from professional life until he or she is genuinely recovered.

The WRAP books recommend things like only returning to work after a month's recovery time from a crisis. WRAP also recommends adopting a four-hour-per-week work schedule at that time of return. It recommends creating a wellness toolbox and using things like going for a walk, or calling a friend, or doing relaxation and stress reduction exercises. There are even things like "look through old scrapbooks and photo albums" in WRAP's prescriptions for returning to health. These are all things that our standard Republicans would probably be appalled by, with their attitude that most mental illness is simply a symptom of being a slacker, that so-called mentally ill people are too often too coddled, and need to just grit their teeth, bear with it, and plow on ahead with their lives.

Lest you think that the four-hour-per-week work schedule should be thought of as just pie-in-the-sky desire, for anyone who has suffered through severe bouts of depression it is clearly a need, as much of a need as the "happy pills" often prescribed by psychiatrists. You just cannot undervalue the little things that keep you from unplugging your cord, your brain, from the wall socket we call life. Checking out professionally, and checking into recovery, requires a rest period. It helps greatly in achieving good mental health.

The Copeland program's downfall is that her recommended time to heal is so costly that, clearly, most people don't have that kind of option. Try to reduce your work life from forty to four hours per week and most of us would no longer have a job to return to. And even if you have sufficient health care coverage to afford the costs of an inpatient mental health stay, getting yourself labeled as having a mental illness is also often a swift route to unemployment. It's only the independently wealthy, who can afford extended periods at recovery ranches, and individuals like me who are involuntary residents at treatment facilities such as the Saint Peter Regional Treatment Center, who when they get into a crisis mode are provided the kinds of time WRAP recommends for recovery.

The kind of recovery WRAP recommends would probably cost someone at least twice the sum of a social security disability check, and wouldn't even be affordable to someone living in government subsidized Section 8 housing. If you work in a high income profession, cutting back to half-time would cost far more.

Our government does not give people the funds to have time to heal. Neither do most private employers. It's an interesting conundrum to think that one of the few professions that gives people enough cash to buy time to heal are the professions selling the very drugs that are addicting many people into the need for Copeland's program: street dealers and legal prescribers both.

Last week, two people from our program attempted to murder somebody. One other person ran away, and there were two knockdown drag-out fistfights. One other male patient, a person generally acknowledged to be a "good guy," was assaulted in the course of one of those fights. Caught in the middle of a fight he neither wanted nor started, he got a huge bruised black eye and several stab wounds from a pencil. The people involved in the fight, him probably included, will each be rewarded for their efforts with a similar set of benefits: more time at Saint Peter, more time to return to a more even keel without the pressures of a full-time job, and more time before they will need to think about their need for income to pay bills, support a family, etc.

A conservative agenda says we need a safety net and not a hammock. Copeland's WRAP program clashes with such an agenda. I don't know, but I suspect that many of the extreme conservative types who have dominated the Republican Party agenda in the last few presidential and congressional elections would sell off Copeland's job to China if they could. Fortunately for us, such an agenda has not yet invaded the halls of academia where our mental health professionals are trained. Copeland's academic credentials back up her recipe for success.

***

Writing in 2010 and 2011, I noted that psychiatric care appears to be evolving in the United States, even in my state of residence, Minnesota, which has long been considered to be one of the more advanced states in the treatment and care of its mentally ill citizens. But even now, as it grows rapidly, it sometimes needs pruning.

As necessary as it is to know about programs like WRAP, it is also important to be aware of one oft mentioned alternative to psychiatry: Scientology, the movement and religion created by L. Ron Hubbard. Scientology is believed to have been created by him partly as a response to the manner in which psychiatric care was being dispensed in 1945, as the U.S. tried to deal with some of the psychological trauma affecting soldiers coming back from the Second World War.

I'll have more to say about Scientology later, but I have one particularly cogent thing to offer the world at this point in my text. I need to specifically point out that Scientology and psychiatry just don't get along. Being a patient who has a more than academic interest in the issues between them, I can clearly say that considering them together would be like a verbal version of watching cats and dogs fight, or maybe the mayhem of a mixed martial arts bout between a couple of ranked combatants.

***

As of the day this portion is being written, I have about six weeks until I go before a Special Review Board at Saint Peter State Hospital, which is sort of like a court hearing that could enable me to get out of what we here at Saint Peter call the "big prison," moving me to the "small prison" where residents have a greater range of personal discretion. This would be sort of like a move from a maximum to a minimum security prison. If approved, I will be physically moving from one end of the campus to the other. I'll just be moving from the south end of the facility to the north, but functionally there will be changes that will be far more significant.

Functionally, the lower level of security will mean I'll be able to walk downtown and get a cup of coffee at a café, and on special occasions actually smoke a cigarette. I'll be able to leave the hospital grounds for up to four hours without an escort, and if I get a friend from outside to come with me I can be away for ten hours. The small prison also does not lock its doors in the daytime hours from dawn till dusk.

The hope I have, with support of the more conscientious Saint Peter Minnesota Security Hospital staff, is that I'll spend my next stretch of time in that mild security environment as a transition to finally being allowed to return to so-called normal life and society. Assuming that hospital staff consider my transition successful, when released I may go back to my city by the river, Minneapolis, or perhaps a smaller Minnesota community with fewer pre-existing connections to my past. However, there are many potential roadblocks and obstacles that could get thrown in the way of that change.

There will be tests, such as the MMPI, the Minnesota Multiphasic Personality Inventory, which I'll have to "pass" to have the staff certify that my diagnosed mental illness is firmly under control. There will be open-ended interviews with psychologists who will be evaluating my responses to their questions against how "normal" people might typically respond. There will be clinical evaluations of how I make eye contact in conversation, how closely my speaking tracks against the subject of a query, how I will or won't be fidgeting during a session, how belligerent they will perceive me to be, how I will be perceived as I speak about and focus, or not focus, on the episode that landed me at Saint Peter State Hospital nineteen years ago.

There can be many reasons why individual inmates will experience extended stays at Saint Pater. At least five people, and possibly many others, involved in a fistfight on unit 800 will not be going home, at least not anytime soon. And then there was the female Saint Peter inmate who tried to strangle her roommate. And there was the man who attacked his mother, the other who got 'happy feet' and tried to run away, still another inmate who stabbed someone with a pencil for no apparent reason, another male inmate who tried to castrate himself with a dental floss tourniquet, and, of course, the so many others involved in any number of less notable confrontations. All of that happened in two short weeks, their actions and behaviors condemning them each to a quite a bit longer stay as guests of the state at Saint Peter.

***

Thinking again of the WRAP model, if the world in general would pay my rent for six months, whenever I needed to recover from a moment of crisis, then I would be well rested and well stocked. Unfortunately the world at large would more likely evict me from my apartment and bounce my checks as I tried to buy food with an empty checking account.

So as I'm looking forward to returning to normal society sooner rather than later, you should probably know a bit more about what happened to land me at Saint Peter back in 1993. If you refer back to my earlier story focused on the two Williams at Saint Peter, the William Dellarose character is an obviously thinly veiled version of me, William Strawn Douglas. Here are a few of the details, not wrapped into a piece of fiction.

I had some issues in 1993. I created what I euphemistically call a small incision, actually a stab wound on one member of a local drug dealing cartel. The wound was small, but its effects on me in the context of my entry into our system of law and order were great. I was hoping to use the incident to put a case forward in a court. The defense that I got was like being a Volkswagen Beetle, with a whole 60-horsepower engine, trying to outpace an 800-horsepower Ferrari in a road race.

During the heyday of drug trafficking, the Minneapolis West Bank community, near the similarly named Minneapolis West Bank Campus of the University of Minnesota, one of its three Twin Cities campuses, had a number of relatively inexpensive cafes. I personally observed that one of them, the Hard Times Café, covered some of its operating costs by selling marijuana over the counter in coffee cups for $20 a serving.

My victim was a peripheral member of one of the local drug clubs. The key trafficker was one of her male friends. If I had any beef with one of his minor player employees, then I should have taken my complaint to him and not to the young scrap of a kid I confronted. My bad!

While my attack on the girl was provoked at least in part by the hallucinations and paranoia of my mental illness, in my mind, at the time, I was taking effective action to stem a drug enterprise polluting my neighborhood. In fact, I was later somewhat vindicated, as my victim's business got shut down in a drug raid. I was no longer deemed to have been hallucinating. I was, however, still considered to be a threat to society.

The State's position on me and my activities underwent a change. The legalities of my commitment were altered because there was now a crucial missing component to the original charge against me. My victim's group was indeed selling drugs. My victim had just not yet been caught at it at the time of our encounter. In fact, she was never herself caught, because when her drug ring was raided and brought down seven years later, she had left the scene and was no longer part of their machine.

To the legal machinations and changes, I have from time to time taken objection to. Now, of course, it is mostly irrelevant. Reality never mattered to the state and it never will. Why? Because the state has one settlement cap and two immunity clauses! They count on violating people's civil rights. They assume such lawsuits would be sought and they've effectively provided themselves with immunity against claims of illegal imprisonment or for monetary compensation.

One of the most damning points to this is that, just to claim your right to trial, you have to assure your psychiatrist for the trial that you intend to plead guilty. This is exactly what happened to me. I had one of the state's top forensic psychiatrists question me as to my intent to go to trial. My examiner told me I had two choices: either plead guilty now or plead guilty later on. I refused both and ended up pleading guilty later on anyway. He denied me my right to trial because anyone who insisted on trial under my circumstances must be crazy. Shades of *Catch-22*, but more about that later. I was intent on going to trial to hand each of my victim's drug associates jail time on drug trafficking charges. My examiner did not believe my statement that there was a logical reason to my decision to stab that kid in the leg to create a court date.

My logic was clearly not in sync with the logic and legal undercarriage of our greater society. Although this crime was created by me as a perceived deed of logic, there were several flaws to my actions. First and foremost was the demographic I found myself a part of. My desire to go to court turned out to be an impossible quest to get civil rights applied to someone considered to be one of society's unproductive alcoholic citizens, a mentally ill homeless person. To people such as I was at the time, the type of crime I'd perpetrated would have made absolutely fine sense. Also, I believe it would have made sense to prison inmates. So all this taken together suggests that my crime, no matter how thoughtful and logical in intent, was the kind of deed only comprehensible to a small population of habitual criminals.

I concede that my actions, though appearing logical to me at the time, were neither sane nor smart, nor very popular.

All that for a moment of twisted logic with a Swiss Army knife. A normal psychotherapist would see narcissism in my thinking, and an anti-social personality disorder diagnosis, plus a healthy dose of schizophrenia.

***

Whether liberals or conservatives are in power seems to make no real difference. This book is for everybody, Republican or Democrat, libertarian or tea partyist, or even people who identify as a Whig, Tory, Socialist, Federalist, Libertarian, Labor or other party member in any democratic state.

Like coping with hunger and AIDS in Africa, you don't question where the food and medicine come from, but you do praise its existence and its delivery to where you are if you are the one who needs it. Even doctrinaire social or fiscal conservatives ought to be able to read a book like this and learn a thing or two.

They probably could all benefit also from hearing Copeland deliver a good talk on WRAP.

Tending to each citizen's unique mental health needs should not be a strange policy for the U.S. We need our nation's consumers of mental health services to get what they need to keep as many of them as possible amongst the ranks of productive and healthy citizens. That does not always require becoming an inpatient. Indeed, the needs of those seeking mental health services should only very rarely require having someone become an inpatient, and even more rarely being detained in that status over a long period of time.

Many people with mental illness can continue or return to being productive people on an outpatient basis if provided with the minimal services needed to promote and maintain mental health. The balance needed to achieve that includes the notion that most people with mental health issues may only need some combination of affordable access to medication, perhaps some oversight to ensure that their meds aren't skipped, or even just some counseling. And, by providing the most limited treatment necessary, we preserve scarce funding and resources for those who truly do need a great deal of help on the level of that provided by a placement in a hospital or treatment center.

The idea of this isn't new to society. It's used in other realms of providing services to those in need. In special education, for instance, providing a "least restrictive environment" is well established as a way for students with learning problems to have the greatest possible access to the mainstream, while still receiving services needed to support individual needs. In a similar manner, providing support to help the elderly stay in their homes has been shown to be both beneficial to recipients and cost effective for society.

A white, male, corporate, suit-wearing Christian may use different services than a half-Black, half-Jewish, lesbian, single mother of five, living with HIV. I use these two descriptions as portrayals of cultural opposites, but recognize that in a major city like New York, Chicago, or even Minneapolis, those might be just two of the sixty people on any given subway car or bus, riding to their destinations together.

Chapter 5: God and Drugs

As a person who has been immersed in our mental health system for decades, it's clear to me that mental health and chemical dependency operate in unison.

Alcoholics Anonymous and Narcotics Anonymous use the idea of a "god of our understanding" rather than explicitly referencing Jesus, or Moses, or Mohamed, or Buddha. But let's start with the obvious. The paradigm behind both groups in the U.S. is the stereotype of "Jesus" in recovery.

With this in mind it should be clear by now that this book is not intended as an academically learned dissertation. It is clearly opinionated about "god" beliefs. The mere fact that you pray assumes you believe in a god. That same god is, however, also the god of science, reality and complexity.

To me the blood of Christ appearing as red wine might possibly be the most visceral ritual experience an addict to drugs can ever experience. Such a heroin addict maybe sees his own blood at the point of a needle and in the bloom of the rose as the backflow of blood appears in the syringe, as blood is pulled in from the vein and mixed with the cooked heroin and quickly re-injected into the vein.

I've observed how communion, as experienced in the consciousness of many participants, is a group ritual of collective drug experience. We all share the same drug. We all share the same diseases as we all drink the same wine from the same cup. We commune. We are the community.

It is as if Jesus were sitting next to each and every one of us and saying: "I knew you were going to drink wine and do every sinful thing from sex to heroin. I knew you would sin every time you drank that wine so I will create a ritual so powerful that every sip of wine would remind you of this conversation you are having with me here and now."

An important thing now is to deal with America's opioid epidemic and the street drugs that too often replace the prescriptions when those supplies run out. The heroin is killing more kids than all the ISIS terrorists ever could. We return over and over again to communion. Every drug ingested, snorted, smoked, eaten, or injected, bathes the brain in euphoria in just the same ways that the communion wine of the blood of Christ ever did.

Is it the blood of Christ or the water of life? Whichever, addicts go to such lengths to pollute it. At that point, whether it's the blood of injection on an arm and the cup of wine in a hand, we look at a god of forgiveness looming over us in the true superiority of being considered by Christians to be the one person who thousands of years ago predicted you would end up with that Burgundy and blood of injection teasing your faith. Christianity says it knew you would end up here, that you would be brought to this point just so you could have this very moment of revelation and hope. Religion maintains that your belief is giving you that chance of redemption. Right now! And that means, it says, it is up to you to pray and acknowledge the existence of an interventionist god in your life.

People like me experienced the meaning of "communion" through drugs like wine and other things more potent. Some Native Americans experience the strangely mystical religious effect from the peyote cactus. Their culture has used that hallucinogen to help put them into a religious mindset for at least 1,000 years.

Whether it be via natural or man-made compounds, there is a common response every time a human mind is exposed to a benzene ring hallucinogen. That set includes mushrooms, peyote and LSD. And curiously, peyote is sometimes used as part of a Native American ritual in curing another mental health impediment: alcoholism.

Heroin becomes a reward cycle for the modified mind. Alternative to sex or pain relief or any other human reward system in the mind, our friend the morphine sulfate molecule goes on its way distracting the human race with a molecular mimic of the reward or pain control function of the normal mind. With it, the mind is distracted by a compound so powerful that the very device trusted to make a decision on whether to consume the drug is the device that is impaired by that drug's use. The mind is literally pouring itself a drink. The mind only minimally interferes with the addiction process as it propels a user to seek more or more power-ful drugs the way a baby seeks more milk. The brain has a sweet tooth for heroin and the brain is the machine trusted with the job of watching over the addiction process. The foxes are guarding the prey.

Whether the real Jesus was actually a religious Jew or the prototypical Christian promoted in the gospels, he probably would have wanted you to pray as this is distinctly a human thing to do. The human organism often just works more efficiently and effectively when a god-based belief system is in place.

An apology is perhaps in order to any atheist or agnostic reader, but when trying to fathom the extremes of recovery from heroin addiction and its involvement in modern Christianity, you have to work with the cultural themes you have been given. Redemption can be a bloody business.

Oddly, sometimes when you get a drug addict to experience some down-time in reference to pausing the manner in which the addiction is satisfied, by pointing out all the parallels between Christianity and drug use, you find them getting just as scientific with their personal theologies as they get with their spoonful of cooked heroin mix ready to be injected into a vein.

They certainly don't start out on a flash feed of miracles. Miracles in-terfere with the common human experience of accessing a higher power or god of their own understanding. Miracles may have been great to ex-perience in Roman times, or even in colonial New England, but they do not fare as well in the post-Vietnam era of helicopter warfare, a military industrial complex, and social role models like Barbie and Ken, sports heroes and internet celebrities.

If you can make it through life without any drugs or alcohol, you will make a great Mormon. No coffee or cigars, and no herbal garden with peyote or marijuana. We need to cut the body count by destroying the profit-based supply network for drugs. That will only happen after the supply chain has been replaced with herb gardens like that noted above. Then we might progress to things like cutting down on mental health oriented issues like mass shootings in schools and other firearms related behaviors.

I don't mind if people grow their own marijuana or mushrooms. We should move to being a society where drugs are only a small concern. In the meantime we should continue to try to de-criminalize the situation in small ways, like we've been doing with the increasing availability of marijuana in states across the U.S.

Regardless, the human mind often seems to work so much better when there is a god constellation in the astronomic anatomy of that mind. Prayer can, for some, perhaps for many, create humility merely by merit of the asking of a god for favor. If we experience a god through prayer we become humble. We see ourselves as something small in comparison to something seemingly endless, vast and deep as the biggest ocean. It can be a balm to mental health to not need drugs, to believe and know that all you have to do to access that power is to pray.

***

The concept of drug advocacy is part of this book, though I personally see no use for opiates other than to treat severe pain issues. Staunch sobriety advocates will say that no drug should ever be tolerated. The sober community, of which I count myself a member, is a small elite group of former practicing addicts. We know things the general population can only intellectually speculate about.

It has taken me almost three decades to get to this point. A text I wrote in the early 1990s discussed weapons and ammunition extensively. This was done from a medical perspective of the wound dynamics that happen in combat and on battlefields all over the world. There was an extensive section on drugs. There were mentions of terrorism including the real world use of airliners as flying bombs that we later saw executed on 9/11. But even then there was extensive reference to religion. There was mention of leftist politics and Native American issues. There was mention of biblical sheepskin birth control. There were many other allusions to practicing medicine at the level of a combat medic or ambulance driver. There was also text on the basic drug culture of addiction at large in the world.

With almost twenty more years of life now behind me, I come to these issues with a more complete and mature perspective. This is derived from extensive reading, therapy for my own issues, and all the objective informational internet downloads I've been able to access, rather just philosophical musings based only on my personal experiences with the criminal street drug underworld as a youth. The internet gives me the ability to download pages of information on almost any aspect of drug use and recovery.

I look at this issue now as one of drug recovery, while my 1990s writings approached it mostly as a manual for drug use, focused on being a survival manual for "working" drug addicts.

There are issues that concern treatment practices for both chemical dependency and mental health. The focus here is on people trying to get completely sober, at least severely moderate their drug consumption, or maybe at least just moderate the damage caused by chronic drug use. This concept is commonly referenced under the political catchphrase of "harm reduction." It is part of my philosophy on the practicing of medicine that it is necessary to keep these doors of communication on use in moderation open. I refuse to just condemn addicts, as condemnation shuts down future possibilities of going sober and gets us all nowhere.

Chapter 6: Catalogues

When we start to talk about various mental diseases and their cures we find that professionals tend to cram all diseases of the mind into four categories: schizophrenia, manic depression or bipolar, schizoaffective disorder, and everything else.

With schizophrenia, you have active hallucinations of the auditory and visual types. You literally see and hear things that are not actually there. You hear voices. You see writing or animals or people that you later find out do not exist.

The worst of these are command hallucinations where you hear a message telling you to do something. These voices or other messages might tell you to do something harmful to somebody else, or to yourself. So long as these voices just tell you to buy a bottle of ketchup every day or bet regularly on the lottery, and you don't spend more than the couple dollars you can afford, then you are relatively all right. It should be noted that you can get into a lot of trouble if you do what the voices tell you to do, when what they are telling you runs counter to society's norms. When your hallucinations tell you to harm somebody, then you are all of a sudden in a very different category than a person in the normal population.

Command hallucinations are common in cases of schizophrenia. Modern cures involve drugs like Haldol and Olanzapine and Clozaril. There were also several older and less useful ones, like Reserpine and Thorazine.

Reserpine is a drug that dates back to the 1950s. It would help people recover from schizophrenia but it would also trade that symptom in for depression. The terrible depression it created caused it to be used only very sporadically, with people for whom such a "cure" would not be worse than their disease. Nevertheless it was a beginning. It was a place for pharmaceutical intervention to start from.

Thorazine became a more popular alternative in the earlier 1970s. It emptied a lot of mental institutions. We hear many bad things about Thorazine, like the *Thorazine Shuffle*, where one "gets on the dance floor and don't move a muscle." But for many it was a major step forward. Another way we think of many of the mental health diseases are as Axis One or Axis Two maladies. Of the three possible Axis One diagnoses that you can have, two of them are schizophrenia and manic depression. The third, schizoaffective disorder, is really a combination of the two polar opposites of schizophrenia and bipolar. Bipolar is the proper currently used name for what used to be called manic depression. With schizoaffective disorder you have the schizophrenia-like symptoms of hallucination combining with the manic behaviors seen in people at the extreme overactive end of the bipolar spectrum. That leaves us with "everything else."

That also means we have to separate Axis Two from Axis One. In practical terms, Axis One problems are the ones they lock you away for and try to use drugs to cure. Axis One diagnoses are ones that can typically be remedied with drugs or with hospitalization for electroshock therapy. Your Axis One illness is the one the state can imprison you for. It is your "major mental illness." It is the schizophrenia, manic depression or schizoaffective disorder that you can be institutionalized for having.

Axis Two problems are the ones they usually try to manage or cure through various forms of therapy or counseling, like the talk therapy used for some personality disorders or psychopathic traits. Axis Two diseases run a gamut through Narcissistic Personality Disorder, Borderline Personality Disorder, Chemical Dependency, and other annoyances of similar magnitude. Antisocial personality is one that is of that order. In fact, just about everything that a pill cannot cure gets lumped into the Axis Two "everything else" category, though I've seen some excessive chemical dependencies treated as Axis One illnesses. They shouldn't be, because that last situation really doesn't fit. It's like entering a Volkswagen Beetle as a contestant in the Indy 500.

As we've noted, the drug Reserpine was developed in the 1950s, and Thorazine in the early 1970s. Olanzapine came along late in the 1990s. All of these drugs had their times in the limelight as their era's wonder drug, destined to make major fundamental changes for the lives of the mentally ill.

Epileptics who also experienced symptoms of mental illnesses often said that a seizure would clear up their mental illness symptoms for a while. Taking note of this, doctors began to induce seizures as a curative. This and early drug therapies were rather barbaric, but nonetheless it was a beginning that helped some people significantly. Now there are many drugs designed to fight various symptoms of the generic foe that we call insanity or madness, drugs like Prozac, Prolixin, Stelazine, Navane, Trilafon, Haldol and Thorazine. Many a side effect is possible with any of these, from serious physical complications like liver failure, and even death, to personality changes, increased feelings of depression, and even thoughts of suicide.

One of the more noteworthy side effects many such drugs have is Tardive Dyskinesia. It manifests as involuntary muscular tics or movements in some people, some minor such as a tongue that twitches, and in other people as major involuntary muscle movements that create a gross inability to walk or stand for any length of time without extreme body movement. Still other people experience almost the opposite, such as a deadening of facial motor muscles. Almost all of the drugs used for mental illness have the potential to cause Tardive Dyskinesia, although more modern drugs like Risperadone and Olanzapine have a much lower potential for causing this symptom.

Trilafon can cause a very different physical side effect, gyrated ocular crisis, which causes a person's eyeballs to roll up into their eye sockets, effectively blinding the person for periods of about five minutes. You probably shouldn't want to drive a car while you are on Trilafon.

Weight gain is also associated with many medications. With Olanzapine in particular, weight gain is a significant side effect, as are pre-diabetes and diabetes. This is a noteworthy problem because Olanzapine is currently one of the most effective drug for controlling schizophrenia and schizoaffective disorder.

Even bipolar patients can get some benefit from Olanzapine. It makes you fat. But at least it makes you sane.

Clozaril presents inconvenient side effects like night drooling and incontinence. It can also have major effects like significantly lowering a person's white blood cell count, a blood problem called *agranulocytosis*. Your white blood cell count goes down precipitously and you lose your ability to fight off infection. While on this drug you also have the inconvenience of needing to get your blood drawn for analysis every week to monitor for *agranulocytosis*. I tried this drug and all of those symptoms were there in me, plus vomiting in my sleep. When my blood work indicated the problem, I was taken off Clozaril immediately. This medication experiment by me then had an additional side effect of causing my sentence to be extended as we worked to establish what new level of my old Olanzapine would now be needed to achieve the previous level of control.

Clozaril was used in Europe in the 1970s with great success. I have also seen terrible things with a new drug called Latuda. I saw two assaults on others and two other major breakdowns come about on people trying Latuda. One man tried to kill his mother. He had been institutionalized because he had tried to do this on prior occasions, but though he was deemed to be cured by the Latuda it didn't stop him from trying again. Another man assaulted his roommate, stabbing him with a pencil while on Latuda, after losing a cassette tape and blaming his roommate for the loss. The third person tried to castrate himself on Latuda, and a fourth had a psychiatric breakdown while being transitioned off of Latuda.

***

Having a mental illness is not the end of the world. If you want to progress toward normality it will require that you take care to avoid flare-ups of your symptoms. I know this to be true. What we have just discussed is, I hope, a foundation of the connection that some of you, as my readers, will have with my content.

In many ways this connection should be a new beginning for us both. We have to learn from each other. If we can do that, then the learning curve will go up exponentially.

We will get a whole that is far more than the sum of its parts. I sincerely hope that I do get something back from you all as we examine the facts of the cases. I am not a professional, outside of the simple claim to be a man extensively experienced with the circumstances of being caught in a particular life scenario. Correspondence would be greatly appreciated.

We have all three major types of mental illness here at the Saint Peter puzzle palace. We have schizophrenia and schizoaffective disorder and manic depression.

I have schizophrenia.

Amongst the trivia associated with my diagnosis it that any children I might have will have a one in six chance of developing a mental illness. You have just as much potential of digging up such facts with your computer as I have with mine. The genetic connection is pretty clear for my family.

Grandmother Jane died in an event we strongly suspect to have been a suicide. Her body was found in the local river. It was a big river, the Snake River in Idaho. We will never know for sure what affected Jane Douglas back there in the 1940s. She is not here to examine or ask, but looking at her descendants we can certainly come to a logical assumption, especially when we look at some of my closer relatives.

My two sisters are dead. One, Carter Lynn Douglas, was murdered by a man she met at a mental institution, and the other, her fraternal twin Cathy Jo Douglas, died by suicide. Both parents are now also gone, though with them the circumstances were a lot less suspicious.

***

While the issues faced by those working to recover their mental health are complex enough for most of those so afflicted, as I noted earlier in my description of the circumstances that led me to be at Saint Peter, there is a public perception that often lumps alcoholism and homelessness in with mental illness. There is more than a germ of truth to this for many people. Self medication with alcohol and prescription or street drugs in not uncommon, and being a recovering addict in a mental health scenario is central to the purpose of this book.

I do believe that many readers of this book will be mental health consumers in a chemical dependency scenario. What that means in practical terms is that you will often have access to all of the niceties of normal life, until some critical event comes crashing through. You'll be interacting with your family, going out to dinner, smoking cigarettes if that's your thing, and so on, until your addictions and mental health issues crash down on you. If you're fortunate your curative program will last you only from twenty to ninety days or so. But as a practical impact of how it could turn out, consider the reality of my program, which has gone on for almost two decades.

And as a practical matter, I have always had a hot temper, and street drugs and mental illness did not help me with those issues at all.

Chemical dependency is found frequently in mental health and poverty. To spend time at a chemical dependency treatment facility is for some people the moment that, for the first time in years, they have a roof over their heads and a good meal to help them along. But to make a transition to permanent health, once your treatment experience is over and you are sober from drugs and alcohol, then you need to begin to recruit people for relationships that will cement you into a less dependent lifestyle. Not all of these contacts are going to be instantly productive.

You will find instability in many of your new relationships, and that should not deter you from seeking out new healthy connections. Chemical dependency and mental illness cut across all socioeconomic, gender, religious and other boundaries, and treatment brings together a diverse crowd. I have seen judges and lawyers at Alcoholics Anonymous meetings. I have also seen paupers and the most destitute people ever deemed to be homeless.

My most specific experiential expertise is with schizophrenia, but I also have some manic traits, so I get all three major disease groups as part of my intellectual diet of things to think about.

The schizophrenic is said to have a break from reality. To call one schizophrenic is to say they have one large break from reality, not that they have multiple personalities. The multiple personality association with the term "schizophrenic" is common but erroneous. It is an older, more popular and less clinical legend of mental illness not grounded in fact. A person harboring multiple personalities has multiple personality disorder. Some schizophrenics have multiple personality issues, but that is not how schizophrenia is defined.

In manic depression, one cycles from a state of being extremely energized with a form of ecstatic joy, to one of depressive fatigue and lack of motivation.

In the manic state, a person's behaviors may seem to make them more productive, characterized by sleeplessness, binge spending, rapid speech, and sometimes bursts of creativity, but often also with manifestations like proposing disjointed ideas, a lack of concentration, and the inability to stay with tasks through completion. Mania can even reach rage and violence.

Crashing into severe depression can leave a person so unmotivated that even eating or something as simple as a short conversation can be a nearly impossible chore.

The cycles can last mere minutes or go on for more months than a typical season. I have even heard of some people diagnosed as depressed who have said the depressive cycle of their illness lasted for years. More typically in manic depression, one cycles from mania today to depression tomorrow, and back the other way again, endlessly. A friend with that problem has told me that at her worst she could cycle between those extremes every five minutes.

Schizoaffective disorder is said to be a combination of schizophrenia with only half of the bipolar as an addition. An ecstatic nonstop high with no connection to a miserable depressive downswing is one way the patient can experience its symptoms.

Having one of the three forms of mental illness most common here at the Minnesota Security Hospital, as a chemically dependent schizophrenic, I can say that problems especially exist for us, the dually diagnosed. Our problems are typically characterized by gaps in memory, limited attention span, absence of abstract thinking, and disinclination to do any planning ahead. Use of drugs and alcohol often worsens all sorts of symptoms of mental illness, resulting in relapses and hospitalizations.

One special celebrity in the world of the mentally ill is Syd Barrett, a very schizophrenic former rock musician whose name is still well known in some artistic circles. He was the first lead guitar player and a primary singer and songwriter for the legendary rock band Pink Floyd. Barrett self-medicated his schizophrenia with copious amounts of LSD and other illegal drugs. Unfortunately for him, the more of these mind-bending chemicals and drugs he took, the crazier he became. The results would be similar for most other people with schizophrenia trying similar self-medication routines.

Barrett experienced an onset of schizophrenia in the late 1960s and propelled his case through rock music society by becoming more and more erratic at Pink Floyd performances. The odder his behavior, the more the band looked for a replacement, which they eventually found in guitarist David Gilmore. Roger Waters took over most of the songwriting and the die was cast with no room for Barrett.

He spent most of the last thirty-five years of his life in a mental institution in England, where he died in 2006. While Pink Floyd was putting together the album *Wish You Were Here* in 1975, a fat, bald Syd Barrett visited his former band mates at the recording studio. The connection was mostly gone.

The maddening thing about a dual diagnosis of mental illness and chemical dependency, like what I have and what Barrett had, is that you never fully know which of the illnesses is acting on you at any given time, in any specific instance. It can become quite a juggling act.

Problems came to us from two directions much of the time. You can go to a meeting for chemical dependency issues and you can take a pill to moderate symptoms of mental illness, but in both cases there is no "one pill cure" to handle both facets, the duality of an afflicted person's problem.

***

The most important lesson the state ever taught me was how to avoid dependence on the state. State care is thrifty and thus dry at the task of filling a cup, and in state care there are usually just a few drops in each cup. Only on rare occasions when the state makes a great error does one's cup proverbially runneth over. This persistent, enforced scarcity has taught me to see the monastic qualities of my experience with mental illness and chemicals, both the positive and negative qualities. Ironically, without that, the experience of Saint Peter would have assuredly driven me mad.

Chapter 7: Chemistry and History

THERE IS A PART of therapy that is little more than word puzzles. It is nothing to be embarrassed about. One has to begin their long relationship with the state at some point. In the professions of mental health, the state is an active partner.

In practical terms, our current uses of doctors in the mental health arena could be just as well described as the employment of drug chemists. The real therapy is what reaches the mentally ill through counselors, therapists and other staff. It's more than just an exercise in semantics. In that sense, one should compare how resources for helping the mentally ill would be, and historically have been, provided by governments dominated by conservatives versus those more liberal. As I've posited earlier, liberal regimes often actually want to try to help you. Conservative regimes tend to expect you to figure out how to help yourself, without providing any significant resources or guidance.

If you were amongst those constituting the mentally ill, which would you prefer? That choice is up to you. On my part I would choose to dispense medication to Republicans and Democrats equally. I should point out that my illegal drug dispensing days were traded in for the privilege of living in the mental health system, the experience of which I will admit has helped me, in fact enabled me to be writing this book for you.

I have gone legit. This means that if you are willing, you all can get the benefits of my experience vicariously, rather than get them in a forced manner as I have over the past two decades.

If you are yourself one of us mentally ill people, maybe you can learn enough from this account to enable you to seek out the medication you need. Then you won't need two decades of imprisonment.

The part that is most crucial for healing is taking time off. As I noted earlier, the WRAP people have demonstrated that time to heal after crisis is crucial. Fortunately or otherwise, we have something of a dichotomy in the state's attitude towards this, sort of how the left hand of the state approves the concept of time off to heal, while the right hand disapproves of providing the funding to pay for it. A big question when every election cycle comes around is where the American people will lead our government in setting its call on resources to be devoted to mental health within the priorities of government spending. Those on the left typically prioritize it higher and provide more resources. Unfortunately, it seems that unless there is a court order forcing the state to provide sufficient funding for staffing and treatment, within the constraints of our government budget deficits in recent years, and the political deadlocks in Congress and all too many state legislatures, even liberals have a hard time prioritizing mental health funding above society's many other needs.

For many of us it seems that economic conservatives would rather provide incentives to allow businesses to open new factories in China, taking jobs of Americans, than to give relief to Americans who need to take time off to heal. Maybe it's oversimplifying things, but it often seems the conservative agenda prefers to spend *their* millions investing in a factory employing hungry Asians to make American flags, rather than actually preserving the rights and freedoms represented by that flag. Then they would like to spend *your* millions on wars to defend their ability and right to do so.

Here's the simple argument for the wars conservative governments seem to get us into, with the military expenditures they generate: defense contractors want a good war to make their fortune on.

That's why the politicians they have bought through campaign contributions always seem to vote for war, though it has been a long time since they were willing to actually legally call one by that name. They use words like "conflict" or "policing action" instead. The companies in the defense industry get rich so the politicians who share their views get bankrolled into office. The whole process repeats itself to infinity. This is how things work in the military industrial complex that former president Dwight Eisenhower warned the U.S. about as early as the 1950s. Behaviors similar to what happens in the military industrial complex also happen in mental health imprisonment industry. The legislature passes a law to commit people to prison hospitals.

Overcrowded, the hospital expands and some new doctor-director gets a new job with a bigger title and higher pay. Officials in the county or jurisdiction of origin, along with the doctor, write glowing reports on progress to the legislature during re-election season, and the legislature maintains or increases funding for its activities and facilities. It is not-so-subtly corrupt.

In fact, an organization called the Center for Responsible Politics has noted that, over the last decade or so, health industry interests spent more than three times as much money lobbying our federal government in favor of their interests than did even the core of the military defense industries for theirs, and those military interests spent more than $1.5 billion over that span. And yes, that's *billion* with a "B."

And while clearly most of the funding the health industry lobbying bought didn't go towards mental health, you can see the corruption in that entire endeavor.

Enjoy your day off. Thus we get back to the Copeland WRAP ethic of taking time off after a crisis period. If that offends a puritan work ethic, then we will see more American jobs going to China. God bless our Marines, because I was one of them. Peace, for a soldier, is a day off from war.

Republicans and Democrats distinguish themselves in Law and Order Incorporated in some unusual ways. Republicans are a bifurcated bunch, tending to be either well-heeled professionals (like doctors or lawyers) and businessmen (owners, CEOs, wealthy entrepreneurs, Wall Street hedge fund managers, etc.), or lesser educated socially conservative religious and blue collar types. Democrats, more typically middle income types, are much more commonly defendants, the accused, or employees in the lower echelons of organizations. Saint Peter State Hospital nurses and staff seem to be about an even split politically.

I have seen devotees of both major political groups in every community, but when it is broken down to socioeconomic groups, it's my observation that we tend to see those who are better off being Republicans, while most of those with more moderate incomes seem to be Democrats. Doctors and lawyers being Republican, and Democrats being union workers! Who'd a thunk it?

Now let's say something positive about conservatives and the military industrial complex, because we might not be here as we are if we didn't have them. We might well have had an east coast of the USA speaking German, with the west coast speaking Japanese. Admittedly, that's an extreme parse of the possibilities, but because it was even conceptually possible, it stands as proof that we need a robust military community, and that means buying toys and equipment for our Seal Teams and Special Ops units to use.

The Navy killed Osama Bin Laden and that's a good thing, in my humble opinion.

Back in the old days of a war in Asia called the Vietnam conflict, because Congress never got around to formally declaring it to be a war, our nation's young people complained deeply about being forced to go to war. Our people had evolved into a culture that wanted to avoid war, especially if that meant some of them were going to be dying in service to that old military industrial complex.

We need them, both conservatives and liberals. Adherents of both extremes have a place here in the U.S. beside our middle of the road moderates and our do-nothing fence sitters and "undecideds." That is to say, even as the complainers recognize the need for our military's protection, the military also needs us, needs at least our tacit approval of them having troops always at the ready with technologically superior weapons. They need our willingness to contribute tax dollars to buy their war toys and pay our generals handsome salaries and retirement benefits. Not too long ago, rich white men sent a lot of men and a few women off to walk patrols in Vietnam and pacify its people. That was bad.

The Vietnamese were invested into a civil war that those in the north were especially devoted to. That meant we were propping up a lesser committed losing side in the south. All the money the wealthy had invested in oil stocks could not stop that war from ending the way it did. When Richard Nixon was president, he is said to have voiced a plan that he would be willing to shed more American blood than the communists could shed.

You can read a great deal more about these kinds of things in the famed *Pentagon Papers*, a large portion of which was leaked to the *New York Times* in the early 1970s. You can still buy their 500 page volume online or through any bookstore.

These days we see similar exposures of things our government would rather not have the public know about at *WikiLeaks* and on similar sites of our present era's Internet information superhighway. For instance, just enter the term "Pentagon Papers" into your search engine of choice and one of the choices you'll see is a site that makes about 7,000 declassified pages, said to be approximately 34 percent of the entire report, available as a massive set of free file downloads.

That's one outcome of our nation's peace movement. In modern times it has largely been conservative administrations that have sent our men and women off to war and into "nation building" conflicts. These neoconservatives often won elections because, of course, we have to support our soldiers by continuing to fund our war factories in the bizarre hand-me-down policy left over from World War II. Otherwise, they fear, instead of speaking German and Japanese, we might now all be speaking Russian or Chinese.

These potential alternative histories are not just good fiction, although writers of popular science fiction have mined these possibilities in many novels over recent decades. Recent discoveries about German World War II technology, from Russian historical archives recently opened for inspection, have suggested that there may have been early use of lasers in Nazi Germany. Since lasers can be used to refine nuclear isotopes, had the war gone on in the favor of Germany a bit longer than it did, it is not inconceivable that they might have also gotten atomic bombs to put on their V-2 rockets. They were ahead of the Allies in other technologies also, including cruise missiles (the V-1), submarines, and unmanned guidance systems.

Fortunately for us, our nuclear bomb program turned out to be quicker. We've also found out that our whole advertised peaceful use of atomic energy was partly designed to cover the manufacture of more bomb material. That history of lying about nuclear being civilian, that it was being kept strictly apart from military nuclear work, was at least in part where our nation's anti-nuclear sentiment came from.

And because one of our former World War II allies, Russia, became our enemy and built its own A-bombs, we had the Cold War. That and hot conflicts like in Vietnam have created a new world for us to live in, with all its conflicts bringing so many of our soldiers home from overseas duty with post-traumatic stress disorders and other mental health problems.

We have a government that is left over from the cold war. It has had the modern end result of people like Copeland and me telling veterans at VA hospitals to take all the "time to heal" they need.

That is a reality that even the most conservative politician should want to get behind, though they rarely do. They seem to mainly focus on funding physical injury care and rehabilitation. Only recently has the U.S. military begun shifting resources into research on and treatment of PTSD, the post-traumatic stress disorder coming home from Iraq and Afghanistan with so many of our soldiers.

Democrats are marginally better at funding psychiatric care. I fear that whenever conservatives might regain control of government in my state, or even just regain the ability to exert major influence over it, they will sharply cut back on funding the already meager resources available to enable people with mental health problems to have time to heal. Obviously I and such conservatives are typically opposites, both financially and politically. I also hope that if they do regain control they will not reverse their most cherished anti-revenue platforms about government taxation in at least one specific area: I fear they would be willing to become avid tax collectors in taking back the VA benefits people like me receive for the parts of our lives we contributed to keeping them safe.

I worked hard to get where I am now. I have at least part of my money saved to be my school money. I am happy that I may soon be able to go back to school.

Regardless of reason for it, I needed the time off I have been forced to take by my incarceration at Saint Peter. Though I have benefitted from having that enforced time to essentially just rest, this whole nineteen-year process has given me gray hairs. But this time has also provided me with the opportunity to learn to write, to create art. "Artistic Integrity" is what the debate now, at least in part, feels like for me. I want more time to do good art. To write, paint, compose, and practice.

So, as a fifty-year-old self-published author and seldom used graphic artist, I want to contribute to my community in a meaningful manner. I feel that the best way to do that is to live someplace other than at Saint Peter and its famous security hospital.

But will I get the opportunity to do so? Will there ever be a peace dividend for the U.S. to invest in helping get and keep people like me healthy? The way politics and the military divide up our nation's economic windfalls, I often have my doubts. I have my doubts because of the closed-loop workings of the military industrial complex. I've said it before and believe it's worth saying again: the politician gets campaign money from the bomb factory; the factory wants to us to go to war so it can make money selling its bombs; the politician pushes the rest of the government to go to war; bombs from the factory are dropped on everyone in places like Iraq, Afghanistan and Pakistan, and politicians get campaign money from the bomb factory to keep the wars coming so it can keep making and selling its bombs. There are lots of casualties, women, children, and animals all killed by the bomb factory. The bomb factory makes money, Iraq, Afghanistan and Pakistan get bombed, and the politician gets more election cash from the bomb factory to perpetuate the cycle forever. The bottom line is there is no motivation for the people who benefit from the complex to stop. The military gets all that the bomb factory can make and then they get glory for a job well done.

Peace and spending money to heal or take care of the mentally ill are apparently just not as much fun as bombing the hell out of people in places we don't like, or as tasty as drinking expensive single malt scotch and sodas at Washington, D.C., bars with lobbyists and at private fund raising parties. Lots of good cigars, lots of scotch, lots of cognac, and lots of injured and ill Americans not getting the money and resources needed to help them heal.

Along with all the neoconservatives who seem to love wars, we get the counterculture out of all of this, the peaceniks and hippies who avoid the wars and condemn the actions of our military. We also get veterans who return to a society which can't find them jobs, that labels their military skills as insufficient or inappropriate for civilian occupations. And we get those other veterans who come back from the hell of a war physically injured and/or mentally damaged, who can't seem to leave that hell behind them.

I want to get Copeland's WRAP program to every veteran, to help them come back from their hell. Conservatives, for all their talk of supporting our troops, don't seem to want to spend the dollars to do that. Some of those veterans come back permanently disabled. How does it mesh with a conservative "help yourself" philosophy, when you're a veteran who isn't physically or mentally whole, who simply can't do it on his or her own?

Our military industrial complex says going to war is a good thing for its stockholders and, therefore, for all of us. By implication they'll say that it's good for the country for us to be at war because of the employment and taxes it provides. That philosophy suggests that we should thusly go to war whenever possible. It's really twisted logic, but that's the military industrial complex for you. They invoke all sorts of real and imagined justifications. They never seem to be able to say that their wars are only good for their investors; with not an iota of good for the vast majority of the people we end up sending to fight them.

That gets us again to soldiers who come home from those wars with broken bodies, broken hearts, and broken minds. Some of them wind up in hospitals and facilities for the mentally ill, like the one where I have lived for more than two decades.

Note the curious case of Guy Harvey Baker. He was a veteran of the First Gulf War, where our friend and president, George Bush, the elder, led a coalition, mostly backed by Great Britain and the United States, to invade Kuwait and liberate it from Saddam Hussein and his then wholly owned country, Iraq.

Back in the U.S., Baker went and led police on a five-block chase from a car in a church parking lot to a wooded area nearby. Baker killed two police officers and a police dog. Ultimately, he surrendered and claimed to be suffering from war-induced post-traumatic stress disorder. This malady in wars past was also known as shell shock and combat fatigue. PTSD is the label we've put on this condition since the Vietnam conflict.

Baker was sent here to the Minnesota Security Hospital's admissions unit for evaluation. While he was here his girlfriend took to throwing pliers, a saw and other tools up and over part of the building, aiming for the smoker's courtyard, planning for Baker to use them to break out of the facility from that courtyard. There is a sturdy cable screen over the top of the courtyard that would make breakout a stretch for even a lucky attempt with the right tools. In the aftermath, his girlfriend got six months in jail for her efforts, and Baker got a thirty-year sentence with his conviction. All that, from the original chase, started with a vagrancy charge and a loaded pistol.

Baker did little except convince all involved that he was far from insane.

Last night I dreamed of buying Indonesian clove cigarettes at a local gas station. Dream on kid. They took free access to our smoker's courtyard away because of Baker.

The military industrial complex protects itself in much the same way as psychiatry protects itself. They shrug off lawsuits. They hide under the mantle of law enforcement. They appeal to judges and legislators as to how necessary they are to the public's health and welfare. They work hard at being indispensable. They see themselves as the first priority for the nation. And it's nothing recent either.

In the days of legal slavery in the U.S., the doctors of that era had a handful of medical diagnoses and labels they could even slap on a slave who wanted to run away to Canada and be free. They would call him or her mentally ill for wanting to run away and be free. Despite being people who were not really people according to the law, their wanting to be free was considered an affront to the dominant society, an illegal endeavor, and a delusionary desire. They were labeled as suffering from *drapetomania*, curiously defining them as being sick simply for desiring personal freedom.

The American physician Samuel Cartwright "defined" that mental illness in 1851, citing our Bible's call for a slave to be submissive to his master. He also prescribed "whipping the devil out of them" as a preventative treatment.

Such labels and treatments were the accepted medical science of their day, and a case can be made that things haven't really changed much since. Doctors still seem to be pretty free to make up a label to define anything against their social preferences as a mental illness. Take homosexuality for an example. Until about 1970, the industry's *Diagnostic Statistical Manual*, used for categorizing and defining illnesses, listed homosexuality as a mental illness. I have several gay and lesbian friends. They do not suffer from a mental illness.

I do. They don't. I have a real mental illness: schizophrenia. But sometimes there is a real light of freedom from medical arbitrariness at the end of a tunnel, not just the headlight of a train coming at you through it. I am now experiencing a new era for psychiatry in Minnesota. Now, all of a sudden, our state government wants to be nice. I am mystified as to how long this is going to last, but hopeful that it will. More on this in a later chapter.

***

As it is practiced in most of what we would call the civilized world, psychiatry has become a wing of law enforcement, and sometimes its need for control has become law unto itself. Psychiatry, as it relates to criminal acts by mentally ill people, seems to not even be a science these days, if indeed it ever really has been. It is an arms race. It is a prison cycle: police, then courts, then mental institution, then legislature, then back to police again. The hospital gets funds to exist. The police get more power to arrest. The courts cooperate and provide more commitments. That is our deadly cycle.

It often seems to me that my time in the system has largely been wasted time. But I am still alive after twenty years of what I consider to be an inappropriate detention. I have become one of the few in my circumstances who have legitimately approached the long desired state of being certified as "cured." Some others who have been here at Saint Peter even longer than me have not been so fortunate.

The insidious nature of long-term indeterminate detention can be seen in the hoops we inmates have to go through to be released from that detention. Because a diagnosis of being mentally ill and dangerous begets an indeterminate sentence, the opinion of the psychiatrist assigned to your case becomes the dictator of when you can get out. No objective measure is available. No calculation based on time served is observed.

In a straight criminal assault case that involved a stabbing like the one that got me committed to Saint Peter, a "sane" person would have received a specific sentence, and probably would have been out of jail in no more than a couple of years.

Chapter 8: The Religious Testaments

THE HUMAN MIND is hard-wired to work better when there is some kind of spiritual belief system in place. The whole Christianity obsession thing is still going strong. Alcoholics and narcotics addicts swear by AA and NA and the god component in those programs. Even today when new groups search the soul, they almost always use a god component.

Some say a religion like Christianity is a form of performance art, or a designer drug, each specifically created to feed an intuitive hunger, like a fear of death at the end of life, or a fear of being alone in the world, or a fear of oppressive governments, or fear poverty and disease. Religion grants miracles and faith tailored and crafted to fit those needs as carefully and responsively as a chemist might create a new designer drug to exactly fit the joy receptors in a brain that they want to feed. Religion and drugs each feed spirituality. It really doesn't matter that reason tells us different. Religion wants you to pray to a god because it's known that your mind will be several gears ahead if you have a spiritual relationship with somebody you can trust. That is the end result.

In the west we prime most kids on a dose of Jesus before they go trotting off to join a human race filled with disease, exploitation and all the other cruel facts of life. We love our kids but we don't always teach them what is wise. We hope they will have success and long life, but there are no guarantees behind often problematic preparation.

Today much of Christianity is largely concerned with soul saving, charity and other good works. However, if you are in forced religion programs like Alcoholics Anonymous and Narcotics Anonymous, then you see spirituality being force-fed to people. But there can be a god entity that is not dependent on Jesus. A god concept can be a part of a mind that accepts as proof of "God" merely a subjective acknowledgement that the need for a god exists. It is part and parcel with the ideology that "god" only exists because "man" invented it.

Think of Jesus as an ambassador of that mindset. For 2,000 years our human race has been on that automatic pilot of religion based codes of compassion and kindness. With all we now know from science we may finally be able to turn the autopilot off, but we can still acknowledge that it has at least on occasion served some people well.

If you are a Christian you don't have to forget about Jesus, but you also don't need to unquestionably accept church dogma as absolute truth. Now in our modern era you can accept the dogmas of particular religions. You can get your faith straight out of any number of versions and translations of religious texts. You can subscribe to simplistic views of pray for miracles and magic-like wishes. You can be an atheist and not believe in anything at all like a god or gods. Or you can believe in a god of infinite complexity that rarely answers prayers, a god that simply set the universe and its laws of physics, chemistry and evolution in place to allow the universe to slowly evolve a human race to a point where our minds could allow the varied instances of religious saviors and scams to be cooked up. Evolution is the real miracle, so to speak.

If a hurricane or earthquake is the hand of a god, then so too has been every savior scam. And so were the Crusades. And so was the introduction by Europeans of diseases that killed 90 percent of the Americas' indigenous natives. And so was the Armenian genocide. And so was the World War II Jewish Holocaust. And so have been all the wars of faith. If you believe in an interventionist god then you should at least be consistent.

***

Rock musician Eric Clapton was once called Eric the Fish because he was said to drink like a fish. He was acknowledged by many to be quite a bit of a drunk. He also reportedly shot heroin, tripped on acid and snorted cocaine. Whenever dour Christians told him to correct his ways he pointed to the ritual of the wine. In his mind he was just as good a Christian follower as were strict "God-fearing" people. In his mind perhaps even more so as he certainly consumed more wine than most.

It seems that the "Old" Testament, particularly the Jewish Torah, the five books of Moses, has many references to holy waters and anointing oils. In a modern scientific paradigm we might categorize these references under labels such as toxicology and topical applications of drugs. The Bible across its entirety is filled with such uses, and be they as goblets of wine or other noxious mixtures and chemicals, they generally have a shared quality. "Take a sip of my glass" typically means share all of my merriment, drugs, and diseases. It may be part of the human communion, as we share all of our body chemistry, hallucinogens and bodily fluids.

This is what is meant by the ritual of the wine. From AA and NA to the seller's door, it all comes together as communion. We share and take as a community. Holy waters and wine and anointing oils of Christianity are all sort of drugs in this consideration. Your real question is whether you have faith that the hangover society is a good thing to endorse. If you say yes to kids taking communion at age thirteen, then give them a sip of wine and stand back as we light the fuse of the alcoholism bomb, then stand back as the enlightened crowd says it's all the fault of the wine and our general endorsement of its associated merriment.

We need to look at these creative interpretations and ask whether we believe the ritual is sound. If we say the creation of the ritual was a good idea, then we call ourselves Christians with the certainly that such creativity is exposing us to the will of the Christian god.

We accept that the so-called New Testament was supposedly specifically written by the various apostles. But biblical scholars are also pretty sure that the Old Testament, the Hebrew books of Moses and other sacred writing were written by live human beings as well, and not just transcribed as anything like recitations by angels. For the later you have to reach out to the Islamic Quran, but whether or not you can validly claim any of the various religious holy books were actually divinely inspired is a question you'll have to wrestle with yourself. Certainly many especially devout Christians do believe their entire bible was either divinely written or inspired, and many of them would not hesitate to try and force-feed other people their literalist Christianity.

Alternatively, we could just conclude that such an interpretation is antiquated and out of touch. For instance, consider this medical comparison: My father once led research on using the drug colchicine to treat pulmonary fibrosis. Colchicine derived from the autumn crocus plant had been around since 1500 BCE (Before the Common Era) as a treatment for swollen joints, but my father was tracking it in a side-by-side trial against the steroid prednisone. After three months the patients on the colchicine were doing so much better that the trial was halted and all the patients switched to the colchicine. The punchline? For all the drama of the superiority of the colchicine, the end result was that barely five years later, still newer medications proved both the colchicine and the prednisone to be antiquated. Newer drugs outpaced both of the drugs my father tested.

Five years in the past the test made sense but now it is obsolete. Other cures got us farther and were certainly healthier than older five-year-old agendas. My father treated the obsolescence of his research as a commonplace occurrence, that all of his work and research would be obsolete within a small span of time. Might a continuing belief in the efficacy of spiritual intervention in mental health be equally obsolete? AA and NA advocates would say not. And for many the success of that approach would be pointed to as proof of its efficacy. But for the mental health component of aberrant behavior it, perhaps, may be less sufficient.

We perhaps need to build something new that's not obsolete. Whether its thirty years or just five, we might need to come together and create something that works for our modern age, getting us all to more nice and healthy days.

In the biblical era, pretty much everything you had for an underlining theme knitting society together was related to various beliefs in gods. There was no radio, television or the Internet, or mass product advertising or political campaigns. We live in a time of social media and cellphones. If Christ were alive today, I'd guess that he would play an electric guitar and be on Facebook.

***

Music, as it is said, soothes the savage beast. Whether it's classic rock, blues, gospel, classical, country, reggae or any other genre, we have come to understand that music is a special language, a language all its own. Rock, for one, is the very lifeblood of modern America. It is the pulse that beats in our blood, as sacred as a drummers' circle sound is to Native Americans chant and prayer.

In the category of drugs, beyond the injectables and powders you inhale, there's the most powerful of communion hallucinogens: LSD. It will either rock your socks off or drive you mad, and maybe both.

Especially stay away from the synthetic drugs, like fentanyl, fake LSD or chemicals claimed to mimic marijuana. They can be especially destructive.

Real hallucinogens can create a feeling of ecstasy bordering on the religious for people already inclined to experience life in that direction. For others they just create euphoria or special senses of wellbeing, unless of course you end up having a proverbial "bad trip." And you can't know what you'll experience until you do. I am approaching thirty years of sobriety amidst a previous lifetime of good and bad drugs. Memories of the good ones I do not regret, but there certainly were some bad days I'd rather not remember.

Narcotics Anonymous likes to distinguish itself from Alcoholics Anonymous. The drug people call sobriety by the name "clean time." NA reflects more the ideas of multiple forms of drug recovery whereas the focus of the alcohol group is closer to seeing it as just another form of bad addictions that could also include gambling, overeating, over-sexuality, etc. In all of these, some can be social, but too much can be destructive. With narcotics, unless you are specifically addressing a diagnosed medical condition, it is almost always a bad idea.

There has to be a new middle ground between hippie heaven and city street life. From experiences I've had in tangles with the law, I can tell you that in prison there is almost always a presence and awareness of chemical dependency. Sometimes there is also the presence of an NA or AA community, but the god component of their spiritual systems often tends to be removed in favor of a DBT (Dialectical Behavioral Therapy) kind of non-god behavioral discipline. More on DBT in a later chapter.

If we are to use an atheist discipline of logic and science, we have to also understand that, under a simple three-step process of becoming part of a NA or AA community, first there needs to be a person looking for a life change. Second requires a leap of faith, of commitment to the new organization. Third is a community of support for any newcomer. But you also need to be careful in selecting your community because dangerous cults operate on a similar paradigm. Those same three parts worked for creating religions and cults. It works for many evangelical Christian communities as well as for cults like Scientology or the Moonies or David Koresh's Branch Davidians (who died at his command in Waco, Texas). There are too many others like them.

People can go to Bible colleges and pay thousands of dollars for the privilege to write papers on subtleties in the history of prayer. They will be just about as substantial a contribution to the world as a paper plane in a hurricane. They often become useless and meaningless followers of an obscure cult of style that goes on, isolated like some huge cult, oblivious to the ways and means of our greater world. Many will contribute little to the modern world, beyond tending the flame of Christianity like the priests in ancient temples. This form of a Christian likely makes for the utilitarian and vindictive parole officers and security staff found in prisons and mental "health" institutions.

Chapter 9: Truth and Consequences, Lies and Rewards

THE GOAL OF this chapter is to show how arbitrary the system can be in evaluating whether a person incarcerated at Saint Peter has healed enough to be released back into the wilds of open society. One of the things the psychiatric staff asks you to do in evaluating your mental health is to replay your crime in your mind, and to reconstruct it in conversations and essays that are designed to show how you have or have not taken responsibility for the behaviors and actions that got you committed to Saint Peter.

They ask you about how your treatments have helped you. They ask about how you'll go about managing your problem behaviors if you are let out. They ask about a whole bunch of similar concerns.

As they concern me, these evaluations of my mental health don't always generate only a single response. For instance, with one round of evaluations I actually created two versions of my response as to how I considered my circumstances, and how I now compared my perception of my "criminal" act to how it was documented in police reports. There was my truthful account, and then there was the version I actually submitted to my psychiatrist.

As I wrote in a 2007 version of a volume documenting my case, *Mental Health Imprisonment: One Case*, the version I published in that volume was not the one I actually submitted to Saint Peter staff. After the published version I wrote in all capital letters: "Be advised that if I turned that assignment in with these ideas in it I would be going to security again. I handed in a different report. This version is to us inmates a high comedy akin to burning our warden in effigy."

***

And lest you think this indictment of the system is only about a single person griping about a perceived personal injustice, I'll note that there's another inmate here in Saint Peter in a similar fix, albeit for the more serious crime of murder. This inmate colleague had no clue as to what he was getting himself into when he killed his father in, he said, self-defense. To that end he expected to go home after the basic legal affairs were taken care of. That turned out to not be the case.

My inmate colleague was given a sentence ranging from two years to fifty years. He was amazed and mystified. He was told he had won his case in that he was found not guilty. He had no idea that the appended phrase "by reason of mental illness" all too often actually meant a life sentence. He now wanders the halls here repeating the phrase "but I got found not guilty." The rest of us just have to tolerate his slow approach to awareness of his life sentence.

My lawyer refused to defend me except under only two possible conditions of guilty pleas. I could straight and simply plead guilty, be sentenced to prison, and then face a mental health court later on to be declared mentally ill and dangerous. Alternatively, I could go directly to mental health court, get declared not guilty by reason of mental illness, and immediately begin the indeterminate two- to fifty-year sentence of life in a forensic mental institution.

It could be argued that these lawyers are essentially letting the system hold their clients hostage to the mental ill and dangerous guilty pleas, allowing them to be held in prison for years waiting to bring their cases to court. It was my opinion that my lawyer was essentially blackmailing me, allowing me to remain imprisoned for two years in an effort to make me capitulate and choose one of the two guilty pleas. My inmate colleague's lawyer simply declined to inform his client of the two- to fifty-year clause in the law. I knew better, but that still didn't help. I remain incarcerated at Saint Peter State Hospital almost three decades later.

The mentally ill and dangerous type of mental health commitment is a legal instrument designed to silence dissent and incarcerate without viable legal opposition. It and the process serve to display the judicial system's pure power and dominance, and usually effectively mean life imprisonment for the accused. Most of the time, unless you're from a family with deep resources or connections, lawyers don't really fight these cases. They seem to only see their roles as moderating the beginning years of a life sentence, rarely asking for any of the various forms of parole that might otherwise be available.

The totality of the hostage incarceration deed, in the absence of any immediate guilty plea, is done primarily through a "competency evaluation." If the competency evaluator subjectively deems a defendant such as myself incapable of knowledgeably pleading guilty, then the defendant is simply declared incompetent to stand trial and is sent to the competency restoration wing of a psychiatric prison. There the defendant will wait until he or she either relinquishes the right to plead not guilty or a period of three years passes, whereupon the defendant is deemed mentally ill and dangerous without a finding of guilt or innocence. Ultimately guilt or innocence has little to do with anything, as you will get a sentence of two to fifty years anyway.

***

I accept now that my crime was serious. I stabbed a young woman in the leg with a knife. To remind you of the circumstances, I believed at the time that doing so would create enough of a crime that I would be granted the trial rights that would allow me to get the legal system to pay attention to the drug dealing going on, from my observation, in plain sight at the Hard Times Café. My attorney was, in my opinion, what has come to be called "ineffective counsel," meaning I had no effective legal representation. Essentially, both my victim and I were petty level drug consumers in an area where there were so many drugs available that the area might as well have been called a wildlife drug sanctuary for people like us to enjoy and to live in peacefully.

I was charged with "Assault Two" and moved to the Minnesota Security Hospital, which has better mental health services than prison but has radically different time schedules for release. I have done nearly twenty years on a six-month charge. I had two years of jail incarceration where a strictly criminal charge should have gotten me out with time served.

The two years served and out would likely have been the case had only my criminal charge been in play. Being found guilty of a mental health crime has proven, in my case, to have netted me a sentence ten times longer than what I would have gotten from a mere criminal charge.

However, doing the assignment as the staff preferred it to be done would have been to blame myself, blame the illegal drugs, blame the lack of psychiatric care and medication, and blame my deviance. They call this "taking responsibility for your mental illness." It is also a key component in subjugation and in displaying submissive behaviors and identity traits. They want dominance and it is your job to deliver that to them.

In this system, pointing out any flaw in the victim's behavior, that is to say in her drug use, is considered to be counterproductive. You are advised to be proactive at prosecuting yourself. That's what "having insight" and "taking responsibility" is all about. More on this later. The insight you are directed to in the process of "taking responsibility" is that she was not the cause of the dispute, but that her victimization was the result of a combination of illegal drugs and untreated mental illness. I take responsibility for all that the state will never fully comprehend.

Typos and grammatical gaffs mostly included, the 2007 version is reprinted below with one short paragraph rewritten for factual clarity.

Sadly, I have lost the original document I actually turned in. Clearly it would have been a serious contrast and counterpoint to this version. The actual submission would have been much more sedate, focused on giving the staff the feedback I felt they expected. I would have written that assignment with a calm reasoned tone and I would have been attentive to the needs of the taskmaster. It would not have included humor and would not have sacrificed a sober perspective in an alternative meaning of the word "sober," not as in sobriety from drug and alcohol use, but as in humble and thoughtful. I would have used the opportunity to try to send the message to my keepers that I wanted to work with them.

***

Compare the sentiment noted in the preceding paragraph against the section below that comprises the bulk of this chapter. I think you'll see some pretty clear differences. Such gaming of the system is believed to be the only way out of the hospital at Saint Peter for many of the people sent by the courts to reside and be treated there.

This is also an example of just how ill and even self-righteous I was in the early experience at being incarcerated. What you are about to read has ugly moments but it is also a clear look into just how deluded a street criminal with an anger problem and schizophrenia can come to be in one contained package.

Within this document there are many inconsistencies brought on by my state of being when I wrote it down many years ago. You can also specifically see the disjointed thinking that can go on in the mind of a person who is mentally ill. Here and there you'll notice an occasional truly insightful statement, but they are buried in a lot of repetition, a lot of trite statements, a lot of stuff that's not too far removed from gibberish, and details about my life and my family that are totally irrelevant from what I was supposedly writing about. I could spend several pages creating an edited version that would clean up all of this, but that would deprive you of the sense of my mind at that time. Be thus forewarned.

***

My Account of Crime vs. Police Report (the 2007 published version):

The police left out all of the behavioral stuff that was auxiliary to the café and the drugs there.

If I was able to find someone capable of bearing witness to the fact that my assessment of the drug scene was not a delusion then things would have been a lot different.

Two points from the police report are key.

#1 My statement that Ms. H was talking about me and that thusly I had a paranoid delusion that caused me to harm someone else.

#2 That my stabbing Ms. H was somehow connected with the stabbing four years earlier of Ms. M, my first victim. I was not the one who assaulted her and stabbed M in the leg.

Conclusion

Without data on the drug scene I had little room for movement. These are the things I thought up and turned to cover up my own involvement in something so clandestine that I could not make reference to it in court until the drug raid of January 2000.

Mr. K knew of the neighborhood long ago but was not part of the Twin Cities justice machine.

I really don't think it's paranoid to say the cops knew about it all along.

I did have a mental illness that interfered with my attorney-client relationship.

My illness had very little to do with my crime. I did not hallucinate a need to stab this person. I did lose my temper.

The behavior chain that led to me stabbing Ms. H began with me directing traffic in front of the café.

I angered those selling drugs because my behavior could have brought in the police.

I will always see me and my family through the eyes of being victims of bad medicine.

The State released Carey Padilla who murdered my sister.

My look at violent crimes is always framed by comparison between known standards. I know that.

Blair W's sister stretched a ninety-day hearing out to three years.

I know that Leonard J. is now on medication at his county's request, not his doctor's request.

I know that James J. is at MSH because things just didn't work out for him at Johnson Hall.

I watched Scott C try to run away. We patients note, observe and compare. We know you don't like us to compare but we do so.

Look for a moment at a stab wound to the lower leg. Clearly this is not a wound designed to murder. If I was psychotic and paranoid I would have tried to really hurt this person badly. That was not the case. I traumatized and hurt this person and I wish I had not done so.

The VA hospital is not going to care whether you all think it is minimization or not. It's going to treat amputees from Iraq and Agent Orange victims from Vietnam.

I am part of that community. I see the wheelchairs and prosthetic legs and arms and I watch the WW II vets smoke themselves to cancer on Pall Malls in the winter in their outdoor smoking glass house.

I will compare MSH to VA to Mayo to Navy Balboa in San Diego. I have no choice at this. These hospitals are in my consciousness and they get compared.

I regret picking on an innocent person. She was not making the big decisions on the dope dealing.

I lost my temper and stabbed this convenient target. I have taken an anger management class but I feel it really wasn't effective.

The missing link was the drug arrest of January 2000. With the bust, my charge changes from hallucinating a need to stab this person to a lost temper between illegal drug users.

That means I don't have to rely on people like Mr. K for input on the West Bank.

Folks like you all discharged Mr. Carey Padilla and he murdered my sister. Your team isn't quite batting 400. I am impressed by transition services and Pexton Hall 1986 in their ability to screw up.

Your professional cousins let Mr. Padilla go and he murdered my sister soon after. That's fact. There is nothing that can be done now to change that.

Impact My Mental Illness Has Had on Your Life, and Impacted Victim?

Like I said, my victim incurred a wound and a traumatic memory. I try to avoid conversing about her with my friends on the West Bank. The more time we aren't concerned with each other, the more time we spend recovering and moving on from that unfortunate intersection in our lives. I avoid her and as far as I can tell she avoids me. She got some stitches. She has a scar. She has a memory. She has her health. She has no lasting injury. Would you all prefer that I did more damage? I hope not.

For me the feeling of being in a personal conversation with radio and TV is a consistent thing. It happens all the time. There is no trigger for this feeling. It is continual from dawn until dusk.

My illness impacted my family as I was unemployed and out of school traveling all around the USA from New York to Los Angeles. My family couldn't do anything about my illness. Olanzapine came out on the market in spring of 1997. So I was impaired from 1983 during my service to the Marines until 1997. That's fourteen years I was impaired.

I could function. I held down jobs and went to school. I expect I would still be under maximum security would it not be for the Olanzapine.

My recovery does include medication. I prefer my medicated state to its opposite. My family and friends prefer my state to be medicated rather than not so.

During the fourteen years between the Marines and Olanzapine my family suffered. My friends were at a loss as to how to help me.

I was very careful to use the word "jail" in reference to my detention here. That's how it's done on the street. Mental health treatment is viewed as being worse than jail.

You got Stillwater. You got Pelican Bay. You got MSH.

MSH is worse than Pelican Bay Supermax of California.

Three Cafés

Of the three cafés only two are still running. Those two are Seward and Hard Times. Riverside closed because of the bookkeeping staff spending profits on cocaine.

The bookkeeping cocaine scenario was a chronic problem for Riverside. Very sad. We of the other cafés did what we could to avoid this behavior.

Seward was very prudent. We kept our dope dealers at arm's length. We never cashed checks for dope heads or dealers.

If you get busted for drugs and you own a motorcycle the DEA can take all your possessions including your motorcycle, your fur coat and your water ski boat. The DEA can take it all.

The DEA can take your café if you're caught dealing drugs on the premises.

My current thinking is that the last two cafés who do this sort of thing are going to be really, really careful. They are self-motivated after the Hard Times Café drug raid. Very motivated.

Managing Target Behaviors

A. Getting enough sleep.

B. Staying sober from drugs and alcohol.

C. Staying on medication.

D. Healthy lifestyle to include exercise and diet.

E. Going to AA or NA.

F. Staying away from cigarettes.

When I am released I hope to become a homeowner and go to school. I plan on taking Chemistry and English with an emphasis on Medical Journalism.

This will include writing fiction for sale in the book market.

I plan on continuing my writing through journaling here and putting together a good book based on the task of being an MSH/transition patient.

Currently I owe the state 1.5 million dollars for my bill.

Had Mr. K been able to cross-reference the drug scene at West Bank most of that cash wouldn't have gotten spent.

Mr. K may be worth 1.5 million dollars to my case, maybe.

I suppose you don't want me smoking cigarettes with Calvin Triplet.

I expect my U.S. Marines t-shirt with the skull emblem of WW II special forces may have to go home.

Yes, am most aware that transition services would prefer my illness to come in the form of a debilitating illness temporarily in remission with drugs. This illness would be the root cause of a violent act and great shame would be felt before one could re-enter society as a penitent obedient mental patient. In my case there is only a very slim shaky connection between my illness and my crime.

In 1993 Ms. H said there was no drug connection to the crime.

In January 2000 there were fourteen arrests made during the drug raid of Ms. H's former employer, Hard Times Café.

It is a common thing for drug traffickers to decline to mention that they are breaking the laws, particularly when talking to police.

I guess the end result is I get to look out at a small group of people and see them as something of a collection of souls played, conned, fooled, and ripped off.

I know I'm not coughing up 1.5 million dollars cuz a treatment team has the insight of molasses.

I am going to send this data to my typist and prepare it for publication.

The section on my sister's death was an appendix or forward section to the main body response.

The point to her death includes many aspects. A wrongful death lawsuit should have been filed. Padilla should have had prison time.

In 1986 Johnson Hall was a chemical dependency center, and Pexton was a mix of both mentally ill cases (MI) and mentally ill and dangerous (MI&D) cases coming from MSH Security.

Mr. Padilla was discharged and soon after he killed my sister.

The point I am making is that the Pexton treatment team was incompetent at determining whether or not Padilla was dangerous or not consistently stable. Your forbearers at Pexton 86 failed miserably at the task of divination. There is significant evidence to put forward the hypothesis that many more cas-

es are no more insightful on SPRTC staff and MSH staff and transition staff that the art of divination is a fraud.

A notable percentage of these cases are unsound and without merit.

I would prefer murderers to do the full complement of their time in prison regardless of their mental state at the time of the killing.

"I was in a bad mood" smacks too much like "Twinkie Defenses."

The point of putting my sister's death into the mix is that I have clear proof that your forbearers were incompetent and that you may be so incompetent as well.

I am a veteran of the Marines. The corps is an extended fraternity of the willingness to risk life and limb in the service of our country.

The corps is a combat fraternity. We are fellows acquainted with the use of deadly force. At the VA Hospital, I see wounds that make me say: "This is as bad as it gets."

Clearly Ms. H is not in that category. These observations are fact grounded in reality. Any deviation from those facts comes as an effort to cover up reality or hide the truth.

To pass a decision and declare these observations to be "Not Acceptable" is to strive to avoid reality and enter a fantasy world.

In the mental health business we generally strive to achieve reality and not fantasy.

On the street amongst bikers, Johns, Junkies, Punks, Hippies, and innocent bystanders, the view of "MSH" as "jail" is not uncommon. Department of Corrections time is counted on as MSH time. A year at MSH takes a year off at prison or jail.

Again, what's distressing is the avoidance of reality in the language used. I choose to not use such a fraud in my life.

Most of the complaints about my writings last week were key points where I did note the Fraud Du Jour or Fraud of the day.

For me it is a case of the emperor wearing no clothes. Ms. H who worked at Hard Times Café during the era of Jason Heissler's employment most assuredly knew about his dope dealing out of the café.

I was told that if I had such a belief I must be crazy and that I should go to MSH because I had hallucinated the whole thing.

Now that it's been proven to be reality, can I go home?

In light of the evidence gathered since 1993, it looks like you have got a *serious reality problem that you like to call "minimization."*

The police raided Ms. H's employer for drugs.

That sort of thing doesn't happen at Dairy Queen or Perkins or IHOP.

Fourteen arrests is not a hallucination. When you're an ex-patient or by other means registered as a troublemaker and/or on parole people tend to threaten blackmail more often than otherwise.

I really do believe all of the benefits of being at MSH could be taught at a two-day seminar.

The rest is fraud and incompetence. A waste of time and money.

If the news camera or politicians ask me what I think of it all, I will say I believe it to be fraud and incompetence.

Bruce W, Doug B, Mark B, Kenny C, Larry D all have a need for some form of care at some point in these last sixty years, but I just don't feel this place is the appropriate venue for them.

It's loop holed.

It's rigged.

It's fake.

By calling it medicine the court can imprison. It's not real medicine so it fails at its mission when real medical needs pop up.

What's going to happen to these people as they get older?

I came from a real medicine family. Grandpa worked for the Army Medical Corps as a general surgeon in World War II. Dad worked for the Mayo Clinic. Great Grandfather had a medical practice in Illinois.

The sex offender program is the real fraud. The emperor's new clothes is key there. Treatment will not cure them.

No ex-post-facto law according to the constitution.

Those are nasty people. I hope something gets changed there cuz as is it may collapse someday. They (mostly) haven't got diseases that can be cured by the use of medication.

I like my medication. It's good for me. It improves my life.

Presently, however, County Attorneys are insisting people be part of a drug regimen against doctors' recommendations. Like the Johnson case. How's that for all those people trying to avoid forced drugging. The county attorney wrote and enforced the prescription, not the doctor. Amazing!

Incompetence means you didn't know better. Fraud means you knew what you were doing.

Governor Pawlenty and Humphrey, State Attorney General, knew what they were doing was wrong so far. I will bet cash you all would agree that on the issue of health care for State employees and wage increases for the same workers, it's not incompetence, it's fraud.

The sex offender program is a fraud. Those devils can't be reached through treatment. Better to give them sentences of 300 years and be done with it in criminal court. It's fraud to deem them treatable.

The MI&D program is only partially a fraud. Some key components are a fraud but it's not alike to the Sex Offender Program which is a fraud from its basement to the tops of its camera towers.

When medically advised, the issue of medication can be a good thing.

Sobriety from drugs and alcohol is also so advisable across the board that if we could get the rest of the population to sober up too our gross national product numbers would go up due to our worker population doing so much better at their jobs. Thus if prohibition had worked it would have been a very good thing.

Some of the counseling at MSH can be of value but it's not worth 550 dollars per day. That's a fraud I will not be paying for.

These criticisms cannot take away from the superb job done by security counselors and nursing staff on the bulk of patients coming in and going through the MI&D program.

Many people have done good work and my criticisms and critical reporting has largely been on or directed at the flaws. These flaws may be many but so are the most of the rank and file of the MI&D program being many good apples, good eggs, and good personnel.

My sister was told to be patient, compliant, obedient and occasionally assertive without being uncomfortable to the staff that worked with her. She was as de-clawed as a "fixed" housecat.

My experience with the Marines has given me some insight into such issues. As we said there, "Getting killed tends to screw up your whole day."

Death shouldn't alienate you. You should be able to talk about death, to embrace it, with hope of gaining insight and understanding. Death is not something we can stop or avoid. It can be delayed and we must strive to delay it as much as possible, hanging onto each extra day as if it were a gift to be cherished.

"Getting killed really does tend to screw up your whole day."

Lawsuit time for wrongful death carries a two-year statute of limitations. Murder has no statute of limitations on it. Murder can be charged forever as long as the perpetrator is still alive. Maybe there could be some merit to an accessory to murder charge.

Well that's probably not going to be time or statute of limitations affected scenario. No sense in hurrying. All the major players will probably still be around.

Why Rush

If you weren't part of PEXTON 1985-1988, then you have nothing to worry about. This doesn't concern you ... much.

If I can raise the money to do so I will pay lawyers to attempt to retry Padilla on murder charges and overturn his MI&D finding. I estimate the cost of this to be at least twenty thousand dollars.

The cost of care bill will have to be dealt with too. Another court experience will have to occur to remedy that. Ms. H is quite well. She has life and wellness. A traumatic memory and a scar.

That's how my illness and my sister's illness have affected me. That's where I am at with the whole thing.

***

My writing is best when it is candid, composed, and not too grandiose, even though the situations I describe are often a bit more so. It's like trying to get a steak out of a McDonald's restaurant. Try ordering a ribeye or a T-bone steak and the counter help will probably just stare at you uncomprehendingly. In a similar manner, over most of the time I've been at Saint Peter, staff has specialized in pacification on a budget. That's the medication. The more valuable therapy is really going to come after I get out to the real world, and have to relearn how to navigate through it after being away so long and missing so much social and technological change. I've already started. I've bought myself a laptop computer that I can use to surf the Internet when the powers that be at Saint Peter permit it.

The real therapy will be in applying all the theory I've learned over the past two decades, and through that creating a stable life. Here the greatest assurance I can give is a sworn effort to not punch somebody or, worse yet, to use a weapon to harm them.

The next chapter, "Forensic Dual Recovery and Religion," more properly known as "Forensic Co-Occurring Disorders: Recovery and Religion," includes elements on what prosecuting yourself looks like. As you read through that, think about what I wrote but couldn't turn in, and judge for yourself what the real needs and pitfalls are in this process.

The central section of this current chapter was obviously somewhat confrontational, but I think it spoke as well for its time and my place as anything could.

The next chapter includes an extreme example of "prosecuting yourself" that is actually a good example of how things worked prior to about 2003. This place has more recently gotten more and more adult in its perspective, largely because of advances in medication, but also because of some important changes in the management of Saint Peter that will be addressed later. The physical changes have effected a change in my emotional well being. The new, better drugs have helped tremendously.

Chapter 10: Forensic Dual Recovery and Religion

THIS PORTION, ABOUT Forensic Dual Recovery (more technically known as Forensic Co-Occurring Disorders Recovery) is in many ways a response to rifts within several care-based communities. These groups include the National Alliance on Mental Illness (NAMI), The American Psychiatric Association, Scientology, Alcoholics Anonymous, Narcotics Anonymous, and a small outfit of critics of psychiatry called mindfreedom.org. I am writing this book mostly for the community that includes AA and NA. At times, the various groups listed above are in open conflict with each other, so I have tried to survey much of the literature and the apparent ways and means these groups put on public display.

Obviously, I have also dealt with these issues as a consumer of psychiatric services.

For those of you who are not professional drug addicts, AA and NA mean Alcoholics Anonymous and Narcotics Anonymous. I sit with the NA crowd, but any meeting will do just fine.

I also come to you with the tag of having a "dual diagnosis," now called "Co-Occurring Disorder" by the psychiatric industry. This means I have both mental illness and chemical substance abuse issues.

In 1983, while I was in the military, stationed in Japan, I began to experience a form of schizophrenic hallucination called "ideas of reference." The exact type of my break from normality was a feeling that all media was in a private conversation with me.

This meant that I saw secret messages in all TV, radio, and print media. Some of those conversations eventually found their way into science fiction stories I've written. I've also written two editions of a book on civil law as it relates to my circumstance, constructed as a criticism on mental health law.

This is as good a point as any to note in passing that, from my writer's point of view, the very notion of science fiction is that it is ultimately a somewhat flawed medium. Like play dough on the beach, it takes on sand and retains it, which sort of means that, if you are the type of writer for whom "writers block" is simply not a functional problem, you can end up cranking out a lot of text. You may double your volume, but that will not necessarily double your quality. This sandy play dough approach to writing just doesn't work for me anymore, and even though I still occasionally write fiction, I just cannot any longer take science fiction seriously. This text is obviously not about bug-eyed aliens and flying saucers.

So how does this reference to writing science fiction relate to AA/NA and publications like this one?

In twelve-step circles, there is a notation that anonymity is important. Sometimes it's good to have and a group will enforce it rigorously. Other times or in other groups, it is a formality discarded easily. The bottom line is that if you are a participant in such a group, you should be careful to not write about real people. Real peoples' stories, if told in any manner that might identify them to any other person who knows them, is invasion of privacy. From that perspective one has to be careful about how one tells a story. That's why so much reality writing changes names and details sufficient to protect privacy.

At this point my counselors at Saint Peter would say about this digression: "Let's get back to symptoms."

While mostly a work of informed opinion, this book is designed to inform in a practical manner on issues that seldom get a good airing out. The ways and means of psychiatry are most often confined to professional journals and similar realms that are out of most peoples' visible range.

To survey this subject adequately requires an aptitude for learning about psychiatry and mental illness, access to relevant professional journals, and the availability of time to do the broad reading necessary. I've tried to become such a person, and I do hope that the way I've digested and regurgitated all that material in this text helps you in your quest for knowledge about how the mental health system works.

In a manner not too dissimilar to how recaptured escaping Black slaves were recommended to be treated in pre-civil war south, with Cartwright's made-up insanity diagnosis, the old ways of doing business in the therapeutic community were to attempt to beat and torture somebody into being cured of their violent or deviant behaviors. I don't believe that many modern readers would find this concept anything but flawed. At its core, punitive health care is nothing but a fraudulently flawed concept. Nonetheless, it has existed in Minnesota since the early 1900s.

Pioneered as "therapeutic imprisonment laws," it has been expanded over the decades to the point that we now have an entire industry devoted to falsely imprisoning the mentally ill, and also the people we identify as sex offenders. I especially call this system a fraud because, in the minds of much of the public, it paints the mentally ill as being in the same cohort as sexual predators. They are most certainly not the same!

As a person with mental illness, I don't like government using a clone of our mental health laws to keep those sexual deviants locked up. It makes things more difficult for us who are ill, not criminal, when the same facility treating us is being used as a prison for sexual deviants in the guise of its actually only being a hospital for treatment. In the public mind, it tends to lump us ill but good guys in with those truly dreadful sexual predators.

***

The creators of text books on dual disorder recovery are medical doctors and well credentialed psychologists. Here at the Minnesota Security Hospital, we have approximately 400 inmates in a forensic forced treatment facility being provided therapy for mental illness. As much as 85 percent of those approximately 400 guests of the state have also used street drugs. Following the principles in the texts, the fine job done by therapists in dual recovery (Co-Occurring Disorder) settings has brought many a person with both mental illness and chemical dependency to recovery and the restoration of good health.

I find the concept of forced care to be similar to many of the ways and means of cancer treatment. In chemotherapy, the drugs are, in a sense, a disease that is designed to fight another disease. In chemo, you are given a drug that tries to stop all cells from dividing, the good along with the cancerous, often killing good cells with the bad. This stops the cancer, but it also stops all those healthy cells from thriving. The hope is that the treatment kills off the cancer cells at a faster rate than it does the healthy ones. Think of chemotherapy as a controllable disease targeted to fight the uncontrolled disease of cancer.

Similarly, mental health "care" in the forensic arena is the disease designed to fight the malady that is mental illness. You treat one disease with another disease.

I could write another book on jails, prisons and hospitals where psychiatric care and chemical dependency treatment are brought together with the intent to create a beautiful recovered person, ready to fly back into the real world, phoenix-like in recovery from mental illness.

Unfortunately, such a book would have to devote equal space to circumstances where the people administering the treatments could, with evil intent, just as easily create a ghastly hybrid more likely to destroy souls. I have seen both.

The word "forensic" means "of or used in courts of law." However, in laymen's terms the use of the word "forensic" has the euphemistic meaning of "jail." Effectively, I have been a prisoner since July 1993. I am grateful for the sobriety it has forced on me, but the situation has long since gotten old and I would like to move on soon.

The core of this book is this section on the dual recovery model in a forensic setting. When the creators of Alcoholics Anonymous were throwing its structure together, they were speaking of it in terms of it being an alternative to their ending up in institutions. We at the Minnesota Security Hospital fill the role of being institutionalized, either because the AA model didn't work for us, or because we never even gave it a try. It's the security hospital reality that makes this dual diagnosis book a tome on the forensic type and variety of incarceration. I've done almost all of my life's writing over the decades I've been a resident in, as I've called it before, the "Saint Peter puzzle palace."

A hospital makes for an interesting prison, and I use that word advisedly. A hospital like Saint Peter is used as preventative imprisonment for crimes not yet committed. Calling it medicine gives the state permission to imprison forever, with no criminal defense rights allowed the accused. It's not criminal court, so why should you need any kind of rights?

My understanding of the whole mental health scene has come primarily through the courts and my internment at Saint Peter. A Hazelden Center book on dual disorder recovery is mainly focused on people who actively seek out mental health care as a supplement to chemical dependency treatment. Our Saint Peter population is largely the reverse, chemical dependency added on top of a real mental illness. Our experience here as patients at Saint Peter is also one where we try to avoid all the punitive care that we can duck or dodge. We consider the state to be an assaulter, and we the assaultees. Our unique perspective is, I feel, quite a noteworthy and distinctive one.

You can use this book to educate the potential candidate for residency in a chemical dependency setting, and this would include a whole lot of young people who just experiment a little with what they consider to be harmless recreational drugs. Young people too often are knuckleheads who think they are indestructible, but even they should want to avoid two decades of imprisonment. To that purpose, here is a text that compiles many myths about psychiatry and substance abuse and mental illness, brought together as a package deal.

One of the myths associated with teen drug use is an easy way to illustrate my point about youths. An affected young person almost always ends up intoxicating to extremes. That's a comment on their inexperience with how drugs affect people, not necessarily a description of their desire for escapism. Such kids should learn in a "scared straight" manner just how serious their situation can get.

***

There is something of a holy trinity to Minnesota Mental Health law: #1, was there a serious crime? #2, was there a mental illness present? #3, is there likelihood that this crime might be repeated?

When the state decides to answer yes to all three, then even if it is merely an accusation, the state can imprison a person until trial with none of a person's annoying civil rights getting in the way. And after a perfunctory trial, the state can effectively imprison you forever, with even less in the way of civil rights.

Less than nothing is given. This is a life imprisonment concept. For me it has been nearly two decades of my life as a detainee. It is not merely MI/CD, as in mental illness and chemical dependency, but MI&D, as in *Mentally Ill and Dangerous*. The *dangerous* label creates the indeterminate sentence which can mean for life. You can get a parole board type hearing every six months but you have to wait a year-and-a-half if you want a hearing before a real judge in a real court. Every eighteen months you can repeat your request for a hearing before a judge. Your likelihood of success is problematic.

Your path is strewn with obstacles and long periods of delay. Here is forensic dual recovery, as it applied to my history, for your viewing pleasure. We start off at the Mayo Clinic.

I actually have several claims to fame as a person with mental illness. I was, in fact, born into the culture of medicine, as my father, William Wallace Douglas, was a pulmonary specialist and physician at the world famous Mayo Clinic in Rochester, Minnesota. Rochester, as you can imagine, is a rather top heavy community with one of the highest ratios of doctors to citizens found anywhere in the world. As a Mayo offspring, I was committed the first time by a former president of the World Psychiatry Association, Dr. Howard P. Rome. His credentials are more than superb. He was president of the Mayo Clinic's medical staff. Ernest Hemingway was one of his patients. He also wrote a psychiatric autopsy of Lee Harvey Oswald for the Warren Commission. In the arena of mental health one is committed for objectionable behaviors. I was provided no exception.

When I was three years old, there were doctors in abundance in my neighborhood. There were so many doctors, in fact, that we grew up as much with Dr. Gentling, and Dr. Robertson, and Dr. Petrie, as we did with Dr. Garbageman, Dr. Mailman, or Dr. Milkman. All the adult males in our neck of the world seemed to be doctors.

The impact of growing up in such an environment is that medicine is important to me. When I can leave Saint Peter I may seek something like a nursing degree, but I do not feel I have either the time or the interest to pursue a full medical doctor degree.

For five generations, my family's men have been doctors, curing illness. I broke from that path and practiced an illegal form of pharmacological medicine without the license. I trafficked in drugs and was party to some dedicated use patterns amongst a small cadre of loyal consumers. In Alcoholics Anonymous people used to say that they had an allergy to alcohol, but the concept of an allergy in medicine is different from the model used in twelve-step behaviors.

Allergies are allergies. Your limbs swell, you have trouble breathing, etc. You don't get allergies to alcohol. You get dependency. While I am not here to lecture on syntax or conjugation to people seeking sobriety, knowing what terms properly mean is relevant.

When your face swells up and it gets difficult to breathe, you may be experiencing an allergic reaction. My mother was allergic to caviar. If she ate caviar, she would get such a reaction, and she would be in serious medical danger.

To say alcohol addiction is as bad as or worse than an allergy is true use of the English language. To say it actually is an allergy is really an abuse of the language, but since it seems to help some alcoholics to be able to say, "I have an allergy to alcohol," for me to take away one of their linguistic tools supporting sobriety would be a sin.

Much of the available literature, and dual diagnosis materials, has been put together in a very academic model, relying on credentialed professionals, funded research, journal peer reviewers, and so forth. By contrast, the traditions of the Alcoholics Anonymous and Narcotics Anonymous networks are such that they come to us from the FUBU principal of "For Us, By Us." As it is often said in punk rock, it is DIY, or "Do It Yourself" treatment.

There is a value to having amateurism and a homemade quality forming some parts and aspects of our psychiatric and chemical dependency curative machine. There are many other aspects where speaking with an expert on brain surgery, or someone with brain chemistry expertise, are valuable too.

The duality of therapy in such circles requires a noteworthy contribution from professionals, but there is a substantial part that needs to be FUBU. Keeping in contact with your doctor can be one of the best and most fruitful associations you have when dealing with the combination of mental illness and addiction. I point out that chemical dependency is classifiable as a mental illness all on its own.

We need sobriety and not just symbolism. We need to be able to take the wreckage and debris of mental illness and chemical dependency and re-forge those pieces of your former self into a dynamic new life. You may well need doctors to help, but the best person and the greatest tool you can bring to the table is yourself.

Hippies used to say, "don't trust anyone over thirty," and Strategic Air Command used to pair a photo of a B-52 with the words, "Someone over Thirty you can Trust." Both perspectives matter and have value. You are here now, so I welcome you. You have made it this far. I hope you continue and garner great success, but just don't trust anybody just because they have credentials or pedigrees (including me). Work with them and if they work well with you, you may want some of what they have. That is a set of choices you will have to develop on your own.

The bottom line is that you are the only one who can deliver yourself to that next meeting. Most AA and NA meetings are psychiatrically friendly and they will not scold people for taking psychiatric medication. Not all are that way, but most are aware of such needs.

I know drug dependency counselors who could write volumes about this. They will also tell you that mental illness is intensified by drugs such as LSD, methamphetamine and marijuana. Also, it should be noted that the green leaf and sticky bud (i.e. marijuana) is already legalized for sale in one form or another in a majority of U.S. states and Washington, D.C. As of 2020, there is legal medical marijuana in 22 states. Another 11 states have legalized marijuana for recreational and medical use. An unknown number of other jurisdictions have effectively decriminalized it by declining to arrest or prosecute people with small amounts clearly intended for personal use. I'd expect that within the next decade or so marijuana will be widely and legally available nationwide, with its use regulated only like cigarette and alcohol sale and use, and taxed similarly.

The reason I point this out is that when it is legalized we will need a national consensus on how new permissiveness about this drug will get added to our accepted ways of doing business. Cops and robbers both will need something functional to replace the ill will generated over the nine decades since marijuana was made illegal.

You'll probably not be surprised to know that I have personally sampled marijuana. It does carry a stout effect. It *effects*, as it is an influence on thinking and behavior that has measurable properties. It *affects*, in that it has an end product impact on an individual, an admittedly less measurable metric. Even as a mild depressant, marijuana can still create dependency behaviors. You may start to wish you were stoned, as the marijuana intoxication experience is labeled, and some people experience the desire of wanting to be stoned all the time. The older definition of dependency was you consume drugs to feel good, to feel more "normal." Your time spent sober is not as desirable, as your time spent under the influence of drugs becomes your desired norm.

According to some sources, more than 80 percent of those hospitalized as mentally ill report that they have used illegal drugs. For some, the goals propounded by AA and NA will be quite adequate. I personally I feel drawn to the NA side of the house most of the time. I've come to like being sober and self-aware, and NA meetings help me stay that way. Finding a dual disorder focused meeting is probably only likely at a treatment center in a larger city.

The medical establishment at Saint Peter says that mentally ill patients cannot have a twelve-step program without a staff member or staff psychiatrist in attendance, which obviously throws a large wrench into a meeting's normal approach of encouraging forthright honesty by preserving anonymity.

The case I am going to put forward is that the mentally ill and mentally accused do have the right and do have a responsibility to create a bona fide twelve-step program for their drug and alcohol addictions. Having a psychiatrist there to help on medication issues may be a benefit and there are times when it is desirable. However, the workings of the AA and NA system, which has gone on quite functionally since the 1930s, demonstrates that within each of us we have a tremendous asset to protect and value, and working with our peers is an important vehicle for doing so.

There is a benefit to be found in a FUBU system, so again, I point out that most AA and NA meetings are already appropriate venues for many of the mentally ill and mentally accused to get their needs met. Some people will also need psych medication and talk therapy with a doctor. Here I agree with the medical establishment in their stress of the utility of using AA or NA meetings in conjunction with a regimen of psych meds.

My addition to this debate is only one of many legitimate viewpoints. I expect the debate to go on for quite some time. If the status quo is to say that the mentally ill and mentally accused cannot have a twelve-step program without a staff endorsed psychiatrist, then I'll maintain that that status quo is inappropriate and not well grounded. Having that AA or NA supplement is desirable; twelve-step programs do work for many.

My assessment of the general situation is that there needs to be a pro-choice element in the provision of mental health services. I know agencies in mental health that say they are pro-choice on medication issues. If you value a medicine regimen, then please do continue with what makes your life livable. Although I have a medicine that works for me, I do acknowledge that for many people this is not the case. I can recommend you find a higher power, but when it comes to medicine, I do recommend a pro-choice platform. This is not a cut-and-dried law. This is only a recommendation.

I hope dual disability people like me will never need a doctor's permission to go to an AA meeting.

When you talk of a dual diagnosis co-occurring disorder, you have two goals that can be thought of as the duality of man. The duality is that, if you are someone living in such a circumstance, you need both sobriety and medication to overcome your mental illness. This can be daunting, as medication is a major factor but not a sole cure, and even when you have sobriety and medication, you can still have breakthrough symptoms. Even when you have stability, the illness can mutate and adapt to whatever remedy you have found and present itself in new and innovative ways that can be difficult to spot. You need neurochemical stability.

There is a need for sanity from two fronts, which means that ultimately you end up being, in part, your own doctor for a lot of the time spent fighting for sobriety and fighting for sanity. "Sober sanity" is what I can call neurochemical stability. In this text we are concerned with clinical stability, and the one term that encompasses both addiction and mental health is neurochemistry.

Going off your psych meds can lead to the return of unresolved mania, depression and psychosis, as well as creating a level of guilt that can be as potent as a drug or alcohol relapse. I have had such a relapse, so you can listen to me for a first-person testimony. I am an author authority on this.

This book is especially for you who have dual diagnosis co-occurring disorders like me. Even bestselling author Steven King reportedly goes to meetings and stays sober. He can write about characters that drink, but he no longer drinks himself. Unlike works by authors like King, my writing is not intended to be a huge commercial moneymaker. It will serve only a small, narrow market of people that I dearly love, occupying a niche that I personally experience.

As I've previously noted, included within this text are small samples of my fiction work. You might as well know just how far my work is from having a commercially centered structure. I am not a treating physician and am only a marginal self-published author.

In the simplest traditions of contribution to a common cause, this work can be a good starting place for a larger conversation, one that is really only threatened when people try to be too abstract. While some reference to professional literature and discussion of medical and psychiatric trends is useful, the greatest lesson is found for many in AA or NA, or even Buddhism. It is often important to avoid getting distracted by the overly intellectual.

There are a few more pieces of the mental illness puzzle palace question to consider, at least as it applies to diagnoses such as mine. One concerns command hallucinations. These are where you hear voices telling you to do something. If the voices tell you to throw a hot cup of coffee at a policeman, then it would not be wise to do what those voices tell you to do. You'll have three choices: you can obey the voices and suffer the consequences, you can with some difficulty learn to ignore them, or you can take medications that make them go away.

There are many medications you can take to remedy this version of psychosis, and finding the right one can be a process of guesswork, and of trial and error. Hopefully, you won't need to first convince any voices commanding you to let you seek this kind of help. I recommend you read up on all your choices and talk to your doctor about your situation. Don't rely on the Internet for your information.

Tempting as it might seem in today's electronically connected world, you cannot alleviate your problems and a symptom with a collection of digital downloads. There are bushels of Internet sites out there hawking and recommending every kind of self-curative approach, and assuming you are reading this electronically, this too is clearly one of them. Even for the few approaches that can be helpful, finding that wheat from amongst the chaff is not a viable task for the novice.

The Internet is vast and so filled with recommendations, one contradicting the next, that I recommend you find a counselor in the psychiatric field in your area of the country to help you sort through all the various options.

Social workers and case management professionals can be very helpful, but I should also note that the folks at www.mindfreedom.org point out that they have a t-shirt for sale which says: "I am not a case, and I don't want to be managed."

In any event, I can't emphasize enough that you should never self-medicate with alcohol or drugs. That is perhaps the quickest way to achieve relapse, and even an intensification of your mental illness symptoms. Recreational drugs will make your illness worse faster than they will make it better. It may not feel that way at first, but time has shown that this has been so for nearly all consumers of mental health services.

Take a fearless moral inventory of yourself, make amends to the people you have harmed, unless you know or suspect that they do not want to hear from you for any reason, and go to AA and NA meetings so you don't isolate yourself, and enable such isolation to allow your illness to fester like a spreading infection. Get out of the house, take a walk, and visit with other recovering addicts to see what works for them. Buy a copy of the blue book for AA or NA and sit down and read up on how to craft a program from nothing. The worst you could get is a blue book for your bookshelf, and some eyestrain from reading that will go away after a good night's sleep.

On the notion of admitting that you are powerless over drugs and alcohol, one need only feel the pull toward a sober life and note that the debris in life left by the opposite pull is strong enough if you look closely, that sobriety is clearly more desirable. If you want to be out of the pool and avoid a bellyful of pool water swill, then the first step is just to get out of the pool. To do that, you have to want to dry off. In the case of alcohol, you have to want to dry out, and this is as close to linguistic gymnastics as we'll get. When you achieve sobriety you will know what I am talking about. Go to a meeting convenient to you, or find the meeting elsewhere that meets your needs and go to it.

One sure way of getting into pure hell is thinking that, since you feel so much better after taking three or four months of medication, you don't need those psych meds anymore. People tend to believe that when they feel their first blush of recovery, all of a sudden they are cured, no longer need any more treatment, and don't need to exercise vigilance to monitor their symptoms of mental illness. Not a bright idea, but one that happens all too often.

Additionally, I expect someone someday will say to you that psych meds are drugs, and you should not eat them because you are not being sober if you are taking any kinds of drugs. To them I say that I take a thyroid pill because lithium destroyed my thyroid gland when a doctor screwed up my medication. I was prescribed the lithium, and now without my thyroid pill I would be fine for only a few months before I would experience physical symptoms like fatigue, weakness and uncomfortably dry skin. When an AA or NA person says I should quit taking my meds …

I think you can see where I am going with this. Don't quit your meds. The specifics of your reactions to them will certainly differ from mine, but as with my thyroid problem, you should make informed decisions before you consider stopping your medication just because you feel better.

Learn what is going on in the treatment of your mental illness, the treatment of your addiction, and the treatment of any physical health effects that might be separate from or have been caused as side effects of the medications addressing your mental health issues. For example, the medication that has helped keep me on an even mental keel for the past several years has a side effect of leading me to a significant weight gain.

I've determined that for me that problem is clearly preferable to being mentally unstable, and it's a side effect that I can also work on through diet and exercise, though I'll continue to work with my psychiatrist to try and find an equally effective alternative without that side effect. If you are so depressed that you want to die, then talk to your Dr. Feelgood and get some Xanax or other happy pills. I don't know as much about depression as I do about psychosis but I know there are several drugs out there that can probably help, though none seem to help everyone and several rounds of trial and error are often needed to find an effective treatment for any specific person. Keep in mind that the alternative can be much worse.

Depression-induced suicide will certainly screw up your whole day. Don't worry about hurting the feelings of Scientology celebrities like Tom Cruise, who is a very vocal adherent of the Scientology line that all drugs are harmful. Some of the pills that are available can do wonders. What we have available has gotten a lot better in recent times, and certainly there are other wonder drugs on their way.

My particular preferred FUBU people are the folks at the Monday meeting of Dopeless Hope Fiends, a group that gets together in the evening at a church basement in Minnesota. Chances are that you will be able to find a similar group you can identify with in your area. Although I will never ask you to be your own doctor, I can and will ask you to be very informed when you make your own decisions, and please do be your own advocate. I will also wish you good luck, although you have just entered a world where it is said of success, that luck usually has nothing to do with it.

Nevertheless, an avenue to avoid is unthinkingly emulating anyone else's approach to handling mental illness, meds, psychiatry, street drugs, alcohol, relationships, and/or changing any or all of these. Our culture being so heavily celebrity oriented, avoiding emulating such people is problematic for many. Resist that temptation.

Let's talk about some of these celebrities for a moment. Brad Pitt had once threatened to vote for a gay marriage and legal marijuana ticket, should there ever be one in any election he can vote in. That need became moot with the U.S. Supreme Court's decision legalizing gay marriage.

Cruise, as we have already noted, has said he is opposed to all forms of psychiatric medication. If marijuana pushed somebody's sanity into the red zone, our friend Cruise and his associates in Scientology would only advocate vitamins and exercise, and of course joining Scientology and achieving what it calls a "clear" status. Hubbard reportedly created Scientology after a bad reaction to being forcibly detained in a naval hospital in Oakland, California. It is said that Hubbard was so disgusted with psychiatry that he created his new "religion" specifically to oppose it. To replace psychiatry, Scientology offers dozens of books, videos and recorded speeches, and an "auditing" process designed to clear out your mind's hang-ups. That it apparently works for some is why Scientology is still around.

One of these days we may actually get to see a real showdown between psychiatry and Scientology. I want a front row seat for that. Actress Drew Barrymore, who was an underaged alcoholic, achieved sobriety before she was even legally old enough to drink. Her underage status obviously failed to be a deterrent to its consumption. Now Barrymore is one of the best representatives of sobriety that I know of. She is a pretty girl with a significant fan following, and her sobriety gets a lot of professional respect. Having it come in the beautiful package she is makes the message more palatable to many people.

Robert Downey managed to fall asleep on the couch of a house he not only did not own, but was also not invited into. The house was unlocked and Mr. Downey's own residence was nearby, but when tested for drug use in conjunction with the crime, it became apparent that Robert's blood contained a noteworthy amount of diacetylmorphine molecules. For the non-chemists among us, I will point out that diacetylmorphine is the chemical term for heroin.

Pig Pen McKernan was the keyboard player for The Grateful Dead rock band, and he died of cirrhosis of the liver linked to Olympian alcohol consumption in combination with heroin use. One of the more serious concerns with substance abuse as it appends itself to mental health is how a drug like heroin attaches itself to three receptors in the human brain. All heroin can really be seen as is two morphine molecules attached together with an acetic acid molecule.

Not many people realize how much damage can be done to the liver from intravenous drug use. Putting needles into your veins can rot out your liver really fast.

Brooke Shields gave birth and then experienced severe postpartum depression. She sought psychiatric help for a deep and quite noteworthy depression. Such post-partum depression happens all the time, but what made her situation stand out was that fellow actor Cruise publically criticized her for a supposed sin of using psychiatric drugs. Most of the nation's celebrity watchers sided with Shields.

Cruise's Scientology view that psych meds are evil was not received well, neither by the medical profession, nor by most of the public or by Shields herself. The proverbial "black eye" Cruise received from that episode was the result of his having come into contact with someone more resilient than him, someone by the name of Shields.

Then there was the Heaven's Gate Cult. They believed that nearly all of the world's science fiction was a description of an actual ideal universe that they had access to. They committed suicide as a group, using a mix of alcohol and barbiturates, called downers, to achieve death as deliberately as if they were punching out of work on a time card at the end of a day. They surely moved from one universe to another, that much is true, but I don't think they are living out the fantasy of being in outer space with the cast of the original *Star Trek*. They are dead, and if you mix downer barbiturates and alcohol, then you too will likely become dead. A bad outcome from a bad cocktail, in my opinion! You don't get to come back from that kind of a party.

Having been part of the drug scene for much of my life before Saint Peter, I've listened to many an associate seeking celebrity, or at least their proverbial fifteen minutes of fame. "What are you gonna write about us, Billy?" I've been asked. "Get my good side, will ya, and get me a check for helping you write your book, too."

I certainly can't grant celebrity to anyone, and how commercially successful any of my writing will be is up to you, the reading public. Most writers don't make a full-time living at it. What I can say is don't be self destructive like the Heaven's Gate cult, and avoid causing any people grief, like Cruise did, when you knowledgeably choose to seek medical assistance for a mental health problem.

***

There are some very special groups of people in this country that are recognized for having special rights. One group worth special mention is the Quakers. Back when the war in Vietnam was becoming a major national issue, we had quite a few people say they did not want to be drafted into the nation's military service. The Quakers were a notable group amongst them.

An odd bunch of peace activist anti-war protesters emerged while we were fighting in Vietnam. Some just didn't want to be sent to a place like that where their chance of being killed was considerably higher than with a suburban trip to the grocery store. Others with a libertarian philosophy said things like: "You can try to enslave us, and we will not go off to war for you, or your employer, or favorite politician." The Quakers were part of a third group which our larger society generally calls pacifists, people who war against all wars, period! Those Quakers were tough in their own ways, brave too, and mostly open to alternative service.

They just didn't believe in war. Court challenges established that you cannot draft a Quaker into that odd form of slavery we call our military. This caught my eye immediately after I voluntarily became one of those "slaves" better known as an employee of the Department of Defense. In my case, I enlisted in the U.S. Marine Corps.

The reason I bring wars and pacifists and military service up is that the whole thing about prisons and mental hospitals, as we have come to know them, was at one time in our nation's history under the almost sole control of cultural and religious groups like the Quakers. They virtually invented the concept of rehabilitation, changing incarceration from being prisons and asylums based strictly on punishment. That often severe punishment was designed to either drive out evil demonic spirits, or instill a fear of the bible and of society into "transgressors." Early puritans also believed madness was brought on by things like being cursed by a witch, receiving the "evil eye" from a questionable person, being a generally shiftless no-good, or a variety of other "blaming the victim" mythologies.

***

I met this small, pretty, compact black girl, about forty years old, and heard her tell a tale of her mental illness. She said she was depressed and that the only cure for her distress was a wonder drug, Xanax, which had a profound effect on people with depression like hers. People it was pre-scribed to began to call it a "happy pill" and it was deemed to be highly addictive, especially so for the clinically depressed. Because of that addictive tendency, getting it was made more difficult, too difficult for my black female acquaintance. One day, depressed and frustrated with an auto re-pair issue, she lost her temper and drove her car through a glass window fifteen feet high and wide.

If it wasn't such a serious outcome, we could be flippant and joke: "Don't mess with that lady's automotive repairs."

Here it might also be appropriate to give another person a moment of special note. I'm referring to the madness of the one and only Earl Steven Karr. He is famous for his career as the "Midwest Pipe Bomber," a label applied to him by the *USA Today* newspaper. He hallucinated that people were plotting against him, which was partly true, as Karr made bombs and other people did try to stop him from doing so. He left his bombs where curious people would try to dispose of them, thinking they were trash, or road hazards, or other such debris.

Karr weighs in at 110 pounds, and has a high-pitched maniacal laugh that causes people to look his way and note his curious qualities. For these reasons, Earl is branded for life as an odd sort of person. He responds to this curiosity by becoming paranoid about people noting his weird appearance and odd ways. He thinks people are out to get him, which is at least true of members of law enforcement. Then Karr gets mad, gets vengeful, and makes and plants bombs. For Karr it goes in a straight line progression: paranoia, anger, vengeance, bombs.

Karr tortures the general population of society, in an equal manner to the way the government tortures him here. Karr validates many of the policies that function as "obedience training for adult humans." For such individuals much of the strict regimentation, and the nearly military autocracy based behavior therapies, actually may have arguable validity.

Karr is one of the reasons we do need a functional medical imprisonment system. I approve of some of what happens to people like Karr. I don't like people blowing up other people. But not all of those medically imprisoned are actually dangerous people, and most of them are mostly dangerous only to themselves.

***

If God exists in your worldview and beliefs, then you are a theist. Let's just call that a nice place to start. My background is something called theistic existentialism. It is a faith in the viability of reality. My view is that God wants you to use your brain and that's why you have a brain. Do try to avoid being too abstract; have faith in the reality that you know, because it is precisely the fact that you have faith in it that causes it to exist for you. Bear with a short digression into my beliefs as to the nature of spirituality, faith, and religion. We'll be getting to their connections to mental health.

You can look at drug and alcohol use as an extension of theology, though alcohol certainly predates all of our modern day religions. Abuse of intoxicants is noted and proscribed in the books of Moses, the Jewish bible, as common enough occurrences to deserve specific condemnation and prohibition. But looking at a few prominent western religions, one could nevertheless argue that a theology of drug use is promoted. It is promoted by the use of wine to represent the blood of Christ for adherents of Christianity, and in such things as the celebration of God's miracles by Jews in their Passover Seder.

Several Christian denominations, most notably the Mormons, are explicit in their denunciation of all forms of intoxication.

Catholics get very serious about the wine drinking and the blood. The blood of the Christ is said to be the divine forgiveness of a gentle, caring God. Washed in that blood, all sins disappear into a form of forgiveness. I cannot second guess anything that someone has as part of their religion, as part of a belief system that they accept as a holy ritual, but to my mind belief in a holy wine of blood every time one looks at a crucifix makes the Christian experience very alcohol centric.

There are parallels in the body of Vladimir Illyich Lenin in Soviet Russia. His corpse was placed into an oxygen-free chamber and has not been allowed to rot into ribbons. This meant a lot to the Russian people, as the bodies of Saints, in their Eastern Orthodox beliefs, are said to never decompose. Giving Lenin this extended shelf life, like a loaf of bread loaded with preservatives, lends Lenin the mythology of appearing to be saintly. He was godly in his own image. So much for the Eastern Orthodox acceptance of "dust to dust."

In Christianity, children traditionally go through communion in white clothes and with a sip of wine. A comparison of the sharing the blood chemistry of Christ to the sharing of neurochemistry of the masses becomes, for me, an almost inevitability metaphorical relationship. When grown, these kids are going to go to parties and nightclubs, where alcohol often flows freely with the tacit approval of adults and society.

Shouldn't we then at least give their consciences a rung up on the ladder and encourage them to want to be sober and away from the disco and dance drug crowds?

As far as I think, that ought to be a main reason for having a religion in the first place, and I have faith that religion is a good thing. At least most of the time I have faith that it's a good thing. The reason I bring this up is that, in my service to the world as a consulting atheist, I once preached against blind faith in that I was pretty certain that all miracles were stretches of the truth. What I had faith in was Saint Peter's "plausible denial."

Now, I have "faith" in my belief that most Christians do generally try to behave well. I have "faith" as well that, on a mass psychology level, the mainstream religious appearance of faith is better for the masses than a faith masquerading and functioning as a cult of personality, or within a socio-economic philosophy like Lenin's Communism. Call that one point for a faith in a higher power.

I don't want to break your bubble if you consider yourself "only spiritual." But, if you have a god as part of your spirituality, then your spirituality is a thing called faith and is thus clearly tied to religion. There are dictionaries that support this idea. To have a higher power may not obligate one toward conformity in any organized faith like Christianity or Judaism or Buddhism, or other brand name faith. You can call it an alternative spirituality, but at the end of the day these things called higher powers are religious enough that they are indeed orthodoxy. It is definitively elemental. The only way you can break it down more elementally is to use subatomic particles as your metaphor.

You can call it spirituality with or without a Jesus or other prophet focusing it, but if it has a god concept, then it is in that category of things that are called faith-based. Added to that, I'll ask if perhaps it is time to ask the folks in the holy of holies business to open up a new department of faith in a god not specifically tied to a gospel or people powered hierarchy.

Strictly speaking, Islam at its philosophical core comes close. It has as a major point that you are a Muslim if you believe in Allah. That's why they at least theologically accept Jews and Christians. While they say Islam is better than its predecessors, they only get to the extreme sanctity of Mohamed as a prophet later on. All the cultural baggage that believers have hung on to that faith in the centuries since Mohamed's death has certainly muddied the clarity of that central belief.

Atheism is having faith that there is no God. Theists are neither agnostics nor atheists. The agnostic believes in a higher power, just not any specific doctrine about it. The theist is a believer in God, just not necessarily that there is a god that has a son, talks to people, or otherwise intervenes with miracles in the affairs of man or the universe. All forms of spirituality where there is a god are connected to those things we call religions. All, including alternative spirituality, are faith-based. There is a cute place in Evanston, Wyoming, where for a small fee you can get a Doctor of Divinity degree, and for that very small fee you are able to marry people legally. There are probably a bunch of other similar places. This one that I know about in Wyoming is a 501.c3 tax exempt, non-profit corporation. In the

U.S., calling an organization a religion makes it a non-profit, granting both spiritual and taxation leeway. It does not matter to me what your own form of spiritual quest is. You can call it "Fred" or a "'53 Dodge" or "the Brooklyn Dodgers," but if there is a god in that formulation, then it is a faith-based concern.

And, as promised, we now turn to the connections of faith, spirituality and religion to our central topic of mental health. The formative events of Christianity predate AA by about 2,000 years. The rituals of wine and forgiveness seem to be connected. Still, enough of theology as a life style philosophy. I will leave most of the god business to the frocked and confirmed.

What I will do with theology is note its value as a practical appendage to aiding people with mental health issues, to include forms of obsession and addiction.

As a free citizen in this world, you have the option to select many of your life's preferences as commonly as you would select clothing items to purchase and wear that match your personal tastes. If I point out that god is a theological concept, I am still just pointing out one of the realities most of us accept as global citizens. As in the United States, many countries provide at least a tax break for religions, and often also for their tax-exempt non-profit satellites, at least for the religion or religions each country variously recognizes. Too many governments, in my opinion, go so far as to have state sponsored religions, and penalize or persecute nonbelievers.

A great variety of help agencies are devoted to assisting addicted people in their quest for sobriety. Their wanting to avoid alienating anybody by not endorsing any specific faith neither absents God for the religious, nor requires belief in "God" by the non-religious. Their real focus is a quest to be inclusive; specifically not exclusive. If you need its help in your journey, certainly bring your religion, but don't wear it too obviously on your sleeve. Because your religious beliefs might not exactly match those of the agency, or those of other participants, be prepared to park your spirituality somewhere between altruism and Zen (A to Z).

I'm definitely not saying you should not be spiritual in your quest for mental health, but providing for the non-spiritual seeking is also necessary, also has value. I personally have faith in the multi-ton qualities of faith. Think about it this way: When you have spiritual surplus, you can ration your excess out to anyone in need who might desire to receive it.

In most modern western nations, the point is stressed that nobody should be compelled to worship any specific religion, or even worship at all. That provision covers agencies such as Alcoholics Anonymous and Narcotics Anonymous. That's why we are having this part of the conversation. If AA and NA were religions, then they would best be forbidden from prescribing recovery regimens for the chemically afflicted. But as nominally nonreligious organizations, AA and NA type twelve-step programs can usually be as ardently faith-based as evangelical television preachers, without themselves being religions. The punch line is not ethereal or esoteric. Just accept that twelve-step programs are faith-based and protected by law, and move on. The law is not going to shut down AA and NA groups meeting in any formal place of worship, let alone in prisons, or even on Skid Row, or at least it shouldn't.

Ultimately, comparisons of twelve-step programs to religious indoctrination programs are nothing more than linguistic gymnastics. Arguments back and forth are not going to stop just because you get chewed out by anyone for being too politically incorrect or illogical in the construction of your argument. In the context of providing effective AA or NA support, even the nonreligious need to be accepted and accommodated. If you consider yourself to be a very religious person, think of it in the context of it being a sin to not embrace people whom you believe are religiously illiterate because they have other or less rigorous religious beliefs.

A worst case scenario would be to say that as a faith-based solution twelve-step programs can and should be rejected. The only case that would carry forward from such an argument would also assail groups and organizations like the Salvation Army for trying to help people become sober simply because they think sobriety is their route to saving souls. So long as they stay away from advocating on broader and divisive unrelated social issues, we should applaud all such sobriety oriented activities.

About 85 percent of the world's population uses a faith-based principle in the daily makeup of their activities, domestic, vocational, recreational, and everything not covered in the above. There is probably only about a small 15 percent slice of the population who would even consider arguing the point, and only a few of them really care about it strongly. Religion and spirituality are effectively protected by the apathy of their detractors.

Chapter 11: God for the Skeptical Addict

A NOTEWORTHY BUT controversial treatment center called "Teen Challenge" is based in prayer and Christian faith. If you aren't a Christian they will do their best to turn you into one. That isn't entirely a bad philosophy. I tend to be a bit more Zen Buddhist of the Tibetan Dali Lama type. I see the Jesus of Christianity as a "lower case" *christian* who emphasized morality and ethics more than just a blind obedience to belief in a particular "God." Teen Challenge will try to turn you into a textbook charismatic evangelical Christian, one of the many flavors of Christianity out there in the world.

Any individual is welcome to practice whatever religious medicine cures your ailments. In my experience heroin use means a need for drastic measures that can even include going to such extremes as turning people into evangelical conservatives. Though I consider myself to be a progressive, I would rather see someone become a live conservative than be a dead heroin addict. The important thing here is to stay alive. If you relapse and drink half a case of beer, then fine. That's survivable. If you overdose on heroin and die, you don't get to come back to another Narcotics Anonymous meeting. If you go get drunk, you just get a hangover and a chance to start over on getting sober, to getting another white keychain for thirty days and an orange one for thirty days after that. After two years you are back in the game with a black keychain, as proud of your sobriety as you were before that half a case of beer. If you die, it's game over!

So long as you come back in one piece, Teen Challenge will be happy to see you. They may condemn you for your sin, order you to pray for forgiveness, and urge you to become an ever better Christian.

I am a believer in science and some faith, not the other way around. I believe that if you physically survive your relapse then there is a core to rebuild around. To employ an analogy, if you destroy the motor and frame of a car, it makes no sense to put on new fenders. As long as the core components are intact we have something we can work with.

A childhood friend had a cocaine moment about twenty years ago and has been sober ever since. He told me he sees Christ as a Buddhist, which is not bad for an Irish Catholic who, like me, is offspring from physicians who were part of the Mayo Clinic community.

Another person I've known—a disorganized, handicapped, Christian extremist, father, ex-husband and a several times drug addict—once gave me a list of bible passages that have come to mean a lot to his treatment for chemical dependency and mental illness. At one point he relapsed in his cocaine habit and subsequently opted for a thirteen-month program with an organization similar to Teen Challenge. Like Teen Challenge, it was very restrictive, but was quite suitable for his needs. He is one of those drug addicts who will always need direction and guidance so Christian conservative guidance is just what he needs.

I wouldn't expect a doctrinaire liberal program to work for such a person. I would trust me to help him even though I am somewhat liberal on many issues, because I am rarely doctrinaire on anything other than that I like the practice of medicine to be based on science. It's very liberating to be at peace with the laws of science first, and the often somewhat arbitrary rules of people only much later on. I have to respect the heroin addict who will say "I can survive this" and rely on science to help them, but I am aware of the careen of destruction they leave in their wake, to their families and the general community before they come to the Narcotics Anonymous community. If they can get sober with us, then the prospect of a Teen Challenge type of program is a last resort not needed.

***

Christianity is an ambitious system of belief designed to combat sin, guilt, grief, and loneliness as well as a fear of a world with no afterlife. It does well for some at combating all of these downfalls of the human experience, and gives some people something to hope for. Does a pretend medically flavored sobriety that is actually based on Christianity achieve the necessary standard of self-sacrifice, community service and caring that typified my father's career as a doctor at the Mayo Clinic? That approach would anger some of the more devout evangelicals. Because I want our evangelical associates in recovery to be happy, I won't require that they discard religion out of hand, but as a science leaning person I assure you that when any but the most narrowly focused evangelicals are in need of bypass heart surgery they will not pass up the science of medicine. It seems that in such instances we can both be in the miracle business.

A believer in world girdling conspiracies, a friend who died in 2017, nevertheless compiled a pamphlet of his favorite inspirational passages from the Christian bible. He thought that Jehovah's Witnesses and Catholic Christians alike were all immersed in cults, and that the Illuminati and other secret governments of the rich and powerful are conspiring to control the world. He very seriously believed they are intent on creating a one world government of the antichrist as described in the book of Revelations of the New Testament. His pamphlet remains, however, a great reference to evangelical Christian recovery from mental illness and drug addiction. He was great at social prayer and had a significant reputation for being able to help people pray for deliverance from their afflictions. Here in Saint Peter he helped a young woman pray her way out of the daily stresses that contributed to debilitating seizures. With prayer her seizures dropped to once a month.

From my perspective, while my friend was a total goofball, he was superb at prayer, and a frothing at the mouth ultra conservative evangelical. But after interacting with the criminal underworld personally, I'm not against the idea that having a few conservatives involved with mental health recovery is not such a bad thing.

In a related vein, meditation can also be useful for recovery. It can aid people in creating a healthful calm and an understanding of inner peace. In turn, this can help people combat symptoms of drug addiction and mental illness. There is hope. Through prayer and meditation many addicts can replace the euphoria of drug use with the tranquility of inner peace. The Dali Lama would prefer you emphasize meditation, while Christians go with prayer.

The Dali Lama and people like the Catholic Pope are leaders in this world, while my friend is more of a drone. But we need drones too, so that's not such a bad thing. My friend expresses the political awareness of a fruit fly, but you don't need to be on top of world politics to be a happy worker bee in the hive. The Pope and the Dali Lama may save millions of people every year while my friend's pamphlet might save only a handful. All efforts are necessary.

Chapter 12: AA and NA and Faith

WHEN A CONVERT to a new religion makes that leap of faith and says "I believe" and prays to their God for help, he or she is doing exactly the same thing that any member of any cult in the world does. You have an individual who wants, or has been convinced to want, a change in his or her life. You have a recruiter looking for such an individual. You get a transforming act of faith where the individual surrenders his or her life over to the care of a group of adherents to a god or belief system. You have a community of support for the new individual who is now part of the group. This invigorates the group and eventually the newcomer can become the recruiter and the process can repeat itself.

Most of us would readily acknowledge such a recruitment process with reference to cults, but we close our awareness to the fact that such a process is also at the core, essentially forms the skeleton of Christianity, Islam and Buddhism, and of Alcoholics Anonymous and Narcotics Anonymous. Modern day Jews are mostly exempt from this criticism because they rarely recruit. That Jews seem to function as a community first and a religion second is not meant as criticism. They have a 3,500-year track record of such a faithful mix of community and belief, and one usually does not think of them as a recruiter-based religion. The rest of our more widespread or otherwise heralded religions have that recruitment oriented flaw, and you also get a version of evangelical conversion focused behavior in AA and NA.

The leap of faith in mental health is just as important as the leap of faith in Alcoholics Anonymous. The day you say that you have a mental illness and you want to remedy that as much as you can, in as sustainable a fashion as is possible, is the day your experience as a student of faith has its beginning. That leap of faith is essential. It works for religions, cults, AA and NA, and can often contribute to recovery from mental illness.

History has shown that, while the leap of faith process has potential for providing great benefit, it can also skew an individual in more questionable directions. If you choose a path less traveled, you could end up selling books in airports like Hari Krishna brethren did in the 1970s.

While a leap of faith is almost by definition an emotional response, that doesn't mean it has to be devoid of knowledge-based influences. Research your leap lest you fall into any bottomless pit of darkness. I recommend you bring some of the light that we all have from our shared Western religions' origins and hook yourself up to a metaphorical power company grid. If nothing else seems to be working for you, try a few kilowatts of faith and see if it helps.

***

Calling AA and NA faith-based might alienate people who are more logic-based and nonreligious, but it really shouldn't. The fact that many of those programs, probably most, are associated with or sponsored by faith-based institutions, often meeting in church basements, should not obscure that what makes the twelve-step model successful has been empirically studied and replicated in groups of people facing other problems. The support of a like-minded community has been found to help many peoples with unifying problems to the successful achievement of common goals, improving their lives just as AA helps its community achieve and maintain sobriety.

AA and NA should be rewarded for decades of what business calls "good will." Such good will moves with a business everywhere it travels. It can move with the company, or with the owner, or sometimes with core employees who move their skills and contacts to competitors. It can even transcend any of these bonds and accrue to an entire industry.

That's why AA will probably outlive any single group that decided to no longer work the program, and it will outlive but include the meetings that do its work. Saying that faith is not part of this would be committing a sin based in fearful thought that the whole program should be assailed for being too spiritual and thus too religious. Clearly, such AA detractors who say this new belief system and access point to god is against the law will fail against the good will that AA has created by decades of successful work within substance abuse recovery communities.

AA and NA are both cut from a Christian model, and their approach represents a belief in spirit that is akin to that found in Christianity despite their general claim to be non-religious, or at least without specific endorsement of any one religion. And while many twelve-step programs avoid direct contact with faith-based institutions, but accept that they are such themselves, others try to strictly deny it.

Those deniers are perhaps best exemplified by the folks in AA circles who pseudo-scientifically call alcoholism an "allergy." That is an unscientific fallacy and a misapplied label. Their tortured analogy may have worked with the 1935 definition of an allergy, but as I said earlier, in more modern application it really is not an allergy as we identify reactions to things like bee stings and peanuts. Nevertheless, to the degree that thinking of it in such a context helps some people successfully use such programs, its conceptual utility should still be accepted.

Let me put forward an analogy. I got a veteran's benefit issue taken care of by a representative. I chose the Disabled American Veterans organization to help me present my case to the Veterans Administration. I could have used the Order of the Purple Heart. I went with the DAV while my pal Lisa went with the Purple Heart folks. The important aspect of picking out a representative is being confident that, whatever the group and person you are choosing, he, she or it will put in the work needed to move your case forward. We both got the help we were looking for. What flavor it came in mattered far less than the worth of our cases and our documents. The VA exists without endorsing any one promoter of its benefits cases. AA and NA exist without the direct connection of a religion itself. The DAV is not the VA but they work together commonly. AA and NA work with faith-based organizations without being connected to any one religious denomination. They are, thus, very faith-based without being a religion themselves. They do not endorse any one door; they have become a door unto themselves.

Trying to avoid the spiritual or religious label is daunting. Spirituality is, by definition, something based in faith. There are worse things to be in this world. If getting sober is aided by a little reorganization of syntax, then please be my guest and completely revamp the English language to meet your needs. I want you sober and happy because it will enhance my happiness to see you doing well. As noted earlier, a definition of the word "religious" includes believing in a higher being or showing devotion or reverence for a deity or deities. That covers higher powers fairly adequately. Dictionaries also say that "spiritual" means relating to religious or sacred things rather than worldly things.

Don't worry about such dictionary definitions. AA and NA can be tasked with getting in line with your program, with your specific individual needs. They don't need help to become "unreligious" as much as we simply need them to be the community that helps us to remain positive and as healthy as we can be.

I have a chemical dependency counselor named Ken. He will ardently argue that his higher power is spiritual and not religious. The revamping and relabeling of religion to being something spiritual, and not an orthodoxy of Christianity or Judaism or Islam or Buddhism, etc., is essentially ethical. Ken does not have a degree in English, but clearly means well. I applaud the spirit behind labeling things as only spiritual rather than religious. People who do that mean well and they achieve more with an ounce of spirit than can often be remedied with tonnage of religion.

We do have things that are religious without achieving goals of being spiritual. For some people, religion can be a dry husk that once contained life but does not any longer. For those individuals, the quest for the payoff of spirit needs no orthodox attachment to the immobile beasts that are many of our faiths in God. In spite of criticizing orthodoxy in spiritual matters, the spirituality of twelve-step programs carries an orthodoxy all of its own. It is a small orthodoxy, and not a huge orthodoxy like that found, for instance, in fundamentalist Christianity, ultra-orthodox Judaism, or radical Islam. While the large orthodoxy works for many, I prefer a small orthodoxy. I prefer Ken's style of spirituality to the official representatives of just about anything.

It's sort of like saying there are chemicals in your water. Of course there are chemicals in your water. There is a lot of H_2O in that glass of water. H_2O is itself a chemical molecule. Spirituality and religion are two access points to a similar product. I can understand when our chemical dependency counselors say it is a spiritual thing and not religious, but ultimately there is a thing where different agencies with very similar understandings compete for the same limited resources. Because AA and NA are FUBU, for us by us networks, they exist without much effort, without the need to compete. They are so intrinsically valuable that we value them without their needing to campaign or advertise or compete actively on their behalf. AA and NA go on where there is no need for catechisms or confirmation or bar mitzvahs, and any advertising that is done for them is largely relegated to announcements of meeting times and locations. Returning to Ken, he may be slaughtering my beloved English language, but I like his work. Given a choice between various faith-based endeavors, I choose AA and NA over all other options.

Some addicts become substance abusers seeking to escape, or subtract from their realities. Others use alcohol and chemicals to add and not subtract, to try to add experiences, to add clarity to their realities.

Those users are trying to have new experiences or put different spins on their old experiences, trying to enhance their lives. I'll put to you their case for enhancement. Such chemical abusers want more than just the nothing and emptiness that cold sobriety represents to them. Such people, and I count myself as one of them, want everything. We want to enhance the good in our lives and not just escape from the bad. To avoid reality is to escape. In our minds, to seek more experiences, or different new spins on old experiences, is to add, to enhance, and not subtract.

Clearly, however, most people can add experiences without the use of a drug. One can live a sober life with no bitterness or emotional emptiness. Many chemical dependency counselors say that there can be found joy in sober networking, in, of and by itself.

For some like me, artistic connections also achieve importance. It is not coincidental that drugs can usually be found at the same places where rock and roll is at its loudest. There can still be good "art" going on there, and while a lot of that drinking and drugging is there to enhance and not escape, crossing the line from the former to the latter is all too easy. You want more and not just less, and though drugs run rampant in the music industry, I know of many sober people as well: Eric Clapton, Steven Tyler, Bob Mould, Ryan Addams, to name just a few.

And people who cross from enhance to abuse can cross back, though care is needed to avoid returning as a dry drunk who avoids all sensations, starving an already damaged spirit.

The dry drunk is somebody who quits alcohol and drugs but never repairs his or her soul from its anger, frustration, and suffering. All that this sober person retreated from through earlier drug use remains unrepaired, never taught to bloom again in a new life, despite the divorce from substance use. Twelve-step programs are not the only answer. Faith comes in many varieties, and returning to being a social person is part of the process of returning healthfully to the real world with a network to call upon that does not require drugs or alcohol.

Reintroducing yourself as a person to your community means rebuilding old connections. Some of these contacts will be so dedicated to using chemicals that they just can't make the roster for future fun. Without himself using drugs, Eric Clapton still plays a user anthem called "Cocaine." He cares enough about his community to give it all he has got. He also cares enough about his community to have created the Crossroads Chemical Dependency Center in the Caribbean.

I guess that means the real estate brokers were right: location, location, location!

Beyond private chemical dependency treatment centers that essentially cater only to the well heeled and the celebrity, several organizations outside of AA and NA have helping people with mental health issues central to their missions. One of those is known as NAMI, the National Alliance for the Mentally Ill.

NAMI has historically been more of an advocacy group for relatives of the mentally ill than for the mentally ill citizens themselves. Sometimes they are saints and occasionally they have shown limits to patiently waiting for things to happen naturally. They put out brochures advising people to turn over furniture in their house, when calling police to intervene on mentally ill family members.

A less financially secure or organized group of people, in Eugene, Oregon, are the operators of the website *mindfreedom.org*. When I spoke last with those website folks, I said I liked my medication. Their reply? "We are pro-choice on medication issues."

I found that sentence very refreshing in a world bounded between NAMI and Scientology.

The Scientology people have created one thing particularly noteworthy. They created a group opposed to all medication, called CCHR, the Citizens Commission on Human Rights. As a Scientology satellite, they are determined to help people avoid all psychiatric medication, and their financial pockets allow them a significant voice on the issue of rights for the mentally ill.

CCHR was cofounded in 1969 by Dr. Thomas Szasz. He is not a Scientologist, but he is a psychiatrist who continually advocates for the rights of the mentally ill, including their rights to choose whether or not to accept being medicated. Definitely out of the mainstream for his field, most of his fellow psychiatrists view him to be a "contrarian."

In all my days as a mentally ill person, there are perhaps only ten or so people I could say were advocates of my well-being. Szasz is one of those ten people.

We, the institutionalized mentally ill, love CCHR. We cherish the thought of somebody being in our corner at the big boxing match in the psychiatric bureaucratic arena. People involved with CCHR are good people who truly mean to do good. I feel, however, that they and we could all benefit by their being a little more pro-choice and positive on medication issues, because the drugs have improved greatly.

Scientology founder Hubbard was a psychiatric survivor. He was detained from September 5 through December 4, 1945, at an Oakland, California, naval hospital for reasons that are said to have included undisclosed mental problems. His physical problem was diagnosed as ulcers. Why he was considered to have psychiatric problems has never been publicly disclosed.

I would like to see Hubbard's "tech reports" from 1975 to his death in 1986. There might be some acknowledgment of medication improving. I feel that once CCHR moves to a more pro-choice attitude on medication, then the world will, in turn, be more "founder friendly."

Despite its overtly oppositional stance toward psychiatric medication, even Scientology looks good when it stands in the shadow of Szasz. The good doctor put out a book in the early sixties called *The Myth of Mental Illness*. He was just the kind of credentialed professional, and his text's premise was just what Hubbard was looking for. Szasz's text framed the conditions of mentally ill people around the idea of ability rather than just dysfunction. He argued that society and the psychiatric industry should take note of the person's talents, such as someone's ability to recite Shakespeare while juggling and grilling a steak to perfection, rather than just focusing on the behavior's manic appearance. It was a much less punitive definition of mental illness. It was, in fact, a redefinition of mental health.

Hubbard loved the spirit of that book. That's why in the mid-1960s, after Hubbard had earned enough cash from his science fiction and Scientology books, and from Scientology, he sunk a bunch of it into CCHR to get it going. CCHR is largely staffed by Scientologists with an interest in anti-psychiatry issues.

One can very easily point to Hubbard's disgust with psychiatry to claim that he did not like anything connected to it. But, when viewed from the Szasz perspective of ability and disability, Hubbard shows a gifted ability to make a huge piece of art of it, creating what we know of as Scientology, while psychiatry has been so modest that it does not really even try to compete with Hubbard's creation in the public mind. Get Scientology strongly behind the activities of people like Szasz and organizations such as the CCHR, and distinct progress might be made in improving the situations of many who are somewhat arbitrarily and at times inappropriately labeled as mentally ill.

It's nice to think of mental illness and mental health in the way Szasz thought about it, but I also recognize that his approach is not going to be appropriate for everyone. There are people in the "mentally ill" population who need more than a redefinition of what ails them. I won't pretend to assign numbers or percentages to this later group, but among them are people like me who truly do need psychiatric medications to approach wellness.

I like some aspects of my medication so you will find me singing its praises in chapters to come, but if you need some alternate views then look into *mindfreedom.org* and Scientology's CCHR group (www.cchr. org) for their takes on the issue. Surfing through either site will lead you to information about Szasz as well. Look into it sufficiently and you may find yourself granting yourself permission to start a personal debate over your medication options. With more information you may decide psych meds are definitely for you, and you'll be able to take those drugs feeling a lot more confident about the benefits of your decision, about the whole psych meds debate. Or you may decide you need to look elsewhere. In either case, at that point you are probably making the best decision that you can formulate, and certainly a more informed one than if you are or are not going to take medications simply because someone in authority has told you to or not to!

Chapter 13: Meditation for Twelve-Steppers

EVERYBODY MEDITATES ALREADY. Whether it is waiting for the bus or quiet time at home or a walk through the forest, you already have all of the skills to be good at the task of meditation. There are formal styles from India and Japan. There was the whole movement in the sixties called Transcendental Meditation. There is yoga and sensory deprivation and Quaker meetings. All of these things come together and give us the ability to wait for the bus with a transcendental smile.

The label "direct meditation" can be used to label the ordinary stereotypical meaning applied to the common ideal of "meditation." This would be sitting cross-legged, back and spine straight, hands near knees, and using yoga-like breathing to achieve a focused trance-like state of pure and deliberate relaxation. "Indirect meditation" can reference tasks and practices that achieve something of a meditative state without the disciplined "direct" practices. This can include activities like walking in a forest, or playing a musical instrument.

Records citing meditative practice reach back to the dawn of recorded history. Anthropological theory tracks it even farther back in rituals at the very dawn of organized tribal societies.

Meditation was revived in Western culture in the 1960s during a time of affection for wisdom from Eastern communities of India, Tibet, China and Japan. The Maharishi Mahesh Yogi, championed by the Beatles of musical fame, especially John Lennon, wrote *Transcendental Meditation: Serenity Without Drugs*. Although filled with nearly indecipherable Hindu/Sanskrit terminology, his book still had a tremendous impact on the movement to achieve inner peace in a world filled with strife, frenetic energy, and general chaos.

Outside of Narcotics Anonymous, there are any number of different groups practicing meditation-like therapies, nearly all connected with a particular religion or philosophy. Plain ordinary meditation allows us each to develop spiritually in our own way.

A basic premise of meditation is that it is difficult, if not impossible, to obtain conscious contact unless a mind is still. The usual, never-ending succession of thoughts has to cease for progress to be made. So practice is aimed at stilling the mind, and letting the thoughts that arise die a natural death. We leave our thoughts behind us as meditation becomes a reality.

Many find that setting aside quiet time is helpful in making conscious contact with whatever one defines as a higher power. By quieting the mind, meditation can lead to calmness and serenity. This quieting of the mind can be done in any place, time, or manner, according to the individual.

Enforced morality lacks the power that comes to us when we choose to live a spiritual life. Most of us pray when we are hurting. We learn that, if we pray regularly, we won't be hurting as often, or as intensely.

We no longer see "God's will" as something to endure. On the contrary, we make conscious efforts to align with higher powers, believing we'll gain happiness and peace of mind in doing so. It can become a cornerstone of recovery.

Consider also a basic understanding of the difference between prayer and meditation. Think of prayer being the times we talk to a higher power, but meditation as the times we listen for a higher power's answers.

***

Both Narcotics Anonymous and Alcoholics Anonymous say that one seeks to enhance conscious contact with God through prayer and meditation. In the NA basic text only four short paragraphs describe this meditation, although it does not describe any particular technique. One can only surmise that it could mean both direct and indirect meditation approaches.

With my nearly three decades of imprisonment in a state run mental hospital in South Central Minnesota, I can attest to a truth that, if you don't learn how to meditate during such an experience, then you are either chronically blind to what is going on around you or you've missed a few too many essential points. I learned a great many indirect meditation techniques along the way which helped me create a monastic lifestyle. Amongst other things, it kept me sane when my cellmates were bouncing off the walls out of sheer boredom.

I am no guru or yogi but take my word that centering and focusing the mind keeps one from the distractions of daily life. Distractions like the ones I experienced can motivate one to find the benefits of both direct and indirect meditation.

Most chemical dependency issues people have who come to twelve-step groups arrive with a Christian, and less often Jewish or Muslim perspective. There are few Muslim alcoholics but hashish and heroin abuse is not uncommon.

Belief in God within AA and NA assumes the believer is at least looking for a small miracle of recovery. In a broader sense, coincidences that become miracles to a believer are only synchronicities to an atheist. Synchronicity is a term attributed to psychologist and psychiatrist Carl Jung in the first decade of the 1900s when he and Sigmund Freud were pioneering psychotherapy. He defined it as those coincidences that religions interpret to be miraculous.

Alternatively, Eastern Buddhist tradition teaches that the individual is responsible for all facets of his or her life. Buddhism teaches to empty the mind and soul of possessions and burdens. It teaches that the desired path is to one of enlightenment, which can be described as an ultimate and desirable form of great insight.

Thus an obvious route to teaching meditation to Westerners is to direct them toward insight and at least momentary inner peace, toward balancing the divide between East and West, toward balancing belief in an external god with inner insight and peace.

Great locations for direct and indirect meditation obviously include quiet places like monasteries, convents, churches, wilderness areas and parks. Curiously they can also include quiet rooms in mental health facilities and hospitals, and jails. Not all jails are quiet but if you end up in solitary confinement the experience certainly would be. Indirect meditation can include virtually anything we call "relaxing." Music, wilderness, common chores, and plain rest can all become meditative.

One Buddhist priest said: "Before I achieved enlightenment I chopped wood and carried water. After I achieved enlightenment I chopped wood and carried water."

My sponsor in Narcotics Anonymous has said: "Christ as a Buddhist? There are corollaries. Connections, if you will. Christ sought balance, harmony, enlightenment, charity, patience, compassion, humility, tolerance, honesty, love, and kindness."

Prayer can in many ways be seen as a meditative approach to making contact with a supreme being. Through prayer one finds humility which is a key tenet in the twelve-step process. In AA and NA addicts humbly ask God to remove their shortcomings. They beseech their supreme being for guidance, advice, and miracles.

Not everybody finds their god. Marya Hornbacher wrote a superb book about using the twelve-step approach without referencing a god. She said her spirituality was found in nature and the human energy of her sharing circle. Marya's book points to the 15 percent of the world's population that without belief in a god might be described as secular humanist or atheist.

A combination of godly miracles and Buddhist unburdening is a key combination for many. Godly people relish a kind of spiritual hoarding that typifies European thinking, Buddhism puts forward an emptiness that most Europeans would feel uncomfortable with. Combinations of these philosophies can provide both a degree of miraculous peace from an external god, along with some inner peace. Combined they form a sort of spiritual housekeeping.

Addicts typically accept that addiction is an incurable disease. It's like having a hole in the spiritual bucket which creates the dilemma of filling it while it also drains away.

Meditation can, it's claimed, plug that spiritual hole. It can minimize the stress of going through life constantly trying to refill that constantly emptying bucket. Put another way, until one consciously heals a wound, a blood supply will be perpetually drained.

Collectively addicts come together in AA and NA to harness the energy of their groups. Personal energy is a precious resource. Participants work the steps and read the literature to effect a process that hopefully leads to a level that provides emotional peace.

And we also acknowledge that we mostly will never get to the top of that proverbial mountain; there will always be new challenges and chores. There will always be more wood to chop, more water to carry, and more meetings to go to.

Often, after a moment of meditative rest, we go back and work all twelve steps again or adopt a new piece of NA literature as an auxiliary reading subject.

***

The concepts I call Christian Rationalism welcome former cult members, teens with behavioral health issues, drug addicts and even agnostics back into the fold of the faithful. It shoots for practical solutions to the complex search for meaning in a world of chaos. It can make spirituality available to the kinds of people who have shied away from it for centuries. We can feed such people forgiveness and love in large helpings with unlimited refills.

Prayer and meditation are free. You can pray and meditate at zero expense forever. What is left to do is the job of seeking out a community of like-minded people for support after making a leap of faith. The only miracle needed is self-forgiveness, and you need not pledge yourself to nonsense to get it. Christ is in a sense reborn to the believer every time he or she calls up his memory. Just the act of pledging your life to being happy and kind bonds you to that legacy. An afterlife may or may not exist, but you can certainly worry first about making this life as good as you can create.

The best revenge you can deliver to detractors is to live well and be happy. And in your spare time, get out there and save the world. Cure cancer with hemp oil. Promote solar power. Feed the hungry. House the homeless.

Harsh Christian evangelicals have carried their literalist beliefs for millennia. They are partly right to have kept the message alive for so long. But to the Rationalist Christian, while Christ did his altruistic and spiritual thing, according to his disciples, recorded history really has been the key to any existential immortality. Jesus would not have been remembered for his activities, for his street theater, if the scribes were not recording it. It may also be worth noting that the Coptic book of Thomas mentions nearly all of Christ's words but none of the supposed miracles.

Chapter 14: Legal and Illegal Chemistry

Psychiatric medication has come a long way just in the years I have been detained. Use of older pre-caveman medications like Haldol and Thorazine are going away. Side effects are becoming a more central concern, and more effective newer drugs like Olanzapine and Risperidone are taking over.

For a side effect example, we can look at one of those older drugs, Trilafon. It creates what is called gyrated ocular crisis. Trilafon may help make you mentally healthy, but it could also cause you a form of temporary blindness, meaning you can't do important things like navigating around your house, driving a car, or generally taking care of yourself. The ocular crisis is that it causes your eyeballs turn up into your eye sockets. You thus cannot see anything but the dark inside of your eye socket. This drug can make you mentally healthy but it also makes you legally blind.

A more modern alternative, Olanzapine, stimulates appetite and tends to makes you fat. You eat your way to a round form that is almost not recognizable. Nonetheless you can be mentally healthy, and as long as you can fit behind the steering wheel you can still drive a car. You just are fat and have that unsightly belly.

One of the key ideas here to note is that psych meds are not one-pill miracle cure-alls. They will keep you sane and you must not put them in the same category as recreational drugs. Mental health patients are in that rare state where abstinence from psych meds is as bad for them as psych patients, as having a fifth of whiskey would be to an alcoholic.

If they are helping you, if it's obvious to you that they are helping, or if everyone around you whose opinion you respect is telling you that the meds are helping you significantly, don't go off your meds. Many of us are going to need our drugs, because if we don't have them at least some of our behaviors could be crazier than a Salvador Dali painting created with him on twenty hits of LSD. If you stop taking them because you can't afford them, or because you feel so good you think you no longer need them, your illness will come back, quite reliably. Then when you try to go back on these medications, you will often find you need more of that drug to get the previously achieved effect of mental stability. Where 30 milligrams of Zyprexa/Olanzapine might have been your stable dose before, after a period without, because of a rebound effect, you might find you need a dose 25 percent larger to reach the previously achieved stability.

That's why folks in the Co-Occurring Disorder group often find they need more psychiatric medication to get to that old place when they convince themselves, or are convinced, to go off meds for a while. I'm a specific example of that effect. I went off my Olanzapine to try a drug called Clozaril. It did not work, and when I went back to Olanzapine I needed a significantly larger daily dose to achieve my previous level of control of my symptoms.

If you have a severe mental illness you don't need drugs to get high and act irresponsibly. You can achieve that end result by merely going quit from your psych meds. For such people, going off meds is like using street drugs for an addict. When you take away the psych meds, your end effect is madness as profound as that any drug can create. We the mentally ill don't need drugs to achieve an irresponsible and impaired state. What the alcoholic calls an allergy, we call a vacation from psych meds. For us, a drugless existence is a very harmful form of existence.

Like with an inebriated driver, a state highway patrol officer can pull a mentally ill driver's car over and give a field sobriety test. As a person with mental illness you'll likely as not pass it, but it should be noted that your illness can make you drive very dangerously.

We don't need drugs to get high and impaired. We do that merely by going quit from psych meds. That type of total sobriety gets us high with a thing called *mania* and it happens in many more cases than just manic depression. I like beer but I don't drink it. I love mania but I take psych meds to avoid it.

Don't ever let AA or NA or Scientology dictate your decision as to whether you will stop or continue to take psych meds. If you don't do your research and come to a knowledgeable decision, allowing yourself to be convinced by one group or the other would just be wrong.

***

In the late 1970s and early '80s, the phenomenon of self-prescribed drug treatment was a new entity that was often irresponsibly practiced, that was recklessly applied in its ways and means. Here in Minnesota, a rock punk band called The Replacements put out a song called "Treatment Bound." It was a work of poetry and melody that stands as testament to the alcoholism that saturated the Minnesota rock music community in that era. What remains today is a sad commentary of a generation that was built on the worst aspects of that culture, built on mistakes that were made in the name of healthy fun. Kids oftentimes drink so much alcohol in a manner similar to alcoholism that they might as well be considered alcoholics. Not true alcoholism, it is a binge drinker's way of life. Nearly all young people who get into drinking trouble seem to start off their drinking careers as irresponsible, binge drinking consumers.

In parallel to the national explosion of drug use, Minnesotans were among the leaders in the developing drug treatment industry in the 1970s. As with the other areas where treatment centers were being established, in Minnesota the treatments being invented and applied were truly experimental. Too many of us were drugged up, to say the least, but at least our local drug treatment centers were a step up from torturous imprisonment previous generations of drug-consuming teenagers probably experienced.

But it was still largely a hostile situation. The ill will went both ways as drug treatment swept through America like a new religion. Not all of it was functional. Much of it was simply ineffectual. The 1970s saw many incidents of drug treatment centers using extremely questionable treatment modalities, such as having their patients wear diapers under theories which postulated that removing a drug addiction could be accomplished by "re-educating" patients through returning them to their childhood.

Minnesota's Hazelden Center did not do this, but it was a real and tangible reality at some other treatment facilities. Sad but true. Hazelden and similar treatment centers chose instead to focus on using a twelve-step Alcoholics Anonymous type format, within which such excesses and extremes are less likely to occur.

This brings up a new problem: What can be said about treatment centers outside of the twelve-step umbrella? A program called Passages, in Malibu,

California, and Recovery Center in Minneapolis, Minnesota, are two of the non-twelve-step programs that I'm aware of. Passages says they try to "heal mind, body and soul" using a team approach for treatment that coordinates services of doctors, nurses, psychologists, therapists, trainers, acupuncturists, and others. Recovery Center uses a similar "holistic" approach, combining acupuncture, exercise, nutrition, massage, therapy, meditation, counseling, tai-chi and yoga to achieve "biochemical restoration."

I know there are many more out there that you can find with any Internet search. If you think those approaches are for you, go use your Google or Bing or other search tool and find them. At Saint Peter, as I'm writing this I don't yet have any access to the Internet, hence no Google, so I can only note the two that I'm already specifically aware of.

Do they work? Do they work any better that an AA model approach? Is AA too religious? Those are all particularly important questions for the non-religious, and also for the non-Christian religious, because for many such people, AA seems to be either proselytizing for Christianity, or presenting a permutation of the Puritan Christian attitude towards rehabilitation. Quakers could be hell to live with, especially if you were making gunpowder or other military munitions, but they were also great reformers in the field of rehabilitation for prisoners in primitive rehabilitation environments and penitentiaries. AA is clearly part of the Christian-centered practice of bearing witness and confession. It goes considerably beyond where Christian doctrines exist, however, teaching non-judgmental self-awareness, individual responsibility, and pure abstinence rather than just communion and forgiveness.

In a sense, AA creates a new level of Christian duty: to self first, and through that, a greater devotion to a greater good that creates benefits that all people who live near, or interact with the AA devotee can see.

This is certainly so for any AA participant interacting with co-attendees. Ultimately, personal changes can begin to affect relationships between the AA attendee and the communities around him or her. The city and nation then presumably begin to take heed that this is a person in recovery, who can thus be welcomed back into society, so long as the portions of society the person interacts with do not encourage the attendee to use alcohol. The context is similar for NA participants.

This is serious stuff. Take it seriously. No toasts or communion wine. No Passover wine either.

Chapter 15: Harder Stuff

WE'VE NOTED BEFORE several chemical characteristics of heroin, and some of the effects it can have on people, and has had on some relatively significant people in the rock music community. While something like the twelve-step AA and NA model is an often effective approach to treatment, for many drug users there is one heck of a large hoop to jump through before treatment can even be attempted. With hard drugs like heroin and cocaine, a user has to first get through an often painful physical withdrawal before setting off on any path toward staying clean, sane, and sober.

From my perspective, heroin is the most difficult drug to defend as having any redemptive qualities. It causes severe addiction and too often leads to a user overdose. It kills some people fast in overdose, and many others slowly from the effects of syphilis, from HIV and AIDS, and from other maladies passed through shared needles and prostitution. Disease comes almost universally and inevitably to addicted heroin users, as it is a filthy drug that contagiously passes infections from hepatitis to AIDS through its user communities.

About 80 percent of New York City's heroin addict community is reported to test positive for HIV or AIDS. Compared to that fate, the problems attributed to crack cocaine seem minimal. Crack's effects come to the user as a gas from vaporized cocaine. Beyond its effects on a user's mind, that means it is no longer a dermatological and circulatory problem, but rather is a pulmonary or lung ailment. I refer to AIDS being a dermatological problem because of the open sores and other problems as the disease progresses and because of the needles required for the intravenous injections that pass it around through shared needles.

Amongst other symptoms are these skin issues, medically speaking. Powerful analgesic drugs, like morphine, when used in appropriate dosages are medications designed only to reduce pain, not induce euphoria.

They may make you drowsy, but won't typically cause a loss of consciousness. Nonetheless, because science has anointed it with a positive purpose, it takes overdose into consideration only as a rare side effect, so we call it an analgesic.

Heroin can cause you to lose consciousness in an act called "nodding off." It is also called Smack, Horse, Boy, Chinese Rock, Junk, Dope, Skag, and a number of other slang street names.

There is another drug, Narcan, which can be used to immediately counteract all of a heroin-user's precious investment into euphoria.

Narcan will take a junkie's use from bliss and overdose to the cold harsh shock of sobriety and withdrawal in seconds. A friend of mine observed the use of Narcan in Chicago in the late 1960s and early 1970s. He saw a junkie go from euphoria to withdrawal in a few short heartbeats.

People given Narcan exhibit convulsions, flailing limbs, and screaming, often screams voicing extreme disapproval of being subjected to a nullification of their heroin high bought with an expensive junk-filled syringe. The name Junk associated with heroin is the source of the name "junkie" applied to street drug users.

Other addictive compounds in the opioid family include morphine and codeine. Codeine is the mildest of those three. Opioids, despite their hazards, have historically gone through periods where their use was socially accepted, and are still used medicinally with prescriptions and under medical supervision. But they can be hazardous, especially when abused and over used.

Howard Hughes, for example, was a codeine addict at the time of his death. Herman Goering was a morphine addict at the time of his capture by allied forces near the end of World War II. Actor Bella Lugosi, best known for playing Dracula in the 1931 movie of that name, was an opiate addict at the time of his death in 1956.

Note that sentence ending: *at his death*. They each used right up to the last moment of life or freedom.

Crack cocaine, also addictive, is called tame in comparison as used by some people, though crack addition is known to exist, and like stronger street drugs it can take credit, or blame, for taking people from their homes, their jobs, their families, indeed their entire previous lives. Paying for the crack can drain bank accounts, lead people into crime, destroy reputations! Name your poison of choice. Choose your doom. And then there's marijuana, for which widespread legalization is clearly approaching, and other common recreational drugs used by many of our youths these days. As of January 2020, so-called medical marijuana is already legal in thirty-three states and our nation's capital, and eleven states have legalized it for general recreational use. Ignoring kids on Ecstasy, or people of any age using medical marijuana, would be writing a book that just wouldn't make modern sense.

The only drugs I do see getting legalized in the near term are cannabis in its varied forms from marijuana to hashish. I also wouldn't be surprised to eventually see decriminalization of some of the milder prescription medications, and possibly some of the more common chemical concoctions like Ecstasy, and so-called "bath salts." These are cheap to produce and have constantly changing chemical variants that make them nearly impossible to effectively outlaw. Because the quality of these street and salt varieties vary so drastically in their noxious and dangerous side-effects, we may eventually be forced to legalize some relatively safe and standard varieties just to keep our kids from killing themselves at frat parties and underground rave dances.

Relatively speaking, some of these drugs are obviously milder with respect to the potential harm they can cause than others. Non-narcotic legal beverages like Red Bull and similar energy drinks can have the effect of a good buzz, but it is like comparing sparklers to bottle rockets, and they just don't have the same appeal to those seeking a high.

To draw an analogy, they long for the affect of the heavier stuff, for that view of bottle rocket ascent and the *KA-POW* at its apex, far more than just seeing the sparks off a wire with a pinch of gunpowder glued to it.

I think it's worth repeating, Ecstasy and similar drugs will probably, eventually, have to gain some limited decriminalization, because they are so easy to make that eliminating their availability will turn out to be as impossible as has been the federal campaign against pot. Ecstasy causes as many as forty deaths each year in the U.S.

Antipsychotic drugs kill people through a disease called malignant neuroleptic syndrome. This affects one case in 1,000 per year, which if extrapolated across all the mental institutions, and mental health outpatients in the U.S. probably kills just as many people every year, though many of those deaths probably get recorded as caused by heart disease, liver problems, etc. Fortunately, not all incidents of malignant neuroleptic syndrome involve death.

Ecstasy releases serotonin into the brain's chemistry. LSD, chemically known as lysergic acid diethylamide, also acts on the brain's levels of serotonin. Dopamine is released in the case of LSD users. Serotonin was first found in the brain and given its name while a chemically similar compound found in the GI tract, otherwise known as your stomach and intestines, was given the name enteramine. Both were eventually found to be the chemical 5-hydroxytriptamine (5-HT). It is a drug very similar to LSD, in that it could be shown to interact on smooth muscle preparations in research labs. LSD is, as we all know, a powerful hallucinogen. It causes massive amounts of dopamine to be released into the bloodstream and brain.

Unlike a narcotic, LSD does not itself get anyone high. It creates a multi-stage cascade chemical reaction that begins with eating a pill or ingesting it in some other way, for instance by licking it off a saturated sheet of paper. It ends with the creation of a hallucinogenic effect after a series of chemical steps. The part that gets you high is thought to be the natural chemicals in the brain that get pharmaceutically "knocked loose" from their traditional locations and residences.

Ecstasy floods the brain with a high-grade designer drug form of methamphetamine, which is, of course, the other common name for methylenedioxymethamphetamine. Medical scans of the brains of heavy users show dark recesses where there should be bright color, all accredited to Ecstasy use. Those dark areas are parts of the brain that are no longer functioning.

One other thing is the potential we all have to self-medicate with drugs like Ecstasy, LSD and other street drugs, or with alcohol and misused prescriptions like oxycodone. While that is not much of an issue in heavily controlled environments such as here at the prison hospital, when you are out in the free world, self-medication does become an issue.

Remember, Syd Barrett medicated himself into an English mental institution.

Chapter 16: Apologies of a Sort

THE LETTER YOU cannot send is partly the difference between a book being written and a psych assignment being done. You are not just a therapy assignment to me. I write to help readers, either by entertaining them with my fiction or informing them with my accounts of the realities of mental illness and my observations of the system we have of aiding people with it.

Any book or song, or play, or piece of art you create, should be done with the mindset that one of the things you can write about is love. Many writers can repetitively harp on themes of romantic love and affection. That is something I cannot write. Because I once harassed an ex-girlfriend, I find that I'd have to tread a bit more lightly than other writers in that arena. I still love my network of friends, but the type of love that I define as the love of getting *work* done or bettering yourself and your community, that is the form of love that I can address.

When you can truly say you are a mature member of your community, whatever community that might be, you can test an idea by writing about it for your community, or delivering a talk, or if it's in academia, a dissertation. In that latter instance, you'd take your final exams, you'd field questions and give answers, you'd graduate, and by doing all that you'd also obtain your professional degree and related credentials.

A fifteen-year-old probably has love in his or her spirit for another person, for a parent or sibling, as "puppy love" for a significant other, or for some aspect of his or her community. We older folk just have more expected of us than singular complete devotion or pure love. Most of us have jobs to do and families to support. We also have more hang-ups and inhibitions. Sometimes it is the kids who know that the king has no clothes better than his or her older cousins do, but not always.

Being an older folk with the personal history that I have, there is something I cannot do, that I can only write about. I cannot contact my stabbing victim and even say: "Oops, I am sorry we did not get along well. My mental illness caused you distress and I am sorry for that."

A person in my circumstance cannot even breathe wrong in the direction of such a victim. In AA they say: "Make amends except when to do so would cause harm to someone." That's essentially my dilemma.

That is the real pivot point, the fulcrum for me and my case. The town is big. I think it's fortunate that it's big enough for all of us. But the result of the situation can be a bit like conversing with a black hole. A black hole is a collapsed star with more gravity than light. Every form of matter and energy gets bent into its cold dark heart. And you can't even get light back out of it. In a similar vein, in situations like mine, you never get an answer back.

That tome of AA where they tell you to not interfere with another, to apologize if the interference would cause more harm than healing; that is the case for me. The way my illness comes to me, I see secret messages on TV. I hear covert messages on the radio. I read concealed messages between the lines in a newspaper. I'm now aware that all these messages are a form of hallucination. Previously, to me it was like assigning a point value to every media moment I encountered. For instance, somehow, some way, the Rolling Stones created a song in 1968 that was written just so it could be played in 2011 for me, with a message that only I was going to be privy to.

Now that's a real mental illness you can sink your teeth into. Leaving the frame of personal experience and switching into the realm of statistics, we find that the incidence of mental illness, with its associated behaviors, differs by gender. Suicide statistics for men and women show that less than 25 percent of women successfully commit suicide. For men, a success rate at suicide is about 75 percent. Men are bloodier and more violent. They use guns. For women, in many ways, taking an overdose of pills is just a cry for help.

In a similar vein, one can also look at the statistics for prison incarcerations, and for criminal degrees of insanity. More than 90 percent of those incarcerated are men. Simple subtraction: fewer than 10 percent are women. These numbers obviously reflect that men are just more prone to violence than women.

Women are just as prone to mental illness, but they more often express it within the limits defined by society as more legal forms of behavior: the hoarder, the obsessive cleaner, the eccentric old lady who seems always to be thinking out loud.

***

I stabbed a seventeen-year-old kid in the leg with a knife because I had a disagreement with a friend of hers. Her friend, Jack, was selling drugs out of their business. I was a minor drug trafficker and user too, so there was no love lost there, but Jack's style of trafficking was a step towards getting the whole neighborhood's drug intake intruded upon by police intervention. The prospect didn't make me happy, in either my sane or hallucinating states. He was sloppy. I stabbed his friend. I apologize, though it's unlikely either of them will read this book, or otherwise ever become aware of my sorrow over the course of events that night.

Jason's business practice was, for $20, to put that amount's worth of marijuana in an empty coffee "to go" cup and clamp a plastic lid on it. He would sell it to anyone with $20 in broad daylight, right over the counter for anyone present in the cafe to see. In fact, anyone looking in through the café's front window could probably see it as well. But that wasn't even the sloppiest part of it. What was sloppiest was that he allowed the buyers to go right outside and smoke the marijuana out in the open in the café parking lot. That whole scene was sloppy. It was such a ridiculously open situation that, if I didn't know better, and was at the time clearer of mind to even think it through to that point, I might have thought he was an undercover narcotics agent setting people up to be busted for possession.

I cannot say I was trying to change anything about it at all. As I noted in my earlier synopsis of the event, with my hallucinations guiding me I thought to change their operation by forcing the courts and the larger legal system to pay attention to the situation because of my act. In practical terms I just have a fiery temper, and that temper was ignited by my mental illness. It is my obligation to learn how to control my temper factor. The two decades of my treatment and incarceration at Saint Peter, combined with the psych meds that help me control my hallucinations, have helped me reach the point where I believe that I can.

Chapter 17: Forensic Mental Health

THERE ARE MUCH better drugs being used to treat mental illness than there were just fifteen years ago. The older drugs, such as Haldol and Thorazine, created a stupor, and many felt that the real goal of these drugs was to get just that debilitating side effect, because that effect would help achieve "patient manageability." For most mental health personnel, tasked as they are with overwhelming case loads, they could probably say honestly that for them there simply is no significant difference between "patient manageability" and a cure.

Not every depressed mental patient is going to write like the next Ernest Hemingway and win the Nobel Prize for Literature. Hemingway may have had some more books to birth from his soul if only he had not killed himself. Many believe that the deed was influenced by his diabetes, high blood pressure, liver problems almost certainly brought on by severe alcoholism, and diagnosable depression.

On my side of the mental illness house, it is all forensic mental health.

The term "forensic mental health," is used to describe the legal aspects of mental health confinement for treatment, and is applied to the activities of people who are involved with the process. On a practical level with respect to incarceration at a facility like Saint Peter State Hospital, forensic mental health simply refers to how people labeled criminally insane and/or dangerous are dealt with.

Forensic mental health personnel includes people from psychiatrists to social workers, people who variously examine, recommend, plan and execute treatment regimens for people like me who are considered to be mentally ill and are accused of a crime. Their purview includes determining our fitness to even stand trial. They may be enlisted to provide expert testimony for either the state or a defendant. They may be outside consultants, or people who work for state health or public safety agencies, or at criminal institutions for the mentally ill such as Saint Peter.

All forensic mental health workers are supposedly there to help patients overcome their severe mental illnesses so they can be allowed safely back out into society without a probability of their seeing those individuals again. In technical talk, the function of people involved with forensic mental health is to reduce the criminal recidivism of our population who have mental illnesses.

Here at the Minnesota State Security Hospital in Saint Peter, we had a case of an alcoholic approaching seventy years of age. His name was Larry, and he robbed banks because voices in his head told him to do that.

I have seen sufferers of Tourette Syndrome speak words of racial insult to people of color. There is a connection between what is said by a Tourette Syndrome sufferer and what is opportune for them to offend. Larry was similar in his choice to rob banks. He had an idea in his head that came from reality as it interacted with his illness, and he grabbed that baton and ran with it.

Larry robbed a bank in his pajamas after he escaped from the Hennepin County detoxification center. In those pajamas, he walked to a men's clothier and bought a suit, socks, shoes, underwear, and a small satchel for the $10,000 he got from the bank. The cops stopped him at the airport because he paid for his ticket to Las Vegas in cash. They were actually there looking for someone else. It almost worked. They found Larry instead.

Larry heard voices telling him to rob banks. I think that he was hearing that because, for whatever reason, he had bank robbery in his mind as his mental illness took hold of him. He was like the Tourette sufferer, in that there was something on his mind that mattered to him that he could not control. Like when the Tourette sufferer says something like "fuck, damn, shit, nigger" while standing in front of a black man, Larry thought about bank robbery and then listened to voices that told him to do that.

The court system and its people who are involved with mental illness are left with an old dry choice of what to do about Larry, and people like him. Do we drug them or let them rob banks in their pajamas?

Such Hobbesian choices affect lots of people with mental illnesses who are being held in places like Saint Peter both for their personal protection and for protection of society at large. Fortunately for the state, they were relieved a few years later of that decision in Larry's case, when he died at the state's only forensic nursing home.

Sadly enough, the story about Larry illustrates well how psychiatric issues were dealt with by society and the courts before good drugs came onto the market and entered psych wards in the U.S. For many, the new drugs aid real and tangible recovery from mental illness, and the delusions that come with many types of it. The older drugs never had that value. The best we could get was a stupor. The various patients at Saint Peter are on a variety of drugs and combination drug cocktails. As I've already noted, Olanzapine is what I've found works best for me. My only complaint about it is that it creates weight gain. We, the group of patients at Saint Peter taking it, call ourselves the "Saint Peter Buddha Bellies." We are all victims of that weight gain side effect. That is, however, a small price to pay for sanity.

***

At one point, I tried to change medication from Olanzapine to Clozaril to avoid weight gain. The end effect was a drastic loss in freedom. I developed *agranularcytosis*, something that causes a white cell problem leading to fevers, sore throat, painful ulcers and reduced immune response symptoms. The Clozaril had to be stopped immediately. There was no tapering off or on after the *agranularcytosis*, a dangerous side effect found exclusively in users like me who are not able to tolerate Clozaril.

In the brief span of time my medication was interrupted, I experienced a behavioral relapse that set me back significantly. I probably added four years to my sentence in my effort to find a pharmaceutical alternative to Olanzapine that could help me simultaneously achieve both mental health and weight loss.

Since going back on Olanzapine, I've initiated a renewed devotion to my physical health. I've lost twenty pounds through dieting while on my restored Olanzapine. I am still sixty pounds over what my weight was when I was first admitted to the Saint Peter puzzle palace, but that's clearly better than being eighty pounds overweight and going in the wrong direction. I continue also to rely on AA and NA type support.

On the face of it, the twelve-step programs of AA and NA seem to be transparent and straightforward. Details of those rules are not, however, always understandable in detail by even their most devout adherents.

Furthermore, it's only in recent times that we see AA and NA formally integrating permissions for medications into their programs. Finally doing so was a recognition that for well more than a decade AA and NA participants were taking things like antidepressants to aid their recoveries, and people were not stridently voicing opposition to it.

The wrinkle that impacts the AA and NA "total abstinence" approach is that some of the new chemical painkillers, drug effect blockers, and mental health medications can be just as addictive as the older, more natural vegetarian heroin and cocaine.

It's perhaps fortunate that our pharmaceutical prowess, which can create drugs with high street value like OxyContin, and painkillers like Darvon and Xylocaine, also create the antipsychotics needed by real mental patients, drugs which fortunately mostly have no street value at all.

One of the medication issues that pops up from time to time is when a mentally ill person stops taking his or her medication, either because of paranoid thoughts that the medication is poison, or feels recovered and either doubts that the recovery is brought on by the medication used, or has come to the belief that it is just no longer necessary. The problem in any of those cases is that patients stop taking their medication.

We had a patient here at Saint Peter who thought his medications were poisons. He got himself transferred to the highest security wing of the prison. We had another patient who managed to get away with "cheeking" his pills, who faked swallowing his medication. He saved up a month's worth of his pills, swallowed them all at once, and died of the overdose. Cheeking meds is forbidden, but in the case of this person, it was obviously done with great skill and utility. He did such a good job that he is now dead.

Sometimes side effects are much more serious for men than for women, or vice versa. For instance, because women often have a more fragile body image, weight gain from something like Olanzapine can contribute to symptoms of depression. If you ever know a woman being faced with the prospect of taking Olanzapine and getting fat, then other alternatives might be better tried first. Some will work well in some cases, though each might be accompanied by its own side effects. For example, as I noted earlier, Trilafon can cause gyrated ocular crisis and make driving impossible, and alter other normal activities. These versus the self-esteem issues that come with being a fat woman, or being restricted from driving. Either could potentially dramatically and severely hamper some people's recovery. If you cannot feel good about yourself then it is difficult to affect a recovery plan. If you live in an area where being able to drive is the only realistic way of getting your medical needs attended to, then that too might hinder a recovery plan.

There is hope. Trilafon is an older med but I have seen two cases where it has done well. Better to lose the ability to drive than to balloon up to 300 pounds and lose the will to live. But if ballooning in weight is what depresses your will, talk to your prescribing psychiatrist. There will be alternatives that only an experienced psychiatrist will know, and new ones come onto the market regularly if not frequently.

Unfortunately, a small percentage, but still too many mental health workers are not really in the proverbial trenches with you for your benefit. Some people are only there for the paycheck. Helping you to feel better is not the core issue for such people. That's why being conscious of your treatment professional's orientation can either amplify or simplify matters tremendously.

It should be emphasized that many, probably most workers in mental health and civil law are moral, ethical, and motivated to help people. How do you tell the difference? I have no tangible answer. Most states use a mental health legal system which imprisons people who threaten or endanger their fellow world inhabitants. It's not well known that, unlike when a criminally convicted person is incarcerated, when the mentally ill get imprisoned, they are typically exorbitantly billed for their own incarceration. Furthermore, they are billed in a way that can only be described as an excessive fine couched in terminology and legalisms that define it as simply paying for the cost of their "incarceration." Theoretically this is considered to be paying for your care and treatment. All of that is legal, and in my opinion it is a growing problem.

It should come as no surprise for many people with mental or physical illness, that physicians are mostly likely to be wealthier and conservative. Clearly, by contrast, most patients institutionalized in public facilities with mental illness are either poor liberals or are individuals who because of their illness are indifferent or languid in their feelings toward their imprisonment and the politics of incarceration. I have one friend who believes conservatives actually want to do a bad job at caring for the poor, so that the poor will all just do the conservatives a favor and die off, vacating the welfare rolls forever. That friend believes these same conservatives will say, "they want free market deregulation," which to me seems only to be a fancy way of saying competition and survival of the fittest, not caring for the least among us.

This is an obviously cynical view of mental health issues as they intersect with politics, but I can't totally discount its validity from my perspective of being a patient inside the system. And with about 85 percent of the people in mental health treatment in the U.S. saying they also have drug and alcohol issues, the conservative approach to dealing with you means you are out there tasked with a huge burden, hoping that the combination of diagnoses doesn't get in your way toward recovery.

For me there is medication that successfully stops about 80 percent of my hallucinations. Another 15 percent is controlled through talk therapy. The final 5 percent of my hallucinations are just something I have been relatively successful in learning to ignore.

In the movie *A Beautiful Mind*, John Nash found he just had to ignore all of his hallucinations. He found that approach necessary because any use of medications ruined his ability to do math. He was a theoretical mathematician who, despite his mental illness, or maybe because of the bursts of creative genius it caused, won the Nobel Prize for Economics. His equilibrium theories proved to be an economist's godsend.

Nash saw codes and secret messages in all print media. My version of the same malady is to also see radio and TV as a secret code. That's all I can say for that final 5 percent of my illness. The talk therapy is the only thing you can change by will and choice. The drugs that control my 80 percent are inert. They have no opinion. If you are like me, then yes, you can choose whether or not to take your medication, but you cannot have a pill talk back to you. If you do, then you may have a new symptom of illness to reason with. Pills do not talk, at least not yet with our current technologies.

NA and AA are all talk therapy and they can be valuable. People work programs with great conviction and deliberate effort. In AA and NA, we put our faith and health into the care of our peers. There is great value in such behavior. A fellow addict may see things that even a professional might overlook.

I have seen mental health professionals acting both like demons and saints. Sometimes the same person is both, in the span of one day. The person who prescribes your medication needs to be the most trustworthy and positively qualified person you can find, someone you can have confidence in, because you are going to be stuck with the drugs he or she prescribes in your body and affecting your brain for a long time, perhaps for the rest of a long life. Because of this, you must select your prescription writer with great care.

There is no magic gun to pick up, no magic bullet to shoot the demon of your illness with. You can only hope to restrain that demon indefinitely.

A friend spoke of the behavior of quitting smoking as being one of avoiding waking up the sleeping dragon. If the dragon does not wake, then the possibility of it annoying you or threatening you is minimized. The saying holds true, I'll maintain, with quitting alcohol and narcotics. The mental illness component is a bit more of an intangible.

As with your medication prescriber, also choose your talk therapy professionals with great care. It should be like checking the credentials of a surgeon for an elective procedure. You want the best you can find.

***

As I've noted elsewhere in this text, I'm presently approaching my twentieth year of sobriety. I got that by merit of having spent all of that time as a resident in a mental institution. Still, my triggers exist and could affect me again. What brought me here was a serious crime.

As I wrote earlier in this book, I scared the hell out of a junior grade member of a local drug enterprise, stabbing her in the leg with a small blade on a Swiss army knife. Just trying to verbalize the event brings up justification triggers and minimization triggers and all sorts of forms of rationalizing the act.

Inmate folklore has it that, in 1937, a then new nationally leading law was created in Minnesota that was designed to contain and imprison flashers and peeping Toms. This law, it is said, is what eventually evolved into today's therapeutic imprisonment laws and practices that allow someone deemed mentally ill and dangerous to be punished for crimes not yet committed. If there has been a significant crime and there is a mentally ill defendant, or even just a credible accusation that the defendant is mentally ill, and there is a belief by authorities that the crime might be repeated because of the mental illness, then the therapeutic imprisonment laws can be engaged, with a result that the defendant effectively loses his or her civil rights.

While this kind of action by the state might seem entirely reasonable on the surface, in practice it can turn out very different. When the person's mental illness has been effectively treated and the danger to society is past, there is no reason for continued incarceration. In practice, however, the standard of "cure" is so subjective, and simply having the condition "under control" insufficient, that for many it becomes a nearly impossible status to achieve. Only in the case of mental illness imprisonment is the person not released when they've complied with effective treatment programs, understand the need to stay on their medications, and are functional people again. Even suicidal individuals are seldom held to that rigorous a standard.

An individual declared mentally ill and dangerous essentially retains only the privilege of potentially being imprisoned forever in a government sanctioned prison hospital. If you are such a person you will have the right to go to prison, and once you are there, at best, you will be allowed to request a hearing on your status once every six months or so. Chemical dependency can also be used as an avenue to getting someone committed. It can be cited as a major contributor causing a person to be mentally ill. All they often have to do is accuse you of a crime for these clauses of the law to become active. This is because in mental health and chemical dependence commitments there is almost a complete absence of the strong evidentiary rules that are present in criminal court. For a commitment hearing, only the subjective opinions of psychologists, psychiatrists and prosecutors are heard.

My lawyer and I have discussed filing a *Writ of Habeas Corpus* to address the issue of jury trials for the mentally accused. A *Writ of Habeas Corpus* is a legal filing that requires bringing an accused but not yet convicted person before a judge or into court to ensure his or her release if he or she were unlawfully detained with insufficient evidence. It comes to us from very old English law, literally meaning produce the body of a person accused and stop trying to hide him in a jail where he can't be found.

My illness had little to do with my crime, but I readily admit my Axis Two type personality disorders made me generally more mean spirited. When I am not on my medication, I am less likely to give anyone the benefit of the doubt or extend mercy or consideration.

I personally have become a medication addict. Because of the dependency my body and mind have for these drugs, I no longer have the ability to live without them. I was not an addict when I came into the system, but I am so now. Fortunately it's an addiction to something that actually helps me.

I do not want an angry crime to be my only memory in the world. I do not want my legacy to be that of a mean-spirited moment and two decades of imprisonment.

I'd like to go down in history as having written a new chapter in twelve-step progress and sobriety. I'd prefer that memories of me be focused on a future of helping the poor, the uneducated, the wounded warrior, the addict, the insane, when I go back to the city, the world, a normal home. Otherwise, without the legal efforts of people like me, we may someday end up with a real society that mirrors the fictional one in the following piece.

***

SIV-P

By W. Strawn Douglas

"The whole thing sounds like self-incrimination. That's against the Fifth Amendment," James said.

"I'm really screwed," he thought.

"The Thirty-First amendment changed all that," she said with her face framed by blond curls.

"You have to look at this sense of entitlement as the key to a good confessing at the review board. If the panel can see that you are taking responsibility for your unhealthy behaviors, then you can begin to work toward a modified release where all the benefits of therapy are supplied by yourself. Once you take over the mission your therapists are tasked with, then their function will fall

away like the snake shedding his skin. It should be an easy transition for you. The biggest hurdle will be getting past those old entitlements from the old-era Constitution. The world we've made is one where a citizen is no longer allowed to hurt himself or anyone else."

James said, "But this program says I have to self-report any infraction of law or behavioral codes that get called therapy."

"Refusing therapy is against the law, and you can be transferred to the crisis unit of the hospital. All it takes is the first little step toward divorcing yourself from that older, illegal, pattern, and you are on the road to a new frontier full of employment and education that won't let the 'old you' fall back into behaviors like drugs and alcohol and antisocial sex. You will get housing and a high-paying janitorial job. You will have everything you need. To get these benefits we need your signature saying you accept placement into the SIV-P program.

"The 'Self-Initiated Violence Prevention' plan is a great program. You should be proud to be part of it. At last you can give something to your nation instead of being a burden."

He looked at her, then out the window. "There are things here that I am pleading guilty to that I haven't done. This says I owe the state $7 million. Isn't that a fine?"

"Paying for the cost of your care is a sign of your taking responsibility for your antisocial behaviors. You still have choices. You can work at a farm, in animal waste management."

"Ever since the doctors took over the behavioral courts the country has gone to hell. And this fine?" James asked.

"It's not a fine. It's a fee. Everyone has to pay their share. This could be the start of a wonderful new relationship for you and your community."

"I am just not accustomed to prosecuting myself. This is the end of my life as a free citizen."

"Look at it as a new beginning." She pushed the pen closer to him.

"Okay, where do I sign?"

He picked up the pen and scrawled his name on the dotted line. "It's confirmed now. I have evidence proving that I am screwed," he thought.

***

You may have noticed some intentional parallels to the theme of Joseph Heller's *Catch-22*. In that book the hero, Yosarian, seeks a discharge from the military. He says that the war has made him insane and he should be discharged from the military because of his insanity. The Army says Yosarian's claim that the Army is driving him crazy is actually a sign of perfect sanity. This means, the Army says, that Yosarian cannot leave because his statement that he is crazy is really proof that he is sane. This "Catch-22" has come to represent every bureaucratic situation where whatever is most obvious is read as meaning its opposite.

An element of Minnesota's mental health *Catch-22* is that there is a settlement cap on suing the state. You can only sue for $200,000. The cost of winning a lawsuit against the state is, however, rarely less than $250,000. Along with extensive immunity clauses in state law, lawsuits to achieve "justice" for an average person are thus made nearly impossible. For Saint Peter's inmates it virtually eliminates a patient's recourse to the courts for claims of maltreatment, illegal imprisonment, denial of civil rights, etc.

Another way a *Catch-22* applies to the mentally ill can be seen with the case of a fellow patient at Saint Peter by the name of George. He was originally detained for punching an abortion doctor, after that doctor had terminated a fetus that George had helped create. He has been detained now for almost thirty years. You could compare his situation to activists involved in opposition to the U.S. Supreme Court's *Roe versus Wade* decision that legalized abortion. Think of George's act in the context of a fifth-degree assault. Instead of a minor criminal assault sentence of perhaps no more than a year, with a mentally ill and dangerous diagnosis George has effectively been sentenced to life imprisonment without parole.

George served with the Coast Guard in Vietnam, in the area just north of the Mekong Delta. He has the long hair that many from that era sport. His beard is gray and he clings to the tenets of his Christianity as an explanation for his crime. In his religious context, abortion is an issue of great national import. For people like him, it is an open national wound. It is an issue with an incendiary effect on the opposite camps of opponents and supporters.

So instead of a simple charge of assault, George was accused of having a dangerous mental illness. This is clearly not the full story. If you could put the right ads in the right publications, or notices on appropriate computer blogs, you could easily fill a courtroom, or even an entire court building with so-called pro-life demonstrators who not only agree with George, but who would themselves willingly punch any abortion provider in the face, just like George did. Would we consider all of them insane and dangerous, and send a courthouse full of them to prison hospitals for thirty years?

If this is a national wound, a national area of contentious debate, then why is a person like George considered an hallucinating madman, while others who do similar things are considered to be perfectly sane? The courts apparently assumed or established that George had some mental health issues before he punched the abortion doctor, but how different was he really than anti-abortion supporters who'd willingly replicate his act? Regardless, for true and for real, the minions of psychiatry do feel compelled to harass and imprison our friend George.

People who are devotees of Scientology can provide no benefit for George, as he is a devout Catholic. To my mind, it should create an interesting paradox for them. They would have little sympathy for George as a theological captive of religious dogma, and yet they'd rail against the medications and psychiatry of the system that has trapped and imprisoned him. And, also paradoxically, while they profess to condemn the trap of religious thought almost as much as they detest psychiatry, they jumped through legal hoops to be declared a religion for the U.S. tax benefits bestowed by that status.

For sure, our man Hubbard wrote a new gospel and it has come full circle from the man from Nazareth, but that does not help our brother George.

***

We, in developed western industrialized nations, are part of a relatively non-violent society. Violence of any sort is not generally considered a good goal or an appropriate way of settling a dispute. Men may be more violent than women and may rationalize violent behavior more, but such violent behavior is rarely productive, is rarely condoned by society. The West Bank community adjacent to that part of the University of Minnesota's Minneapolis campus is not the Vietnam battle of Khe Sanh. You just cannot stab someone and expect the state to tolerate such conduct.

When you are in the throes of an episode of mental illness, however, you just don't recognize your behavior as being dangerous or criminal. I believe that you'd have to be an extraordinary soul to be able to seek knowledge by yourself on how to cope with mental illness, when that mental illness is present in you, along with chemical dependency and various self-medicating behaviors, before being forced to accept professional forensic medical intervention.

Richard, a former patient at Saint Peter, drowned in a swimming pool when he had a seizure. He had inherited a house from his mother and rented out rooms to pay the bills and cover the mortgage. He had strict rules for residency in the house, including absolutely no smoking in the building. When one tenant began to smoke a cigarette in violation of the rule, Richard got into an argument with him, grabbed a large kitchen knife and stabbed the tenant in the butt. The tenant ran out into the street screaming, where a citizen witnessed his plight, came to his rescue, and called for police and an ambulance. This incident caused Richard to be labeled mentally ill and dangerous, and made a Saint Peter inmate.

In his mentally ill state, Richard didn't see anything wrong with his behavior. In his mind at the time, in his mental illness, everything Richard did was absolutely normal, not dangerous or criminal. He just wasn't able to recognize that he had a problem there. There are an amazing number of people at Saint Peter with similar incidents in their past.

A mind is like a parachute. It functions best when it is fully open. To achieve that opening, I recommend that you buttress any existing philosophy of life that you might hold with lots of Oriental philosophy like Tibetan Buddhism and Zen. *The Tao of Physics* is my favorite. It's an approach to life that tries to merge mysticism with the physical realities of our world. It asserts that physics and metaphysics can both, in fact, inexorably lead to the same knowledge.

We need to also consider a few important things, so let's create a special label for the moment: the duality of man. I'll define this duality as the combination of, the crossroad between sobriety and medication. These should be your points of duality: avoid drugs from your dope dealer and liquor store, and actively seek out drugs designed to stop your symptoms of mental illness.

I will confess that I am very attracted to the possibility of eventually being out of Saint Peter and supporting myself with an actual paying job, possibly even one in the mental health recovery business. Upon my release from this imprisonment, I might pursue an LPN degree so I can be a "low paid nurse," otherwise more correctly known as a Licensed Practical Nurse.

The absolutely truth about this that I can't tell you often enough is that the two quickest ways to get you into a relapse are to forget to stay on your meds, or to begin or return to messing around with drugs and alcohol.

The Scientologists will say to stop your meds, get yourself "audited," and then treat your mental illness with vitamins and exercise. Many devout Christians will, for their part, tell you to give your heart and soul to Christ, their martyr, and that then the power of your heartfelt prayer will bring you to him and cure you.

Neither of these outcomes would likely have provided any real benefit for George in his legal fight over his assault on the doctor. I would personally love to crowd George's courtroom with 500 ardent supporters from the right-to-life community, and the cynical part of me says using medical law to achieve political ends is very unethical.

Another case in point is the Minnesota Sex Offender Program.

Barring major legal change, virtually nobody from that group will ever get discharged from that side of the Minnesota Security Hospital at Saint Peter. In 2012, however, a class action suit brought on behalf of those inmates resulted in a court order requiring the state to alter that program to create a path to "cure" and freedom. Running such politically sensitive criminal cases through the mental illness machinery of the state gives practical immunity, to doctors and the state, from being sued for the structure of mistreatment that they are so obviously immersed in. Again, George can turn to his belief in Christ for personal relief, certainly not to Scientologists, and probably to nobody and nowhere for any actual legal relief.

You are entitled to your own higher power. Accepting medications, therapy or peer counseling to supplement whatever you can personally enlist religion to do, to accelerate your return to mental health, should not be perceived as being in conflict. Consider religion to be a supplement, not a replacement. Here we add and not just replace.

Many behavioral scientists do believe that the human mind works better with the influence of a god and higher powers than it does without such belief. They believe that people tend to behave much better toward each other when they can envision a divine or higher or more perfect overseer to the life experience that we each have. To appeal to such a power and ask for something better or more functional is seen to be beneficial.

I can sincerely say that, even if your higher power is dramatically different from mine, I have faith that the human mind, and my mind in particular, works better with a higher power concept in place. For my part, the most important definition of spirit as it pertains to spirituality is the definition of a "life force of person." This refers to whatever that thing is that makes you alive. To me the concept of life force is valuable and it goes beyond the ability of language to explain. The concept should be of more value to the person with a damaged spirit than it would mean to those who feel they have most of their spirituality intact. It is a thing that has to be experienced before it can be described, and according to most twelve-step people it is a valued asset. They believe that it can be rebuilt, revitalized, reinvigorated. They believe that if it is lost, it can usually be found.

The only times that I have any real problems with God or religion, or even misapplied spirit, is when adherence to it is hysterical or inflexible, or is abusive to self or others. If a faith message cannot be trimmed to meet the unique needs of the people it is designed to help without harming others, then in those circumstances I cannot embrace it in my life. I hope that the definition I've arrived at meets your needs as well.

Chapter 18: Scientology and DBT

SHIFTING GEARS, WE need to return to some discussion of Scientology and Hubbard, its creator. Hubbard was so angered by psychiatry that he wrote the book *Dianetics*, and then created Scientology to deliberately confront psychiatry with what he considered a clear real alternative. Because Hubbard created his text in 1947, by any estimation it should be considered woefully out of date. It was, after all, basically a diatribe against the psychiatry of that era, and its practitioners were largely still using the sexual repression model left them by the preeminence of Sigmund Freud's ideas.

Hubbard's invented religion was a masterwork of modern words negating Christianity's two millenniums and Judaism's five millenniums of historical evolution. Fortunately or otherwise, it's easy to agree with him in some ways because psychiatry in 1947 was very primitive and quite barbaric. There were no real effective medications for mental illness back then, so when Hubbard published *Dianetics* it was something of a breath of fresh air. However, it soon became outdated as other approaches began to take hold.

One of the early approaches to therapeutic services for mental health issues appeared when mental health workers noticed how mentally ill epileptics tended to feel better for a time after experiencing a seizure. This led to seizure therapy using insulin shock, and then later electroshock therapy, now properly known as ECT or electroconvulsive therapy. With ECT, a small voltage shock is coursed through the brain. It only takes a very small electric charge to bring on the seizure.

Users of electroshock therapy often experience small amounts of memory loss and side effects like incontinence. The payoff and benefit is that suicidal patients forget why they wanted to commit suicide. Of course, there's more to it than that, but that's how I generally think of ECT.

Dianetics defined a status called being "clear," where one is supposedly no longer going to be bothered by yesterday's anxieties, misgivings or sins. It described a process called "auditing" which replaced rituals like confession and prayer. Being audited in Scientology is a ritual as much as are religious prayer or communion. It consists of a question and answer pattern and is designed to remove anxieties.

On the up side, it is valuable for being what it is not. It clearly is not antisocial. It involves no predatory behavior. Nobody gets hurt. It seems to reinforce positive aspects of the person being audited. It creates self-confidence and peace of mind. These are all good things.

Hubbard came to see himself as an opportunist, but as an ethical one. Various governments and courts around the world disagreed. Britain, Greece, Portugal, Spain and Venezuela closed their ports to him, a court in Australia revoked Scientology's status as a religion, and a French court convicted him of fraud. Nevertheless, he felt his creating Scientology, writing the series of books that defined it, was a step in the right direction for society at large. His being one of the relatively successful early twentieth century writers of pulp science fiction, he was acknowledged to be a creative type. His creation of Scientology gave him a flock and great wealth in the process, so then why not create?

Hubbard's conceptualization of Scientology and the software created for his auditing process are achievements that stand tall, like the ENIAC computers of that era. But, those were computers filling rooms the size of tennis courts to a height of ten feet. We now have smart phones with apps you can buy for one dollar that are orders of magnitude better. Modern Psychiatry can be a demon for sure, but Scientology is not well equipped to deal with that devil. A cult that has been flying on automatic pilot since its leader died in 1986, the main gift remaining from Scientology to the mentally ill is a well-worn, out of date, sixty-year-old copy of *Dianetics*.

Cruise' faith in Scientology is cult-like, and though Scientology is now trying to be an ally with the anti-medication forces in improving laws affecting the mentally ill, there are problems. It is not a perfect fit. Scientology was couched in all sorts of pseudo-scientific terminology, and it created a community of people who had similar experiences and who felt collectively liberated. That community was a social group supporting a newcomer much as veteran participants in AA and NA groups support their newcomers. In the process the veteran is strengthened and becomes a leadership figure. In 1947, this was truly a step forward. This was also the recipe for a cult.

Nowadays the Scientologist flock calls their book collection a form of "software for the human computer." Nonetheless, the software they speak of is more than sixty years old, dating back to the era of vacuum tubes.

A great deal of Scientology, in my opinion, is outdated mumbo-jumbo. But, while I think I can safely say that a lot of *Dianetics* no longer applies to the real world or the world of the mentally ill, it is important to remember that at its beginning it really was a step forward. Since the 1980s, there have been significant progressive steps made in developing psychiatric medications for the treatment of various mental illnesses. There was the drug Thorazine, which was one of the first true anti-psychotic medications. Later came Haldol, and finally, in the current century we have Clozaril and Olanzapine. Despite these advances, the whole Scientology thing has never adjusted its opposition to all medication.

These new drugs work much better than their primitive ancestors did.

I noted earlier that a payoff to the use of ECT was, amongst other things, a reduction in suicidal tendencies. That's a good point to also relate to antipsychotic medication.

The book, play and film versions of Ken Kesey's *One Flew Over the Cuckoo's Nest* each had our hero, McMurphy, undergoing ECT and being turned into a vegetable. This is an extremely exaggerated scenario.

What I get from *Cuckoo's Nest* is an honest and verifiable attitude that parallels how I've seen core modern day providers operate. ECT is not used to lobotomize. The reality is very different from that.

Nobody gets lobotomized in that way anymore, or even surgically. They use drugs to accomplish similar effects now. The adversarial relationship between the provider and the patient and power control relationships are, however, accurately portrayed. The Nurse Ratchet behaviors portrayed do exist, but are much more subtly nuanced in the reality of present day practice.

The petty tyrant issues portrayed are also real and tangible. It is behavior we find in the military, in prisons and in mental institutions.

***

One pet peeve is watching young people be bullied by family and state, labeled as being "behavioral problems." Such kids may get involved in drugs and alcohol, street crime, unwanted pregnancies, and truly dead-end jobs. Such kids are often faced with forced evangelical Christianity, ordered to pray their way out. It's tough to make coherent career decisions at the age of seventeen, or even much younger.

Daniel Sheehan was a lawyer and liberal activist. He founded the Christic Institute as a non-profit law firm to go after CIA indecencies in South and Central America under the Reagan and Bush the Elder presidencies. The Institute was ill fated as a court judgment issued a very large fine that forced it into bankruptcy. It reformed as the Romero Institute, named after civil rights crusader Archbishop Oscar Romero, who was assassinated in El Salvador during that country's civil war.

By the ritual of communion in Christianity you may be said to be pre-forgiven of your sins by God, but you may have still broken criminal or civil law. You'd be advised to be careful to not anger a judge as he or she may well be your only possible savior and delivering angel in our worldly arena. If you are under the age of eighteen you can become an emancipated teenager through the courts. You will need a job and a place to live, and usually legal assistance in such an effort. Though this "emancipation" is possible, it is often not easily granted in many states.

***

Delivering a recovery message to drug addicts from all points of the religious globe can be a daunting task. I come from the same largely Christian background as do most Americans. My approach to life therefore is neo-Christian, Christianity tinged by the reality of science, and my love of science fiction, good music, and the best drugs available to me. I have fortunately found a few drugs that are less harmful than others, and other legal ones that have actually contributed to improving my mental health.

While I consider marijuana to generally be one of the good drugs, it disagrees with my current mindset of having a mental illness that forbids me from ever again being a marijuana user. I have had to put it aside. It's not called loco-weed by random mistake. Generally it is mild stuff, and in my old age I try to preach "the call of the mild." People are now looking to marijuana as a cure for intractable pain and the shell shock of PTSD. As such it is being lauded as a cure for many illnesses from seizure disorders to shrapnel injuries from combat in wars.

The best thing I can say about crack cocaine is I run into a lot of people who complain about it but are in perfect health because that drug did not give any of them AIDS or a heart attack. After quitting the drug, their health improves and their survival rate is very good. The trick is to quit and survive.

The use of cocaine, opioids, fentanyl and heroin has been sweeping through American culture faster than a wildfire, and with the impact of a blaze in an oil refinery. It's bad news. In 2019, overdose deaths hit a new high of 71,000, driven mainly by fentanyl and synthetic opioids such as OxyContin. They spread AIDS and kill through overdose. It is a modern perpetual problem for which there appears to be no quick cure. There are detox drugs that can get an addict through withdrawal sickness in as little as six hours under sedation. There is the antidrug Narcan that can stop an overdose in minutes. Narcan has been around since the 1960s and it still works quite well. A shot of Narcan can save a life.

LSD can drive you insane. It can fry your brain like an industrial chemical, but it can also create the feelings of religious ecstasy that kept Timothy Leary fascinated for fifty years. More recently it and related drugs have found some medical uses in trial studies on treatment for PTSD, the post-traumatic stress disorder that, for instance, affects many veterans of combat.

Cocaine continues to be a go-to drug in many celebrity spaces. Though I preach a variant of Christianity that helps people recover from drug and alcohol use, I'm hard pressed to successfully argue a case against it without getting drowned out by a cheering demand for that drug.

The devilish thing about drugs is it wouldn't be a problem if there was no attraction factor. If they weren't fun, nobody would use them.

***

Any god should, I believe, want you to be happy. If you assume a god exists you should probably also assume that such a deity should want you to live without a crippling dependency on anything. In a sense you might say you are already addicted to food, water and air. Creating other artificial addictions, to opiates and amphetamines, starts a drift into some of the most crucial points a religion like Christianity seems to have been designed to deal with, or at least ought to have been.

Christianity is, at least in theory, big on forgiveness. Clearly it's meant to help an insane world find peace and fulfillment. Currently our religious institutions want people to avoid drugs other than the proverbial opiate of the mass, religious belief. Most western religions strongly counsel against drug use, a few ban absolutely any use of mind altering alcohol and substances, and one even totally bans medicinal interventions.

I, on the other hand, am very aware that drugs do get consumed. My take is to get a message of forgiveness out to that population of users. So drafted and conscripted into the drug use army, these people inevitably constitute an army of the walking wounded.

The best message is that there is hope. There's hope for veterans who get hooked on opiates overseas, even from conflicts in heroin country designed to fight the international movement of drugs. There's hope for people with lost limbs and chronic pain who get hooked on opioid pain killers. There's hope as a "softer" drug, marijuana, which is better, less harmful than heroin, is seriously becoming a legal alternative in more and more states.

Walking into a biker group's clubhouse with a stack of King James bibles and a lecture on temperance just doesn't work. But if there can be any path to forgiveness, it probably has to start with giving yourself some forgiveness for the mess you have gotten yourself into. Other forms of communion can be an alternative route to forgiveness for some. It can be a sharing of food, drink, and even drugs, spit and other body fluids, but such sharing can be as much a portal to the spread of disease as a joining together in community.

Some will thrive while others will die. In religion we accept this with a spirit of forgiveness. With drug use, as often as not we condemn the users to social oblivion. All would have been equally tuned to the practice of mental health being an application of the arts of biochemistry.

When we tell kids about Jesus or Moses or the many other figures out of religious history and mythology, we feed them miracles and folk tales. That keeps them theologically well fed mostly until about age twelve or so. That's when most people stop believing in Santa or the Easter Bunny. That's when many get the story switched to more "adult" theology, or are just told that Jesus was simply a man with some cool ideas and a somewhat suicidal bent aimed at getting his point across.

***

Behavior therapies often try to address mental health both as stand-alone treatments and in combination with medical chemical or other therapies. DBT (Dialectical Behavioral Therapy) and Scientology are two of the better known of these approaches, as greater America strives to reach a broad definition of behavioral health.

Both Scientology and DBT feature behavioral exercises designed to create healthier humans. Scientology is old and DBT is new. Scientology's patterns of harassment and assault are becoming public, and people are increasingly beginning to see it as a cult.

Scientology "simplified" human psychology in postulating a belief that there were two halves to the mind, one half analytical and the other the source of all emotion and troublesome demons. This later half it called the reactive mind. The entire school of Scientological thought was directed to the process of attempting to control this troublesome half.

DBT constructs its theory more complexly. It breaks its analysis of behavior into four parts: mindfulness, interpersonal effectiveness, emotional regulation, and distress tolerance, but also teaches that behavior is the outcome of a two-mind system. Much as with Scientology, DBT postulates that one half is the rational mind and the other is the emotional mind. Where the halves intersect is where DBT identifies a third focus that it calls the wise mind.

Thus it can be said that Scientology started some basic concepts that are still used today.

Scientology, regrettably, suffered from an artificially constructed power structure in a top-down dictatorship originally run by its founder, Lafayette Ronald Hubbard (or as he preferred to be known, L. Ron Hubbard). He once proposed the idea that the surest way to achieve power and riches would be to invent a religion, and so he did. He just got a bit carried away.

Hubbard was a prolific writer of mainly adventure and science fiction novels. He began his religious endeavor by mining his previous works of science fiction to develop a founding creation myth, however absurd it appeared on the surface. He told his followers to believe the myth of ghostly spirits that infest humans to this day. The technical and expensive process of going "clear" was how an individual could be rid of the infestation and become a success in life.

Neither Scientology nor DBT is actually a mainstream therapy today, though you can still find the later in use as a behavioral therapy. What I have found is that present standards in psychiatric care and community resources often force those accused of being criminally mentally ill to live without or with strictly controlled minimal human contact. Therapists and doctors keep a distance and the accused rarely has a chance to bond with anyone in the process outside of, perhaps, other felons. And this is even without considering the abusive use of solitary confinement to control those with more dramatic mal-behaviors.

This makes for a population of people so starved for human contact that they become vulnerable to both legitimate medical as well as cult-like therapies found in groups like Scientologists, Moonies and other harsh charismatic Christian-like churches. Whether truly Christian or quasi-Christian, cults should be seen as an evil permutation of all the good that can be found in faith.

***

In addition to my base schizophrenia (that's things like hearing voices, not having a split personality as it's commonly defined in the public mind), I suffer from something called "psychiatric trauma." This is a form of PTSD created by too much psychiatric care. The very concept of "forced care" implies psychiatric trauma. Psychiatrists don't often admit to being the cause of a disease, but I assure you that concepts like this are assuredly valid.

The Narcotics Anonymous Blue Book covers many mental health issues in a doctrinaire and dogmatic manner, but it is written with a sense of purpose and practicality that transcends those aspects. It is written by people who care about helping people involved in addiction issues.

One person Narcotics Anonymous helped was a person I know who became addicted to injected opiates. He now has a business career and has been sober for more than a decade. A success story, he attends NA meeting regularly. He has come so far in those twelve years. In that time a new career, a divorce, and a new "family" through NA have saved his life.

Before NA, despite a drug injection incident that almost cost him one of his arms, after the damage was fixed in a hospital, he went right back out to using. When he became part of the NA community, he found a wealth of people to help him through the cravings and the longing for the drugs of his addiction. This became a key element of his recovery as his new career actually provided access to some drugs. The NA community met his crises with love and compassion.

With this kind of help addicts who starve themselves down to looking like concentration camp survivors can give up the addictions that consumed their finances all the way to their food money. They too came to the fellowship of NA and found the energy needed to surrender that addiction, letting them embrace an addiction-free way of life.

NA type therapy is neither easy nor a quick fix. When NA was founded in 1953, there were few drugs to choose from. Now there is a cornucopia of compounds to choose amongst, and the list seems to grow daily as medical and chemical scientists come up with new drugs and compounds.

Because there will always be people who are going to do drugs, there is often nothing that can be done except wait until someone crashes and then help pick up the pieces. When that happens you can try to help them sort the debris and pick out the parts that still work, but the seductive pull of the drug will still be there. They will often keep going back no matter how hard they crash.

It's times like that where I actually put my atheist ways on pause and recommend the option of a god connection the individual can relate to and use to start a climb out of the hole they dug themselves. Nearly all of us in America come from a Christian/Judeo background. When you need faith you can see many positive aspects to the old cure of Christianity. In faith, people can fly over the barrier of convention and reason in times when a spiritual connection is one's only realistic path to reason.

NA has never been a place for a devout atheist. If you want to recover with them, ultimately you have to make peace with its religious roots. Eastern religions and Native American spirituality may or may not work similarly for any given adherent to those traditions.

***

To my way of thinking there is a distinct possibility that Hubbard's creation myth was actually a channeling of megalomania, itself a mental illness.

In many ways an upgraded and modernized version of Hubbard's invention, DBT nevertheless sometimes seems to be becoming a law enforcement standard for categorizing criminal mental health. This being the case, Marsha Linahan, who wrote and created DBT, may well inherit the evil potential found in Scientology. I can only hope that if it makes her rich it doesn't go to her head as "power." And also that DBT perhaps helps deprogram Scientologists.

Many times in the current mental health/chemical dependency system, you find people who are not so much mentally ill as they are feral. Wild and "out of control," as the state would say, those people are being arrested for not having a suburban settled safe homogenous lifestyle. The state takes over and turns them into drones. Oddly enough, many people are happy and fulfilled with that role in life. They eat their drugs, be they medicines or street illegals. They study their DBT literature. They show up for their appointments and work. It's just like the '70s, where Sergeant Friday on *Dragnet* tells the kid to get a job and a haircut. Oddly enough, many people love to fit in like one of a thousand bees in a hive.

Underneath it all, society accepts that the mass of humanity really want to be drones, to fit into a suit and a tie, enjoy a barbecue with other drones, drink the same beer, drive the same cars and listen to the same music. An English translation of Matthew 5:25 says: "Agree with thine adversary quickly, whilst thou art in the way with him, lest at any time the adversary deliver thee to the judge, and the judge deliver thee to the officer, and thou be cast into prison." We are getting to be safe, non-confrontational drones, happy to receive our small share of suburban bliss.

That's certainly not a revolutionary commitment to fight power or any status quo.

Other New Testament passages could be read as suggesting a type of peace pact between the "powers" and moral, ethical practices, like between the Pharisees and Rome, or a non-aggression pact like the one between Hitler and Stalin. The contrasting points suggest a duality that must be reasonably considered.

As noted earlier, in courts around the country, DBT seems to be increasingly used to parent the feral behavioral type, and reclassify a growing litany of crimes as the manifestation of disease. Crime seen as illness? Some will say this is an upgrade from a penitentiary's penitence and enforced remorse.

There was a gathering of "hippies" that challenged their open and forgiving ways, of ultimate freedom and forgiveness practices. It seemed a wolf had infiltrated those sheep. A child molester had bought and modified a school bus into a classical hippie-look camper, and was caught trying to lure children into it. The hippies reacted by calling local police and getting him hauled off to jail. This odd behavior from the seemingly perpetually forgiving was like the passage from Matthew about plucking the eye from the body and casting it out to protect the larger body from contamination that would "cast them into hell." In special cases like this, even the most tolerant of peoples can resort to using an unforgiving legal system. Even the most permissive of peoples carry a standard of decency and fairness.

This is the duality that can exist between tolerating an obscenity and forgiving with mercy. The hippies transcended their own identity as scofflaws and committed their "sin" of endorsing and using the powers of law enforcement to maintain their own healthier communal body.

In this sense justice has a place. We make judgments and live with the results of our choices, our collective votes and consciousness, whether we are considering "pure criminal behavior" or similar acts moderated by mental illness. Is it better to pray for a revelation to stop the dictator, or just the heart attack?

There were similarities between the early hippie and early Christian communities. Each had a group consciousness and group dynamic which focused on shared resources, pacifism, and on creating a loving opening to a peaceful group goal.

These dualities are the core of this book: war and peace, meditation and combat, emotion and logic, intoxication and sobriety, and often, mental health and illness.

The real goal for all such dualities is seeking balance, such as what those with mental health issues often seek out. This is sort of like what one finds in Asian martial arts, where the violence and intensity of combat is balanced by the spirituality found in meditation.

This balance is transcendent. If we can go from being "all on" and take all of that energy and give it away to the universe through the calm and peace of meditation, then those with mental health issues may be able to live a balanced life. Rather than go "all on" and then "all off," the goal can be to bring a peace and calm to the combat in a person's brain. An energetic and peaceful presence might be achieved by some through to the exercise of meditation.

Chapter 19: Spycraft

AN IMPORTANT ASPECT to the way mental illness is managed in the U.S. is the reaction of case managers and psychiatric staff to imagination. To the world outside of a mental hospital, imagination and creativity is quite often a much valued character trait that can be channeled into research and invention, and into art, music and storytelling. By contrast, inside a mental health facility a creative imagination can be a cause for a case manager to write negative comments into your permanent medical file. Bear with me through a slight digression to set the scene.

Many pieces of fiction have tried to describe secret lives. Good film directors like David Cronenberg and Terry Gilliam have made the surreal into the remarkable, and the marketable, in films like *Naked Lunch* and *Brazil*.

Drug addicts often use imagery from books and movies on spies and other covert enterprises. We would call ourselves "sneakers," and get ourselves around by taking seriously our need to be drab, colorless little people. On those occasions when we would be moving a pound of marijuana from one part of town to another, we would try to take off all our cultural defining tags, become as mundane as possible, and try to blend into the everyday background in the world around us.

We became students. We became housewives. We became clerks and waiters. The long hair got stuffed into stocking caps and the political buttons came off our lapels.

We carried a backpack for the look of a student. We put a shoebox inside the backpack. The drugs went inside the backpack or shoebox. We took a cab or drove our own car. If we drove we drove a Chevy, Honda, Ford or Toyota, and nothing near their showy high-end or sporty models that you see drug dealers driving in the movies. We avoided bad neighborhoods for any chance of a breakdown.

We would put on a suit or a dress, wear a tie and carry a briefcase, or carry a shopping bag or that backpack. If the courier is a woman, then the shoebox containing the pound of marijuana resides in a Target or Macy's shopping bag. Such a woman would be casually but well dressed, like a reasonably fashionable lady going about town or on her way to a social activity downtown or in a nearby suburb. What policeman would stop an everywoman carrying a Target or Macy's shopping bag?

We really did become secret agents, and we took our smuggling very seriously. It didn't matter if it were coke, heroin, or hash. Long hair was a hazard. You did not bring your drugs to a political demonstration. You didn't go to political demonstrations. Looking too much like a political leftist or hippie or punk was bad for business. There would be time enough for that form of anti-social behavior later on. We wouldn't do it when we were being a courier of drugs. The more drugs we had, the more invisible we needed to be.

You also always carried weapons because you always carried cash.

We created safe houses. We used weapons and chemistry equipment.

We talked our own language. Heroin junkies would talk about blood and roses as their drug would back pressure blood into the syringe and create a rose of blood in the clear fluid of the heroin-water mix already in it.

Junkies would seek out acetic acid, which could be used to extract heroin from morphine.

Gay heroin addicts, like William S. Burroughs, wrote about secret agents and secret gay sex and drug hustlers.

Junkie poet Patti Smith wrote a song called "Horses" for her album titled *Easter*. Her Easter reference was used to separate drugs, like heroin from the Middle East or Far East, from more homegrown drugs like Columbia's coca. Coca is from the Western hemisphere whereas heroin is from the East, and thus "Easter." Horses are a reference to junkies calling their drug "Horse." Thus we get *Easter* and its song "Horses."

In a not dissimilar vein, John Lennon says, "I dig a pony" before the song "The Two of Us." Coca is said to be the white pony, while heroin is the white horse.

At the height of his group's popularity, The Rolling Stones' Keith Richards, who liked heroin, frequently visited France while driving his Bentley automobile, which the group named "Blue Lena" after Lena Horne, a popular jazz singer. They found they could unbolt a spot on the car's frame and store their drugs there. It was like being a spy who would hollow out anything convenient to stash microfilm, or to stash their stash in this real life.

Other people hollowed out books, replaced the stuffing in children's soft toys, or wore their drugs in special pockets under their bras or around their waists.

Depictions of mental hospitals in *Girl Interrupted* and *Awakenings*, and even our "Cuckoo's Nest" were all very realistic.

Generally, this has not been the case. TV and movies have made it all look great for the camera, and that's where John Q. Public came in. We needed you all to realize that drug use was not how it looked on film or TV, at least when it's glorified. Some of the more sordid scenes of destitution and prostitution were more accurate.

We took it all very seriously back then. When it was invisible, then it was functional. We were all very professional. Thus, we get to my letter to my case manager that said I thought I was a secret agent practicing medicine in a vast organized crime network.

We were not too far from the truth.

We had it all and it was a paradise of sorts, at least as we compared our lifestyle to those not in it. We had rock bands like Soul Asylum and Replacements and Hüsker Dü all putting our humble Minnesota scene in the music forefront. We had a national exposure. We had nurses and doctors at our call no more than a three-block walk away from our downtown homes. We took all of our drug culture and medical facts and we tried to practice as good a form of medicine as we could. We were very good at our spy craft. We could move ten kilos across town with no problem.

The Talking Heads tune say: "We dress like students. We dress like housewives. We ain't no foolin' around." That is from a song called, "Life During Wartime."

Whenever bands would go on tour to New York, they would bring back souvenirs like heroin or coke. From Seattle would come stuff like Hong Kong heroin or Vietnamese opiated hashish. From California, they would bring back cannabis and eight-inch by five-inch sheets of blotter paper soaked in LSD.

We bought sheets of LSD from San Francisco. One gallon of laboratory pure LSD could dose a significant portion of the entire United States. Like nerve gas, it is very potent stuff in its pure state. We could get our cost down to thirty dollars per sheet in San Francisco and get our cost down to about $600 for a pound of smoking herb.

There was an entire subculture to this. My contribution was *spycraft*, though I was not as colorless and drab as I could have been.

Ordinary people only see the flagrantly ostentatious who spend money visibly. The invisibles rarely get caught. The real operators are the invisibles who don't go out to high end clubs, or buy expensive clothing and fancy cars. These low-key people are the ones who have three kilos of contraband in their attic in South Minneapolis, or they may be a local organic farmer growing more than just edibles, or a worker at a retail store marketing a few other things on the side.

Hustlers were everywhere. You never trusted anyone with money. Drug transactions were always in cash.

Drugs were herbal, vegetarian, Native American. The cocaine was Incan. Marijuana was herbal. All were vegetarian.

Those were the days. We were really good secret agents.

We mostly also used ourselves as pharmaceutical guinea pigs. We saw ourselves as test pilots going up or down in new and innovative ways. But as with test pilots, the experimentation was deadly for at least some.

We satisfied our curiosity on how to grow mushrooms, experimenting with an autoclave, and growing marijuana in the backyard or in a foil lined grow-box inside a closet. We pioneered home growing, and head shops now sell grow lights ostensibly for February tomatoes and other gardening uses.

I take great pride in the professional way we worked our craft. Our craft was locked on and rock solid. We were really good at what we did.

I also take great pride in my military career. I brought military knowledge from a Marine Corps that smoked its way through Vietnam with cannabis and opium. We did not value or see its potential when we were over there.

For the most part, however, our drugs did not come locally from Wisconsin growers, or even nationally from California. We mostly got Columbian and Mexican marijuana. We knew it came from organized crime, but that was part of its appeal.

We had real organized crime connections. We thought we were very professional at our craft. My contribution was to connect buyers to product if they had the cash and the right pedigree. I got a small commission.

We used every trick in the law enforcement military smuggler playbook. We went back to medicine reprising the Civil War morphine addiction called "soldiers sickness." We used Sherlock Holmes' seven percent solution for cocaine. We read the 1909 book called *Pearls, Arms, and Hashish*. We had it all, from the rare Thai stick to the Sensimilla variety of marihuana.

Our drug culture also included money laundering and works of charity. Since we had money to burn, we would get generous at Christmas time. Did you ever put a hundred dollar bill into a Salvation Army kettle? Some of us did.

Money laundering was done similarly to our business setups.

We filed our taxes as self-employed private contractors. Our cooperative/communist cafes helped us with this. You did not pay social security, and you officially earned only a few dollars above the minimum wage. The biggest payoffs were that you could smoke pot in the basement and you were your own boss. The group managed it all collectively. We had an entire subculture that surrounded the idea that we were very professional about our drug trafficking behaviors. It was no joke. We took it very seriously. We used spy stories and mafia movies as our inspirations. We looked at movies and at characters like James Bond and said those people were absurd and silly, because we were the real things. Wear a suit. Cut your hair. Carry a briefcase. Become invisible. Remain functional. We were the real things, while 007 was a fantasy. We spoke in codes and rarely used phones to do our dealing.

Those who stayed with it became truly professional. The rest of us just did enough to supply ourselves and pay our bills.

We flew like we were astronauts. We skulked in the shadows and maneuvered around the "system" like spies and secret agents. We were hallucinauts. Of course, part of my problem was that the hallucinations continued when the drug was gone, like a permanent hallucinaut. Like being stranded on Mars with limited oxygen and a crashed ship, your time was going to be limited if help failed to arrive. My mental illness was certainly intensified by my drug use. I sometimes could not tell where the "professionalism" of the trafficking ended and my illness began. Pretend paranoia and professional paranoia often got blended into my mental illness as one great big paranoia.

I personally did not like the white powders: heroin, cocaine and methamphetamine. Marijuana was another thing completely. Because it feeds hallucinations and encourages paranoia with people like me, it did not improve any of my mental illness symptoms.

For me, having a mental illness with a secrecy component carried over into the drug community and its secrecy behaviors. One day, you're carrying a pound of marijuana across town on a bicycle. You also have a mental illness. You would separate those two activities if you could. They are both rooted in paranoia.

With my mental illness and my behaviors crossing over into paranoia, I'd spot key phrases in songs and understand them in my unique context. Songs on the radio took on different, secret meanings. The paranoia had me mentally recreating my courier missions over and over, looking out the window again and again, to see if I'd been followed, to see whether the two fortyish white males in a four-door nondescript car outside my front door were undercover cops. Or was the paranoia again getting the better of me?

When your paranoia has reached that point, then what do you do? What happens when just sobering up makes for an incomplete change? What happens when your paranoia is still there long after the drugs have gone away? Wrap all of those factors together and you might well reach the conclusion that both sobriety and medication are clearly suggested as a prescription for future sanity.

As for being a secret agent of the drug cartel, then that is something I may someday write a novel about. If you are interested, I already have three fiction novels, *Black Hole Drive*, *The Joy Engineers* and *Ultra Murder*, and two editions of a nonfiction book to my credit. The nonfiction work is *Mental Health Imprisonment: One Case*. All are available for purchase online in digital and print editions.

The novel *Ultra Murder*, about drugs and secrecy, borrows generously from my experience with the behaviors of my drug days. Set in the secrecy of drug trafficker based realities; I'd recommend it to drug addicts who are vacillating between sanity and medication issues. For an addict, changing your behaviors to incorporate swallowing pills to feel normal may be a problem. Quitting other drugs may also be challenging. Sobriety requires that both be done.

Often times, just being involved with the secret world of drugs can be seen as symptoms of mental illness. Sometimes this is clearly and obviously open. Other times, one paranoia gets confused with another. When I was talking about writing about some of these things, my county caseworker once said: "Oh great, now you're going to do everything I tell you to do because you're telling me about your career as a secret agent and that means you want me to take control of your life." She underestimated how much depth there was to my secrecy behaviors.

It has been important to me to be accurate when talking about my paranoia. The book you are currently reading would probably be more to the caseworker's liking than some of the stories I related to her.

When I told my case manager that we saw ourselves as secret agents "practicing medicine to the mob," there was this feeling being put forward that I thought we had national importance. Any such idea would obviously be only a delusion brought on by my drug use and mental illness. As my hallucinations were bathed in small pieces of reality, I said I thought that we thought our realities were unique. I have since learned that many mentally ill people think they are secret agents. The actual reality for us was probably closer to only meaning that we were trying to be sneaky and careful and stealthy.

While we were indeed at the end point in several chains of drug distribution, there was no vast criminal conspiracy, at least not one that I had any effect on. Lots of people take drugs. My actions may have affected a few hundred, but that's all.

Those are the delusions I meant when I said that I practiced medicine to a vast criminal conspiracy. In my mind, I was a secret agent. In my mind, I practiced medicine. In my mind, I administered to a vast criminal conspiracy.

Certainly, my involvement with all the "Fat Tony's" in our nation's criminal underworld was pretty close to minimal. I was a small spot on the soft underbelly of America's organized crime scene. I was so drug addled that my contribution was probably more properly labeled "Disorganized Crime."

***

Those are my past life's delusions for you to peruse. Knowing how my delusions and hallucinations influenced my behaviors will, I hope, give you some insight into one individual's plight, how that person's mental illness, interacting with and being reinforced by substance abuse, led him eventually to an overtly harmful criminal act. It will, I also hope, encourage you to seek out and work a treatment plan for your mental illness or substance abuse, and enable you to get out of any personal or institutional prison you might find yourself in as soon as possible.

Now, I rep for the sobriety scene. It is not always a perfect fit for a person historically inclined to individualism like me, but at my age I'm running out of time to argue the case. When I came here I was thirty-one. As I write this passage I'm in my fifties. That means I won't have a lot of time left to argue any finer points in the debate. There may be power in numbers, but the disorganization factor goes up exponentially. Maybe I and my crowd just went to more spy movies than were good for us.

At this point in my life I have completely lost my appetite for any treats from the street pharmacy. They simply no longer make any drugs that I want. Those were the days. Gone but not forgotten.

Chapter 20: The Proffitt Effect

First, a little background on the State Security Hospital itself, and its operations.

What we now know as Saint Peter State Hospital opened its doors as a hospital for the "insane" in 1866 in temporary quarters. Its first permanent building was completed in 1875. An Asylum for the Dangerously Insane was opened on its campus in 1911, to receive transfers of people from other prisons and reformatories showing signs of "insanity." It was also to receive "such persons from the various criminal courts of the State who are adjudged too insane to stand trial, as well as those acquitted because of insanity; and finally, to receive such persons from other state institutions who show homicidal or dangerous tendencies," according to the 1914 Biennial Report of the Superintendent. The "Minnesota Security Hospital" name was adopted in 1957. Other facilities were eventually built to increase the state's capacity to house such people.

Thorazine, the first effective medication for the treatment of mental illness, was introduced in 1954. It and subsequent medical interventions contributed to a nationwide deinstitutionalization trend beginning in the 1960s. Along with these medications, the establishment of community nursing homes for elderly and chronic patients reduced Minnesota's security hospital MI&D populations from more than 2,500 in the mid-1950s to fewer than 400 by 2015. The other part of the facility, housing Minnesota's sex offender population had 288 "patients" as of September 2020.

In the early 2000's the philosophy for adult mental health treatment focused on person-centered treatment for patients. However, this focus changed in April of 2006, when convicted rapist, Michael Dale Benson, and three other patients escaped from the security hospital. Law enforcement and Minnesota Department of Corrections personnel were assigned to the hospital to make it more secure, and sophisticated security and monitoring systems were installed. This created a closed campus with restricted access through checkpoints and guarded gates. High intensity lighting, cameras, motion detectors and razor wire installed around some of the buildings turned the hospital into even more like a prison. Patients were required to wear electronic monitors.

All these physical changes in the hospital's environment contributed to overt changes in the facility's culture. The once therapeutic milieu of the hospital transformed into a hostile, punishment-oriented environment based on adversarial relationships between staff and patients. Security-oriented counselors who were already hostile, antagonistic, provocative and malevolent toward the patients became more so. Rules were enforced arbitrarily and restrictions were doled out liberally. A patient's good behavior meant nothing to them.

In this new confrontational environment, the Security Counselors were viewed as constantly scheming to entrap, goad and provoke well-behaved patients into acting out in anger. That was so they could slap on restraints and throw them into seclusion. Subduing violent patients who were acting out often resulted in serious injuries to staff and patients.

What was left of the therapeutic model was at best a process of self-flagellation, with staff freely exercising their domination over patients. I had personal experience as a victim of all these changes.

***

When I talk about life here in the "off the books prison" at the Minnesota Security Hospital in those early high security days, I have to focus on what I call competitive self-flagellation. This model was used to dominate the so-called therapy process. It was a process of trying to break people down, of dominance and subjugation. I remember well the faces of murderers and rapists, each petitioning for mercy and deliverance. I remember all those damaged souls who tried to harm the world and got that harm reflected back on them. While you can call it karma for them, for the rest of us it was simply a not so subtle form of coercion and torture.

When I arrived at Saint Peter in 1994, I saw cases that were old even then. There were cases like that of an inmate I'll call Ben, who had killed his mother about ten years earlier. And there was another, Earl, who had put together a couple of dozen packages of explosives and left them in corporate buildings and at children's playgrounds.

In the winter of 2011, we were told of a black fantasy that could affect us if put into law. It was a perspective on mental illness held by some of the more conservative members in Minnesota's legislature. Whereas authority and direction of patient procedures had come to be focused in the facility's medical director's office, the proposal would have turned absolute decision making authority back down to the vagaries of individual psychiatrists.

It seemed that supporters of the legislation were seeking to have Saint Peter, not even then known to exemplify the most humanitarian approaches to caring for its residents, return to an archaic torture mode of so-called treatment. Such was an approach too many of the older staff found to their liking because it would give them absolute control over their individual charges. This was in the aftermath of initial patient-centered changes brought about by the hiring that year of David Proffitt as the new CEO of Forensic Services.

Prior to hiring Proffitt, a report by regulators had described the hospital as "unsafe, unaccountable and dysfunctional." The report documented a "pattern of willful violations by staff and administrators who were incapable of changing the culture." The CEO at that time, Larry TeBrake, was asked to resign because of safety issues.

The search for a new top administrator began with the Department of Human Services looking for a "change agent" and "visionary" with excellent communication skills. Proffitt was hired with the mandate to reform the hospital, and do it quickly. He was to retrain staff to use more behavioral tools to help patients modify their behaviors and sharply reduce the use of restraints and seclusion.

Proffitt had come to Saint Peter as something of a delivering messiah, from Maine, where he had already reformed another punishment-based mental health institution.

We'd had an incident here at Saint Peter where a man had been locked in solitary confinement for twenty-five days without even a mattress. It seemed he tore up every mattress he was given and used the pieces to block off the window to his cell. Every time they gave him a mattress he tore it up and blocked off the window to his cell. The staff said they needed to see if he was still alive and breathing, so rather than trying to find out why he was destroying the mattress and covering the window, or leaving the window covered and putting a small camera in the cell to monitor him, they just quit giving him mattresses. He went on like that for twenty-five days.

In an incident in 2011, a patient was put in seclusion in handcuffs and stripped naked. That led to the firing of one psychiatrist and the resignations of five others, including the state's Forensic Services director and the hospital's Director of Psychiatry. They all said they felt they had to leave because they feared they'd lose their medical licenses, claiming new director David Proffitt was abusive and his mismanagement "toxic." None of their claims focused on their "toxic" approach to treating their patients.

Proffitt fired all the people who had been involved in the incidents: the psychiatrist, the unit director, and line and nursing staff. All were suddenly gone in one clean sweep of his administrative broom.

That is when the shit hit the fan. All the other psychiatrists at Saint Peter resigned in support of the one that was fired, at least all those on our MI&D side of the facility. They left us without medication prescribing psychiatrists for six months. They rose up because of the challenge to what had been going on since the beginning of Saint Peter, an arrangement that put the individual psychiatrist at the top of the decision pyramid. The psychiatrists were the ones who gave the orders. Having one of their insider set fired was a serious blow to their authority.

When Minnesota Governor Mark Dayton toured the hospital with his Commissioner of Human Services in February, 2012, he found a "crisis of patient abuse" at the facility due to a lack of training and confusion over the use of restraints and seclusion. Taking a closer look at Proffitt's credentials, the DHS commissioner found that Proffitt's doctorate was from an online, non-accredited school, there were discrepancies in his resume, and that he'd been arrested in 1992 for domestic assault.

Soon Proffitt's composure began to crumble. He pounded fists on tables, yelling at employees and threatening them. In short, his behaviors degenerated to the point that pretty much all the people on the staff at Saint Peter took a disliking for him very quickly.

After an independent investigation concluded that Proffitt was being verbally abusive to members of his staff, refused to listen to dissenting views and threatened to fire employees who disagreed with him, he was asked to resign after only about seven months on the job.

While Proffitt got himself canned after seven months, the positive patient centered concepts he brought to Saint Peter, emphasizing a non-pu-
nitive treatment experience, have mercifully lingered. It was a ghostly
imprint left in the aftermath of the departure of the less than profitable
Proffitt. Like the continuation of a great experiment, the punitive part of
our experience has remained on hold, for now.

But it must also be acknowledged that not all has been positive. The
negative side of these changes is that some of the more violent offenders have been emboldened by them. Previously, when they had become
aggressive, they'd always been put into restraints and or solitary confinement. But now they can get aggressive knowing that they will be let out of
solitary after only a very short cooling down period, often in no more than
an hour. So, being put in solitary no longer provides the respect-provoking
consequence that it once had. The consequence is that serious injuries to
staff by violent patients have sharply increased.

This, of course, brings us back to the torture regime that had been
stopped in February of 2012.

Until the advent of anti-psychotic and other chemo therapies, violent
patients could only be controlled with mechanical restraints, by dramatically increasing the numbers of staff, or by the use of padded cell seclusion.

As noted earlier, mental health treatment has historically been a torture-based system. Read your history. For example, one form of treatment
that was used in the past was "blistering" on a man's penis to prevent mas-
turbation. Toxic purges were used as treatments, and there were, of course,
the variety of restraints used from the late 1800s until 2012: chains, shack-
les, straight coats and jackets, and wristlets. A five-point restraint on a
board and a restraint chair were used as late as 2012.

Most people have seen straitjackets in magician escape routines. They
allow the patient to walk about, as do wristlets and two-point restraints
that secure a patient's wrists to a waist belt. A straight coat, for those un-
informed, was a tube of fabric that would be slipped over a patient's head,
extending below the knees, and tightened with leather belts in the back.
It left a "patient" angry and deprived of effective motion. The five-point
restraint secured the wrists at the waist, and locked chains secured both
ankles. A large wooden restraint chair would hold a patient seated and
upright, while securing his or her waist, legs and arms.

And there were other types of restraints for out of control patients, such as the 'Utica Crib,' basically a large solid box with one side made of slats – at Saint Peter, some patients were kept in these cribs for months at a time – and the hospital even kept an iron "crib" for patients strong enough to kick the slats out of a wooden one.

***

There is no disputing that staff at places like Saint Peter have generally only wanted one basic question answered: If not torture, then what do you expect us to do? And by torture, we need to include both the actual and the threat of physical or chemical restraint. I note the current improvement, in that, because they have been forced to seek alternatives, they have found other things they can do outside of severe coercion and torture.

Their shift from a punitive approach to more humane treatment was hindered by a lack of professional staff such as psychiatrists and psychologists, existing staff who lacked human services backgrounds and had too many years in the security focused environment, a lack of effective training in patien-centered approaches to controlling violent behavior, and generally antagonistic relations between labor and management. All of this led to an increase in the number of serious patient and staff injuries.

Reasoning that patients getting high quality treatment would be less likely to become violent and require restraint or isolation, in 2017 the legislature appropriated $23 million to increase staff and improve training and the physical facility. The entire therapeutic focus of the facility was changed.

***

My current concern is how long will this last? My current hope is that all those former practices will not visit us again. Looking at earlier times, I'll note that they used to label rule infraction punishments under the term "restriction." More recently, they've adopted a more oblique nomenclature, calling problems "level C" infractions. Being hit with either label meant you were going to lose privileges for one or more days.

I'm now passing my twenty-seventh year of this psychiatric torture, twenty-seven years during which doctors and staff could arbitrarily choose to withhold anything they might construe to be a privilege. They could and did deny tobacco addicts access to cigarettes. They could and did deny patients access to televisions or other forms of entertainment. More recently, they could and they have denied people access to the Internet, limiting the ability for those sufficiently motivated to be able to keep up with the tools of modern society they will be faced with should they ever be "cured" and released. They could and did withhold basic rights to know and understand the realities of this very pattern of torture.

Historically, psychiatric care has always involved degrees of torture, as we have come to understand the term today, often under the rubric of "forced care," an oxymoronic concept if there ever was one. In the 1970s, an individual by the name of Homer Jarvis protested the notion of forced medication. He had been admitted to Saint Peter in 1977, and after a legal challenge he brought wound its way through the courts of Minnesota over about three years, his case found its way to the Minnesota Supreme Court. That court issued its opinion in 1988, saying that doctors would indeed be restricted in what they can do to patients, but not prohibited. The Civil Commitment Act was amended to include the Jarvis Petition. The Act established that a patient must be committed before doctors can force neuroleptic medications on a patient without their consent.

Homer Jarvis lost his case to totally avoid psychiatric medication, but he won the right to limit doctors' sole discretion and their previously unlimited control over their psychiatric patients. The power of doctors to torture was finally limited. They could no longer legally torture people, or annoy them into submission.

***

Back in 1975, Amnesty International included a "Chart of Coercion" in a report on torture. The chart was compiled by sociologist Albert Biderman. His chart categorized the variety of methods that could be used to break down a person, rob them of their humanity, and make them pliable and subject to another person's will. Biderman's chart was based on how American war prisoners had been interrogated in several conflicts, but many of the techniques he enumerated were just as well known to inmates of mental institutions here in the U.S.

Biderman's chart encompassed eight general categories of coercive approaches that could be used against people to break down resistance and make them compliant to their captors' wills, and a whole bunch of specific techniques. These were things that were just as routinely being employed on patients at mental hospitals like Saint Peter, before reformers like Proffitt came on the scene, as they had been applied by foreign forces to captured Americans.

A "panic" is an old codeword for an assaultive pacification of an errant prisoner. The "panic" would be sounded as an emergency call to attack and subdue the person with all force available. People would abandon their posts, leaving only a skeleton crew to watch the residential units, and run from one end to the other of our two-acre complex to pile on and assist in taking down an errant prisoner.

I have seen virtually every aspect of the conditions enumerated by Biderman demonstrated at Saint Peter over my years there. During the time before the current "Incident Command System" was put in place at Saint Peter, there were takedowns executed so violently that one even killed a fellow inmate, Jamal Rice. His death was the tipping point incident that caused the "panic" approach to be re-addressed under current procedures as an Incident Command System event.

I have labeled how these behaviors get used as "obedience school for adult humans" and "preventative imprisonment for crimes not yet committed." I told you about "bait and switch" behaviors in an earlier chapter of this book. Everything on this chart was part of the pre-Proffitt era. Now many of us at Saint Peter tread lightly and hope that we never experience a return to that mindset.

***

BIDERMAN'S CHART OF COERSION*

General Method	Effects (Purposes)
1. Isolation	Deprives victim of all social support of his ability to resist Develops an intense concern with self Makes victim dependent upon interrogator Variants: Complete solitary confinement; complete isolation; semi-isolation; group isolation
2. Monopolization of perception	Fixes attention upon immediate predicament; fosters introspection Eliminates stimuli competing with those controlled by captor Frustrates all actions not consistent with compliance Variants: Physical isolation; darkness or bright light; barren environment; restricted movement; monotonous food
3. Induced debility Exhaustion	Weakens mental and physical ability to resist Variants: Semi-starvation; exposure; exploitation of wounds; induced illness; sleep deprivation; prolonged constraint; prolonged interrogation; forced writing; overexertion

4. Threats	Cultivates anxiety & despair
	Variants: Threats of death; threats of non-return; threats of endless interrogation & isolation; threats against family; vague threats; mysterious changes of treatment
5. Occasional indulgences	Provides positive motivation for compliance Hinders adjustment to deprivation
	Variants: Occasional favours; fluctuations of interrogators' attitudes; promises; rewards for partial compliance; tantalising
6. Demonstrating 'omnipotence'	Suggests futility of resistance
	Variants: Confrontation; pretending co-operation taken for granted; demonstrating complete control over victim's fate
7. Degradation	Makes cost of resistance appear more damaging to self esteem than capitulation Reduces prisoner to 'animal level' concerns
	Variants: Personal hygiene prevented; filthy infested surroundings; demeaning punishments; insults and taunts; denial of privacy

8. Enforcing trivial demands	Develops habit of compliance
	Variants: Forced writing; enforcement of minute rules

---

*"Biderman's Chart of Coercion" in *Amnesty International Report on Torture Revised Edition*; 1975; Gerald Duckworth & Co. Ltd., London, in association with Amnesty International Publications; pg 53. [British Spellings]. Used with permission.

***

The psychologists at Saint Peter particularly encouraged a form of torture describable as competitive self-flagellation, officially known as group therapy. They encouraged people to confess to the crimes they were charged with, whether real or imagined by the court, to get the patients to criticize themselves in a harsh and unforgiving manner. This supposedly helped provide us patients with what the doctors call "self-insight" into our need for treatment. This was an especially favored technique prior to 2004.

In the proverbial best of all possible worlds, group therapy would be integrated into comprehensive individual treatment plans thoughtfully and therapeutically. In a good therapy group, eight or so people would come together in a safe and neutral location to express feelings, share insights, try out new ways of behaving, and generally interact in an environment where the level of trust would allow them to talk personally and honestly. Because such a group would often have members who are at different stages of treatment, seeing people already coping or recovering would theoretically aid those early in the process.

We had anything but that best of worlds here in Saint Peter, when it was the land of competitive self-flagellation. We had days where group therapy sessions would become a disease all on their own. Usually we've had ten patients in a session, with two staff members guiding the process.

Here is an example of how our group sessions would proceed prior to changes initiated during 2003. When the meeting was convened, one of the staff members present would ask if anyone would like to take "focus" and be on the hot seat for the session. We patients would all beg to be given the option of being on the hot seat as this would be seen as "progress," a progress that could potentially, at least in theory, get one slowly, gradually closer to an exit from Saint Peter. Staff would pick out one or two members of the group to serve in that role and then the process would begin. The begging to be in the hot seat is the "competitive" part of the "competitive self-flagellation" exercise.

Questions would be thrown at the person in the focus. He or she would have to respond to questions like: "What benefit do you notice from your medication?" And: "What difference do you notice from being on meds as opposed to being off of medication?"

Thus would begin the patient's performance of self-health introspection, the self-flagellation part of the performance. We patients knew from experience and the grapevine that we needed to invoke speeches and responses indicating how much we were terribly afflicted and truly dangerous to society, but that now that we were recovering with the use of medication we were feeling so much better. We would also need to say how we planned to stay on our various medications for the rest of our lives, devising and disclosing plans that would supposedly help us assure that we would.

Some of the people participating in these groups are rapists and murderers. Those people know they have no hope of going home without the Saint Peter staff first determining that their maladaptive behaviors would never happen again. They know that this is the end of the trail for them, their last possible chance for clemency, relief and possible eventual exit back to society. They know that beyond here lies nothing. They know they have to game their performance to meet the staff's expectations. The group therapy objectives, as they are called, are designed to reinforce dependence on staff as part of a patient's exit strategy. Staff, in turn, call this being "invested into treatment." Patients slander themselves, prosecute themselves, confess to all manners of behavioral sins, but always in the pattern of "those problems bothered me once, but now I am cured, so please let me go." This is seen as "insight into illness." This is how we patients are trained, through mild to severe torture.

An objective might read like: "Mr. Erickson will talk about how his crime impacted his victim." This is actually not a bad question in and of itself, but when it is part of a punitive behavior system of mild to severe torture, a question such as this can be part of a very aggravating scenario indeed.

The "Mr. Erickson" in the example above, a real person, was actually a rather bright individual, but he lacked the social intelligence people need to achieve healthy mental lives. At a first glance, Erickson would appear to have the actual intelligence of an amoeba or tomato. In reality, he could function quite well intellectually, at around the education level of an average high school graduate. Furthermore, because he had an air of simplicity to him, and was always accommodating, the staff were more forgiving to him than to most other patients, as he presented neither a threat nor challenge to their authority. In other words he was docile. For those reasons, he moved through the program rather quickly.

Patients like Erickson would never complain about their treatment being an obedience school for adult humans. In fact, they would rarely complain about anything, because they only rarely found themselves at odds with the rules of the Saint Peter road. They'd show up for group sessions on time. They would not break any of the twenty or so primary behavior rules. They would not often find themselves put onto restriction. Patients like Erickson were sufficiently naive and compliant that they would clearly epitomize what staff thought of as an ideal patient. I find parallels to how behaviors in Stalin's Soviet Russia, that humanitarians in the west railed against, are actually applied here. The terrorism aspect is certainly similar. Random arrests create fear and terror.

Random restrictions of freedom in psychiatric facilities do as well. Also of note is that the attorneys who deal with this area of law are rarely invested in being advocates for the rights or desires of the types of people who are their clients, the mentally ill. As often as not, if they are in the courts for a mental competence hearing, these attorneys seem to be there only to make sure that the sacking and looting of the "defendant's" rights happens in the appropriate due process manner as prescribed by the court. They are not there to prevent an assault by the court, nor are they there to protect the defendant. They are only there to ensure that the assault happens in the proper legal fashion.

Amongst our other desires, to argue our cases for us we, the ill and accused, want better lawyers than even Scientology has on retainer. It's clear that institutional mental health care has always been a torture-based system, but we also find torture, at least in milder or benign forms, in virtually all forms of forced behavior modification. Sometimes it is significant and obvious, as with trying to fix the mentally ill, or change behaviors of imprisoned criminals. Other times it presents itself in a much more benign guise, as with training soldiers to act on a battlefield without questioning a superior's orders, or when we require children to cooperate in maintaining an orderly learning environment in schools. We find it in prisons, schools, the military, and in mental hospitals, and we find it in so many places because it does have some functional value. We end up putting a lot of people into good colleges after tasking them in a challenging manner in their elementary and secondary school experiences. Work hard in high school and maybe you'll go to Harvard, Yale, or MIT.

We get our military missions done by an air force, army, coast guard, Marine Corps and navy that are each populated by people who live in tightly regimented, rank-based systems. Essentially caste-like systems, they deliver a wall of force to protect us Americans from evils like North Korea, the Taliban and Al-Qaida. It is sad and frustrating, however, that our military is also used to defend some of the most exploitive people in the world, like middle east oil billionaires and the avenues of ocean and air commerce that support their excessive wealth. Too often, such military regimentation assures that our army's privates and sergeants will lay down their lives before admirals and generals need to lay down theirs. That's one of the downsides to military life, or more accurately to military death. It's similar to how people like the late Osama Bin Laden used misinterpretations of Islam and the Koran to coerce and convince other people to kill themselves in suicide attacks that they would never dream of participating in themselves.

In prison, we bully people around who have murdered or raped in the real world, and even in the artificial reality of prison itself, in the rationalized hope that we might "cure" them of their propensity to perpetrate such acts. Real world rape of children is considered especially onerous. But the research is at best sketchy on whether "cure" is even possible. Neither peer-to-peer inmate action nor professional psychological and psychiatric intervention has seemed to do the trick on more than just an exceptional few. "Control" of urges to do such mayhem may be the best society can reasonably hope for, and even that may often be unachievable. Thus one can say, not only has there been torture in traditional western care for the mentally ill over the past many centuries, masquerading as "control" it exists as a reality in psychiatric and mental hospital care today.

It's an interesting contrast that in many so-called primitive and aboriginal cultures, people whom we in the "modern" world might consider mentally ill were considered to be prophetic or shamanic figures of stature in their communities, and some are still revered widely today. Were a biblical prophet like Elijah, Isaiah, Jeremiah or Ezekiel to appear today, if we didn't just ignore him, we'd probably either call him a cult leader or just throw him into a mental institution.

For the mentally ill or accused, another real and tangible difficulty should also be noted. We face the problem of undesirably funded mandates. We may often understandably mistrust and dislike government because we see mandatory health care as something assaultive to our community, at least as it is practiced and applied to incarcerating us in the so-called hospitals that are really our prisons. If the states have money, for instance, from the federal government to spend on our imprisonment, then many of us would contend that it's time to move to Canada or somewhere where our treatment would be less egregious.

For at least several years in some states, and now in national health insurance requirements as the result of the Affordable Care Act, an undesirable funded mandate is the requirement that mental health care be provided on parity with the provision for care of physical maladies. This "parity" unfortunately creates a "disparity" when the element of forced care is introduced. If mental health parity includes more funding for mental health commitments, then such a health care plan could be considered most undesirable to many of us. Parity could open the door wider to imprisonment flying under the banners of being acts of healing medicine.

With the rare exceptions of people who are unable to give consent because they are a minor, may be unconscious, because they have ceded power of attorney, or have registered a living will, physical medical care cannot be forced on someone. If someone breaks a leg, he or she cannot be forced to go to the hospital to have it set, though it would be a rare instance indeed where someone wouldn't who had the opportunity to do so.

Similarly, a doctor might prescribe rehabilitative services, but the choice to use them would be up to the individual.

By contrast, if you have a mental illness like depression, severe psychoses or schizophrenia, and it is determined that you are "dangerous to yourself or others," the courts in many jurisdictions can order your involuntary incarceration in a local locked hospital psychiatric ward for up to 72 hours, to assess whether you meet the criteria for a longer involuntary civil commitment. Then when you meet those criteria you can be transferred to a distant institution and incarcerated there for any crime committed due to your condition.

Sometimes those authorities can even extend your incarceration based only on a fear that you *might* commit a future crime because of your mental illness. And with funding parity between physical illness and mental illness now mandated more widely, it's not impossible that we'll see the health care system able and willing to incarcerate more mentally ill people profitably.

Regrettably, as we move towards funding parity we may also be moving towards where parity for mental health also enables politicians to fund more treatment for any imprisonment-based illness they would like to think of as criminal behaviors, or a plentiful source of funding to keep people already committed, there longer.

If rich doctors or lawyers want to surrender their money in higher taxes to fight poverty created by severe and chronic illnesses, then I would be happy to help them redirect some of their cash in that direction. But that's not going to be where any expansion of funding is likely to come from. It's going to come from the middle class in higher insurance costs, or from subsidies funded by tax increases on everyone other than the wealthy.

California literally pays the mentally ill to go away and not bother its rich Hollywood stars. When I lived there, I received less than $800 in Social Security and other benefits, but absolutely no assistance to manage my medical condition. All I could do was just show up at the bank with my checks and then take my cash and, California authorities would hope, disappear into the undergrowth. If you were in some rural agricultural communities, you might supplement your checks by gleaning foodstuffs in fields left over from where the migrant workers were picking fruits and vegetables.

California dumped its mentally ill onto the streets when Ronald Reagan was governor. California, a state with eight times as many people as Minnesota, nevertheless, has a single state hospital for the criminally mentally ill and no state hospitals for other mentally ill citizens in any of the rural valley communities. California saved about $12,000 per month per patient by avoiding parity and sidestepping the issue of care or responsibility for their citizens with mental illness. It will probably still save almost as much under the Affordable Care Act's requirements because of federal subsidies.

Many of my friends here at the Minnesota Security Hospital in Saint Peter would be homeless in a state like California. They'd be sleeping on the streets or under bridges instead of being guests of the state in a facility like Saint Peter.

Chapter 21: Reality and Unreality

WE HAVE THIS great invention called written language. It gives us the ability to store information today so it can be used tomorrow. Added to the concepts integral to our major modern religions, personal writing and internet publishing potentially gives each of us some sense or expectation of a type of immortality. Spirituality in turn encourages morality and aspects of behavior designed to make all people behave better. If they fear God, then they will treat each other better. At least that's how the theory goes.

That thriving for better behavior becomes not just the plan of the day, but as well the plan of the last year, and of all the past, and for all the years to come. Passing all of this down through generations becomes more possible for more of us with our written language. It causes the divine to be truly immortal in a way that is easier for many of us to grasp, even as it allows the more mundane a similar immortality.

How many people declared themselves to be divine conduits to God before the Romans wrote the name of Jesus into their military records? We know a few of them from archeology, mythology, and tracts handed down by each of the various religions. How many more of them there actually have been has obviously been lost to the veil of pre-written history. Moses was fortunate to be part of a culture that valued its oral history and continuity, and managed to survive into the Common Era. Jesus had the fortunate timing to be doing his thing in a cultural context that paralleled the beginning of more widely disseminated, durable written language.

Passing over the question of belief in Jesus's divinity, and also of any possibilities of wishful distortions in the reports of his miracles made by his apostles in their accounts of his life recorded in the Christian Bible, a significant portion of modern humanity can theoretically achieve at least a sort of "immortality" in the way we use and have expectations about the posterity of our messages.

In our very modern world, proliferating cell phones, tablets, laptop computers and digital cameras are all around recording sound and video, and sending much of it automatically to the great Internet cloud of servers, where expectations seem to be that they will forever then reside. But for people in places like Saint Peter, whether that will ever happen is questionable. Those devices are forbidden here. In fact, it wasn't until 2013 that any of its residents in the minimum security area were even allowed to possess their own laptops, on which they can at least now write about Saint Peter's "goings ons." The Internet is, however, largely still forbidden or restricted here.

Were residents allowed to take and upload videos and recordings, the immortality of the recorded world would mean staff could be held accountable. Their coercive and arbitrary acts would be matters of record. In situations of competitive self-flagellation it could mean that the institution of that torture practice would be threatened by its potential exposure to the proverbial "light of day." The news, the truth, the reality of the torture that has gone on forever in medicine could be exposed for posterity and could come to a final crashing halt.

Regrettably, one former Saint Peter inmate who assaulted his mother, stabbing her, blinding her, actually did come back to our domain. In December of 2013 he won the privilege of avoiding prison incarceration by being re-admitted to the Security Hospital.

In a newspaper's Sunday comics section you can always find characters that most of us would have no difficulty defining as being outside the orbit of average and normal. For example, one of the comic strips, the Dick Tracy crime drama, historically featured an abundance of very strange villains. One who comes to mind is "Mumbles." Our friend Mumbles could barely talk. In spite of that severe handicap, however, Mumbles managed to achieve enough of a payoff from his criminal schemes to employ a slew of evil henchmen.

If he were a real person today, his high criminal profile would throw a huge crew of law enforcement agencies onto his tail, and with today's technologies I'm sure he'd be caught. I'm also sure that, if he were a real person today, well before he got anywhere close to the heights of crime the comic strip environment allowed him, he'd have been caught and more than likely sent to a place like Saint Peter.

I'd probably end up welcoming him to Saint Peter because we welcome all sorts of people to our facility that in ancient times might have been seen as anything from followers of the devil to prophets in communion with God. Today those could include charismatic godly proselytizers to leaders of murderous cults like Charles Manson. Certainly, Mumbles could qualify as a delusional cult leader of thieves and fit right in here. Having a cast of memorable characters, a plot that is advanced in social issues and technologies to play around with can be antithetical. Mumbles cannot speak. Maybe he can write, but I have yet to see his plan of the day put onto paper.

Dick Tracy and Mumbles and their assorted contemporaries are unreal immortals, and their unreality is the very reason they can be on a newspaper comic page in the first place. Significantly, unreality triumphs over reality all the time in our culture. Soap operas, science fictions, faked dramas, situation comedies and staged so-called reality shows rule a television medium that increasingly seems to avoid serious news and real reality. Unsurprisingly, people would rather be entertained than informed. Even if they chose to be informed, there would be the issues of how and why the news that existed had actually gotten to them, the consumer. People just don't understand how media gate keepers operate because most people don't think that way.

We end up with young kids dreaming of being police officers and arresting people like Mumbles. Only as they grow up do they find out that real crime is sometimes done by celebrities they look up to, and more often by otherwise normal people or by gangs, or by junkies looking for money or things to steal and sell to pay for their next fix. A lot less frequently, headline crimes are committed by sociopaths, sexual deviants, or people who are depressed, otherwise identified by society as the mentally ill, or by people we later learn were victims of bullying.

It is difficult to record the style and voice of a real criminal in a book, because real criminals are often pretty much like other real people. Unlike the criminals you might see on what are called criminal procedural television dramas, outside of perhaps a courtroom or when they are interacting with other criminals, they generally don't speak in particularly distinctive manners. You could be standing next to one of them at a bus stop having a conversation about the weather or local sports team and never know what they were about.

Look also at real police officers. They have an all too often thankless task, and much of the time they seem to get treated no better than the same vermin they thought they were in their profession to fight. Most of them have never fired their weapons outside of the police firing range. And, solving crimes takes months or even years. Real reality just doesn't fit conveniently or commercially into an hour-long television program.

The reality of crime and punishment is usually so tedious and boring that no major network seeking a broad audience could ever sell the necessary advertising time to support broadcasting it. Who would want to try selling eyeliner or canned tomatoes on a show where the only thing going on is a detective making call after call on his phone chasing down a hundred fruitless leads on a gang-related shooting that killed an eight-year-old bystander sitting on a couch, unseen by a shooter, behind the wall of a house a poorly aimed bullet just happened to go through?

It seems that people generally have to choose between a reality which is tedious and boring, and fantasy which has, at best, limited public service value. It seems also that people who watch TV or Internet videos actually think that what they see is the bulk of reality. That's dangerous. Such people actually think the extreme views of extreme politicians are actually mainstream because they see them so often, because they too often also only choose to watch stuff that supports what they already think they know. That is not the actuality of the reality that most actual humans actually experience. Those caricatures of reality push out real reality. Real reality is far more tedious and boring than fiction. In "reality," people go from jobs in retail, insurance, food service, education and transportation, to homes where as soon as they walk through the door they turn on their television and escape their repetitive lives, not recognizing the irony of the repetitiveness of their escapist TV preferences. The television fantasies are their respite from their reality before repeating it all the next day.

We at Saint Peter have a similar routine, but with a lot less opportunity to break out of our boring life repetitiveness. We are at the mercy of the staff as they decide whether we can even have the privilege of lighting up a cigarette.

In about six months, as of this writing, if I'm transitioned to a lower security area and program at Saint Peter, as I've petitioned for, I will have

enough freedom to actually go out to downtown Saint Peter to get a cigarette and a cup of coffee. Saint Peter is a town that has been significantly
devoted to insanity for longer than Rochester, Minnesota, has been dominated by the treatment of physical disease at the Mayo Clinic.

Recognizing that in terms of the potential for lung cancer I'm probably
better off physically being denied access to cigarettes, I nevertheless will
probably avail myself of the freedom as soon as I'm able. To all of this I will
dedicate at least one cancer coffin nail. One cigarette, or at worst a few,
and I will make a donation to the American Lung Association. Nonetheless, I will give in to this craving. I will acknowledge it as being a symbol
that I might be approaching full freedom.

***

Mental illness can be very unbecoming. The fiction composite that was in
one of the earlier sections of this book had a patient assaulting his mother
with a steak knife. He had unsuccessfully tried to kill her ten years before,
when he had succeeded in killing his sister. He had spent about a decade
at Saint Peter before being declared cured enough, obviously erroneously,
to leave us.

Another patient left the confines of the Saint Peter without permission. He escaped. In mental health language, he "eloped." It's not like he
married anyone, but an escape is called an elopement. To many of us, that
particular terminology is simply hilarious.

Our current state of understanding into mental illness and mental
health leaves a lot to still be understood. This isn't a revelation of any sort.
Even most psychiatrists would probably admit this, because currently, any
given psychologist or psychiatrist is free to apply his or her understandings
of the philosophies of people like Carl Jung and B.F. Skinner and Sigmund Freud and Jean Piaget and Friedrich Nietzsche and Georg Wilhelm
Friedrich Hegel, amongst others, to support their preferred prescriptions
and treatment plans.

You can ponder those great minds, use leftover time for Jean-Paul Sartre and Simone de Beauvoir, and still have no better understanding of
how the mind really works than a doctor in 1900 might have had. While
concrete, controlled biomedical research has begun to actually find chem-

ical and hormonal imbalances in the brain, and researchers are finally beginning to gain some real understandings into how some portions of the brain work, outside of improved pharmaceuticals such knowledge seems to be taking its time getting down to helping people buried largely out of sight in the trenches of mental institutions.

Such uncertainty does lead to people being declared "cured," some of whom return to society where they relapse and do harm. Another example of this uncertainty, one that is particularly relevant and personal to me, was a former Saint Peter patient who while back out in the world met one of my sisters and bludgeoned her to death with a pipe.

I specifically and honestly believe that I am a person who is truly no longer any threat to any person, to greater society, or to myself. Despite my mental illness, because I've accepted my need for sobriety and perpetual medication, I believe I am now part of an ongoing nonviolent community. Presently, however, I continue to languish at Saint Peter with my "dangerous" diagnosis. My goals are simple. I want to get out of Saint Peter. I want to go back to school. I want to publish more of my writings, and seek the widest possible audiences for my thoughts, perspectives, theories and conclusions.

The criteria being applied for considering me to still be dangerous are sketchy at best. Is it an existential thing or is it experiential? Or is it both? Jung, a psychotherapist, would point out coincidences and call them synchronicities. Freud, of psychoanalytic fame, would point out the sexual angle and symbolism. Nietzsche, a philosopher, would say there is no hope in ever trying to educate the masses, as they are cattle to be led. Sartre and Simone de Beauvoir, among other philosophers, would say that God created reason for a reason.

Their perspectives all have merit. But how can they help the mentally accused, when in a real sense they seem to exist in no more of a practical reality for a state mental hospital patient than do the lane marking guide lines on the bottom of the swimming pool used in the last Olympics?

Freud points to sexual motifs in everything and so connects his imagery to so many things that his concepts become overly universal. You can only point to columns supporting great weight for so long until you find yourself looking at many columns clearly being built not for symbolism, but for engineering simplicity.

Jung and his symbols and synchronicities are at least a bit more warm and fuzzy. With synchronicities, you at least have the god motif that is comfortable to a whole planet of Christians and other religious believers. Providing more belief for god-centric people will sell a lot of books.

Erich Fromm wrote about the dilemmas found in pop culture and he called the interpersonal conflict between conformity and authoritarianism versus freedom and democracy a desire, or at least willingness, to "escape from freedom." This means that after struggling for decades to create a free society, people still retained a drive to create commitments in personal life that far outweigh whatever gains in freedom they created earlier. Originally conceptualized in a book he wrote in 1941, the concept still typified much of the psychological profession's views of people's internal conflicts for many decades. His book *Escape from Freedom* (published internationally as *The Fear of Freedom*) was still regarded highly as mainstream psychology as late as 1975.

Eric Berne created the text called *Games People Play*. There one can find simple games like a woman proposing a combat between two suitors as a game of "Lets You AND Him Fight." Games like this are common. When the games are benign there is no problem. Men playing the game of "how General Motors could improve their sports cars," and making related small talk about cars generally, creates no problems. Fighting, however, is a real problem that's all too common.

There are points of wisdom to be found at all levels in this vast storytelling. Often the criteria for being deemed dangerous is in flux from one week to another. Concrete expressions like Berne's "Games" are easy to grasp while Freud and Jung are historical, outdated, and esoteric. The practical usually, but not always, out rules the merely thoughtful.

Our society has the resources and capacity to create a very modern reality to better serve the mentally ill, and at present, many of the customs and legalities of indeterminate mental health sentencing are up in the air in Minnesota. As this was originally written in 2013, Minnesota's indeterminate sentencing of criminal sexual predators, our legal cousins who occupy the other side of the Saint Peter facility, was under assault by a court order that recognized the reality that the way their "therapy" was arranged, literally no one was ever going to be considered cured and released. That was securely written (pun intended) across the entire history of the program. No matter their criminal sentence, the actual sentence for everyone sent to Saint Pater was imprisonment for life. It subsequently fell to the courts to impose changes because neither the state's legislature nor its administrative agencies were willing to take the political heat that would result from creating a fix for this.

It is worth noting for this edition, that as of the end of 2019, this new legal regimen has allowed nine convicted sexual offenders to be fully discharged by the court and released from Saint Peter, and another twenty-five have been provisionally discharged.

Fortunately or otherwise, even the courts' ordered revisions will not likely empty that part of Saint Peter State Hospital by discharging all the sex offenders. I'm personally thankful for that, because I have always felt such people should get 300-year sentences in criminal court, rather than the sham of a civil mental health commitment. Because of the sexual motif of their imprisonment, and a statistically demonstrable likelihood of recidivism amongst such people, the process of release orchestrated by the courts has been a slow and calculated one, with extreme levels of parole officer type oversight for anyone actually released. Perhaps for many of them it will in the long run turn out to be somewhat less than the "escape to freedom" they might have anticipated.

This new legal paradigm about to envelop the sexually mentally ill may also conceivably impact the rest of us residing at Saint Peter. The new definitions suggest that, once an inmate has *successfully* completed his or her course of therapy, the burden of proof for needing to keep that person incarcerated will be heavily shifted to the state. Should a similar standard be subsequently applied to my community, those *only* labeled mentally ill and dangerous, then many of us may also see a clearer path to rejoining larger society.

Ending Notes

I HAVE SEEN a rare few who are detained by the State and are on no medication who do get out of the clutches of the government. I saw one patient readily admit he had used a shotgun on a man and had killed that person. The extra special quality of his crime was that, while it did not call for any medication, the county insisted that the patient be on medication. The county usually has no say, or even interest in medication issues, but in this case they broke from tradition as readily as the hospital had avoided usual patterns in not issuing medication. Usually, county input concerns the legal affairs and leaves medical issues to the hospital. Just as the hospital broke from tradition in declining to prescribe medication, so also did the county in insisting that the hospital reverse its decision. Other than that, most of our discharges are routine.

The average stay here is about six years. People seem to either leave in only a few months, or never at all. That rounds off the average at six years.

There are a great number of conformity issues surrounding the whole larger discharge issue. One individual, whom we will call Devo, took his hat off in conference with his county case manager and a bag of marijuana fell out of it. Not a very smart idea to drop his stash onto the desk of his case manager, and pretty clear evidence that he was not conforming to the terms of his discharge.

Most of those discharged as cured don't encounter problems like Devo's inner city urban jungle issues. We have people who come from rural areas, where there are few people around to threaten their lack of sobriety and self-medication issues.

And halfway houses in large cities have problems. A big one is that no neighborhood wants to have one near them, but in my view the biggest problem with them is that these places want all of your money. The halfway house will charge patients $4,000 per month to reside there, or they will help the patient get a menial janitorial job, and then charge that person 85 percent of his or her earnings. Most patients do not have a lot of money to toss about. No cash to spend makes each dollar more precious.

For the few who have inheritances or other money sources, it becomes a very careful undertaking to plan your finances so that you do not have very much available cash, so you can avoid getting charged at a phenomenally exorbitant rate for your care and treatment. The system's approach to acquiring a patient's money constitutes what I consider an excessive fine that should be declared unconstitutional. Criminals don't have to pay for the costs of their unwilling incarceration. Why should those of us who are similarly incarcerated against our will in mental hospital facilities be treated any differently?

When I die, I hope to leave no cash for the state to seize.

Another constitutional issue includes double jeopardy, which means being prosecuted twice for the same crime, as you might be when first tried and committed as mentally ill, and then for some, later tried criminally when they are declared cured. A fellow inmate by the name of Gary died of cancer here. He was the belligerent type who, not doing his personal case any good, would threaten staff here all the time. He did twenty-five years in our prison here and then was stunned when he found out that being here was not technically even being called being in prison. Under the laws of Minnesota, because the prison hospital is not legally a prison, they can keep you here as long as they want, and you have no legal remedy.

As I said, Gary died of cancer before he could get back to the real world. They strapped his arms down. They took his clothes and shoes, and made him wear a paper dress because he smeared feces all over his solitary confinement cell in his rebellion against his situation.

Other relevant constitutional issues include being denied the right to avoid self-incrimination, and being denied the rights to trial, speedy trial, public trial, trial by peers, and open trial. I relate. I had recourse to none of these things.

We need better lawyers. Public defenders are awful; they are really nothing more than public pretenders. A public pretender is there to make sure that when you get screwed by the state it is done in the correct due process manner. They are not there to defend you.

Regrettably, if you are ever in the situation that I was, your public pretender will look at the demographics of your case and, if he sees your voter's block of origin is homeless alcoholics, or a former resident of a state and federal prison, then that public pretender will not raise a finger to help you.

***

Reference to the Fourteenth Amendment to our constitution is important. One of several amendments enacted in the aftermath of the Civil War, it affirms four things: state and federal citizenship for all persons born or naturalized in the United States regardless of race; that no state is allowed to abridge "privileges and immunities" of citizens; that nobody is allowed to be deprived of life, liberty, or property without due process of law; and that no person can be denied equal protection of the law. Due process and equal protection are the salient rights here. The Fourteenth Amendment was enacted basically to say the states could not create laws just for one subset of the population.

You need only look at how, even after the Fourteenth Amendment, Blacks were effectively kept from voting or being counted as citizens through Jim Crow laws, cattle prod justice, the lynchings and terrorizing tactics of the KKK, and a simple cultural refusal to obey the amendment. Essentially unrepresented, the subset of Blacks continued to be deprived of their rights to be full citizens of the nation. This is not dissimilar to how the mentally ill are deprived of their rights in society today.

The mentally ill and mentally accused constitute two of the modern day subsets of people who are deprived of their basic rights. One can also say that all criminals are another subset. Those deemed mentally ill and dangerous inhabit both of these subsets and accrue a compounding lack of benefits from each.

Mental illness has special legal qualities to it. No person ever woke up one day and decided: "Today, I am going to incur schizophrenia and have a lifelong handicap. I really want to suffer." People just don't think that way. People do not vote to become mentally ill. They do not buy a mental illness, except perhaps as a byproduct of their purchase and abuse of alcohol and street drugs. Parents do not get to return a child to a birth center because they notice he or she has a mental illness.

The mentally ill have many points covered in the sentence, "I never asked for this." Mental illness indiscriminately drafts the young, the old, men, women, children, and from every other group in humanity. You can be Hutu or Tutsi, Communist or Fascist, Rich or Poor, White or Black or Hispanic or Asian, Christian or Jew or Hindu or Muslim or Buddhist, and mental illness can befall you.

And isn't it an oxymoron how we talk about forced care? One must observe with intense curiosity other unique moments of the system at work, as if you were watching a messy process, like if we had the government adopt kittens with the sticky fingers of a young schoolchild. Our group here at the Minnesota Security Hospital in Saint Peter sort of has one of these house pet type people, a person who seems to truly have diminished capacity. He is, to use a current reference, cognitively impaired. This person is rather slow. To be blunt, in times past we would have called him retarded. I am not sure if he really is a mentally ill person, but his status as dangerous stems from swinging a bicycle chain around over his head in a Hennepin County detoxification center. For his crimes, our man, I'll call him "Slow B," has been imprisoned now for a decade. Slow B is probably actually somewhere between mentally retarded and extremely uneducated. At least one of the other patients calls him "Nostra-dumbass." Using a chain as a weapon is not the kind of thing that really warrants a fine of $150,000 per year, the cost of his interment here for his round the clock incarceration.

Very interesting!

Our law system punishes based on demographics at least as much as the word of the law. Slow B will always be a client requiring the attention of others, and not a true participant in his own life. His detention at Saint Peter points to some inherent problems in our legal system. He probably should be in an appropriate supported living facility for adults who have his type of intellectual deficiency, not in a hospital prison. While we sit and attach names like "Nostra dumbass" to Slow B, the state holds him close and apparently cherishes his idiocy. The state entertains him. The state medicates and cares for him. His detention is a mix of beneficent dictatorship impounding a human life, and the care and feeding of a living entity that cannot manage for itself. It is like the state adopting and caring for a person just like we might adopt and care for the above referenced pet kitten. Only in this case, the "cat" is grown into about 200 pounds of toothless and arthritic human.

In the forced care system, the state picks up people who, through the variety of circumstances not usually of their own causing, end up being housed to the end of their lives at a state prison for the mentally ill. This happens too often, in my opinion, especially in the face of evidence that many such people could be served better, less expensively, in their communities, if resources were made available.

***

There are similarities between many of my thoughts and the big blue book of Alcoholics Anonymous. I feel good about what I have been able to put together. The blue book has many different stories in it, and its stories have changed from one edition to the next. For instance, the third edition has a story called *Bondage* not found elsewhere, and the fourth edition has a similarly unique story, *Resentments*. The format for the blue books is visionary. They were well put together before my life began. I hope this book is similarly received.

This book, being on and about the connection of mental illness and chemical dependency, obviously goes into territory beyond AA. Normal alcoholics have no need for psychiatric medication. As for other approaches, I have no idea what alcoholic Scientologists do to try to sober up and get their brains into one coherent package.

It was late in the year 2013 as, working with my editor on the original 2014 edition, we finalized the manuscript for that book. That edition and this revision are texts that have evolved through thoughts and versions that date back well more than a decade. Getting the several messages it contains out has been a focus for me through my upswings and downturns, as I've battled to control my issues. At this time my mood is good. My energy level is normal. I feel neither over-energized nor exhausted. Talking and writing about these issues helps me visualize them and bring them to the forefront of my mind. That is the therapeutic point to all my writing. It's far more therapeutic than tracking concerns in the popular press about insanities like thinking our world as we know it will come to some spectacular catastrophic end, like the meteor that put the period on the end of the era of dinosaurs, or that last-day event of the Mayan calendar which only existed because the people who recorded that calendar simply stopped bothering to count it forward past the end of the 5,126-year-era of their "Long Count" calendar.

I am lucky and well enough to have access to a computer, and to have enough of my wits about me to use it to do my writing. Most of my fellow inmates simply use the computer as a DVD or CD player.

For people who have something to say, the computer has become the great socializing typewriter of the now global community. Those who don't have Internet access restrictions can use it to call up friends in Europe, send e-mail to acquaintances in Asia, and keep track of the doings of Facebook friends in Africa or Latin America. And of course, we can use it to write serious stuff on issues meaningful to us, like this book. I haven't been sure where it really belonged in a book like this, but I think it's important for readers to understand a bit of my writing process. Before it even got out to my professional editor, who did yeoman work rearranging dispersed segments and adding copy to tie my thoughts cogently together, my writings passed before other eyes. And so, before I end this book I'd like to introduce you, my reader, to my Saint Peter gatekeeper crew, Lynn and Ken. They've watched as this manuscript came together, as they did for others before it and may possibly do for ones to come. Ken would look over what I've written and ask: "What about feelings?" Lynn would say: "I'd like to see more on symptoms." Both of their concerns have merit. Both of them are honorable and caring people.

Lynn and Ken look over journal entries for many hours per week, like prospectors sifting through pans for gold dust that are filled mostly with worthless dross and debris. A lot of writing is done that has varying and lesser degrees of quality. Ken gets warm fuzzies when he sees that a project like this of mine is coming to an end.

I copied my manuscript onto a disk and sent it off to an editor I engaged on the recommendation of a friend whom I once worked with, back when I was a cook many years ago. My original idea was to simply have him get some of my grammar cleaned up and bad punctuation fixed. Instead I found a professional who saw beyond those basics, who saw that with a bit more work my mostly stream of consciousness writing contained the potential to be a bit more than just an outlet for one author's somewhat rambling thoughts. He pointed me also to several places where I could valuably expand my existing text to make it a more valuable commentary for readers to spend their time with. He also added significant additional material that has helped me flesh out my thoughts.

I feel like the ship that is about to dock. Soon this textual ship will dock and its metaphorical crew will disperse out into the town, but given the subject matter, there will be no drunken sailors in this unique and special place.

Soon it will be time to end this project, and begin another. The last collection of journal entries that make up the finale to this book are for Ken and Lynn as much as for anyone else. These last pages of my book will therefore get written that way. I usually write 1,500 words for the local kids and 40,000 words, or more, for a publication's larger audiences.

Because of whom their audiences are, the best publisher for this book for me seems to be one associated with mental health issue as they impact the vulnerable adult community. Keep in mind that I said at the beginning that it's something of a memoir, self-help and exposé mashup. But, for this book an equally reachable audience ought to be some of those in the paranoia business.

This manuscript speaks to the paranoid community, with its Trilaterals, its gold, its black helicopters, and its secret societies. The paranoia publishers especially make the best venues for libertarians who oppose mental health imprisonment. Those same libertarian presses print books on conspiracies surrounding assassinations like that of President Kennedy and, subsequently, Lee Harvey Oswald, and about CIA heroin trafficking. They print books on Hitler's last days, putting him not in Berlin but in Argentina, that the moon landings were all a hoax, and how the Illuminati is getting set to brand everyone on the planet with "The mark of the Beast," 666, for people to buy and sell like they believe is foretold in the Bible's *Book of Revelations*.

The data here is for the whole world and is there for many to use.

I actually find the scholarship on Hitler's Germany to be bold and well focused in books by Joseph Farrell and Peter Levenda. And, William Cooper has written what I think is one of the best paranoid books in *Behold, a Pale Horse*. That text presented chapters that told of freaky phenomena that Cooper had encountered in his short life. He died after being hit by a car, and his fans, being the true conspiracy paranoids they are, say he was assassinated.

I find Cooper's book available everywhere. It's in Barnes and Noble. It's at Amazon. It is also in the collection of books here in the low security section where I live at Saint Peter. The symptoms I feel most when I think of Cooper are surrounded with the legend by which he lived: paranoia. My own paranoia is associated with my past drug use and trafficking behaviors. There is often a distinct paranoia that lingers in habitual users of drugs like marijuana. Long after the drugs are gone and out of the body, the paranoia remains. That is one of the kinds of paranoia we call mental illness.

This manuscript will also go to the core vulnerable adult care community, with their concern for how people like me, and for those with both lesser and more severe mental impairments, are treated, too often mistreated out of the light of public scrutiny.

I really did experience that form of illness. I took risks, and I made others pay the price for some of my poorer choices. The kind of crime I did was protected, in part, by the way those with mental illness are affected by some interpretations of law. I poked a hole in the skin of a seventeen-year-young person with the blade of a pocket knife. The drug dealing crimes of her people were numerous, but ultimately the mistakes I made back then were mine.

I should have chosen a different path. Because I didn't, I became a person subject to an insanity plea that I did not want and certainly did not agree with. I don't believe in the ethic of insanity defenses, and at that time, in my thoughts I was looking forward to having a day in court as an opportunity to present my "case" against the drug dealing. I had a sister who was murdered by a resident of the same prison hospital where I now live. He found Jesus and Clozaril and they let him go. He ended up doing another eleven years on a murder charge. I have spent decades in the system and probably have at least a few years left to go.

I feel anticipation. I feel anxious. But I feel my paranoia is now well managed. I have a good appetite. I sleep well. Last night we were awakened by screaming sirens that indicated a fire alarm, but there was no fire. In a more paranoid day I would have interpreted the siren as a plot to annoy us all, and me in particular. Now I accept it as faulty equipment or a false alarm prank, shrug it off as easily as a loon would shed water from its oiled feathers, and go back to sleep as soon as I can. I sleep well.

Maybe my most significant current symptom is something called *Hypergraphia*, which is a drive to write. This means I would probably write even if I had nothing to say. Fortunately, I have a lot to say. I think this is a good book and I have some good reasons for thinking that. For instance, the book *One Flew Over the Cuckoo's Nest*, and its widely viewed film version, was a powerfully written story, but it was far too mild and forgiving of staff who only rarely even consider things like civil rights. It might best be thought of as the Harlequin Romance of mental illness. It also portrayed patients as cartoon figures who do no real harm. I've lived with murderers and rapists, and they are a rough crowd in their own right.

Cuckoo's Nest was a good book in the same way Batman was a good comic. It titillated and entertained its readers, who laughed and cried all at the same level and tempo of a person with a sixth grade education. It was a not overly intellectual book whose characters all had, at worst, unique traits that we would typically only call idiosyncrasies. When writing any book you have to, of course, consider who you believe will be the audience who will buy and read it. For popular fiction like *Cuckoo's Nest* you have to run it all through the mill of pulp writing and see if it makes sense to the flora and fauna of its community of readers. It has to be written so that they can accept your completely fictional world. It's just that, as a person who has been living in the world of the *Cuckoo's Nest*, its poignant and true descriptions of torture disguised as therapy, coercion disguised as therapy, the arguably sick agenda of Nurse Ratchet and the equally criminal negligence of the supervising physician, were all sugar coated in a way that diminished their contact with reality and their ability to generate outrage in audiences that, after all, considered it all to be fiction.

I just read a Mickey Spillane novel, and found it to be a pathetic male fantasy of gorgeous women stalking the male lead character for sex and plot development. It demonstrated what is not real and what is used by the book business for selling what in the 1880s were called "dime novels." I'm not a professional book reviewer, but that's what I thought about it.

Spillane's type of writing is clearly not what I intend to send out to the world at large in what I've written here. Even when I return to writing fiction, there are points of reality I will try to retain to keep my characters grounded.

My male leads will not be hard driving private eyes who smoke hard, drink hard, have sex with their beautiful clients, and solve cases with a gun and a left hook punch. They will be more like normal people, who will act like normal people might behave given the situations I will put them in.

If life were as simple as most fiction portrays, we would have an easy time of it all. Too many novels at best are cartoons of the realities we deal with every day. If I ever chase ambulances, it will be with a nursing degree, and I'll be doing it only to look for real people to base my stories on. My real test as a writer of fiction will be to make my Dick Tracey, my Mickey Mouse, and my Tom and Jerry types look real across a slow, sleepy, year long journey through a murder investigation, like what we might actually see in the real world.

Moving on from writing themes, I'd like to suggest that there needs to be an accounting done on the financial ways and means of our mental health system. The best way to shut something down is to hit it at its money source. If I choose to earn a nursing degree, it will be to be better prepared for, and have better professional credentials, writing about the facts and figures of mental health and hospitals in general. Getting an overview of a large financial concern like psychiatry requires an appreciation of what good it can potentially do for some, as well as what an evil it can become for others if used wrongly. That enterprise should be interesting. It's something I believe my life at Saint Peter will have prepared me well to do. I am clearly not there yet. I have much to learn, much work to do to reach that point.

It's important that people like me, who have a personal stake in improving the system for patients, begin tracking and publicizing the abuses and excesses that medical insurance and others with financial stakes in the system are paying for: what and where, and what the psychiatric machine is doing with all that money it is collecting. Once you make public such an assay on all these finances, I believe those results will provide practical visibility to that system for the first time in ages. I believe it will actually show how insanity defenses bring in more money to psychiatry in a state like Minnesota than it does in states with nonparticipating governments. I believe it will show that, in states with an insanity plea option, you will find a larger psychiatric establishment, and a greater propensity to spend medical dollars to detain and imprison people in ways not legally supported in other places.

Remember that the medical financial complex is similar in many ways to the military industrial complex. Doctors are just doctors, wherever you go, but in a state where you have an insanity defense plea, I believe you will have a bigger collection of professionals and doctors who have a vested interest in keeping insanity pleas in the system. Why this will be so is obvious. Ordinary greed is often its own motivation.

Additional benefits to the system are intangibles like control and complexity. Simplicity is the enemy of the complex. If a jury trial had simpler rules, then maybe we would have simpler cases. Does a more complex system route people more frequently to insanity pleas and requirements to be medicated? Are cases even noted as mental health status derived cases in states with more difficult standards for submitting insanity pleas? Would they even record such data? Answers to such questions will only be generated by dedicated people diving through statistics in states with and without access to insanity pleas. Assuredly this would make sense to prison pharmacists. Would it end there or would a new chapter begin?

That is where we hopefully are at now. This will be our beginning. This will be a brave new world where we, the actors, can affect the stage on which we act, and thereby become more than just actors. Living in the mental health system has been a multifaceted experience for me. While here, I've found a medication that works well for me, and learned that it and other medications do not always work so well for many of my peers. Because drugs like Olanzapine and Risperidone have changed my life for the better, I can honestly say that medication will be a key component in many recoveries. It will, however, also fail to deliver any benefit whatsoever to others. It will be a real crapshoot. Some people will win and others lose.

Would, should, and could are all kind words, but I'll put it to you, the reader, that if you are experiencing mental illness, I hope you win more than you lose. That is why I hope that this text finds its way to the William Cooper appreciators of the world. I trust I won't get assassinated for it.

Living proponents of more intense scrutiny for the ways and means in our world, for everything from Nazi runaways in Argentina to the cultish ways of founders of modern religions, all breathe easier when spotlights are focused on the dark corners of the world. Neo-Nazi and Scientology leaders alike need to be in the same evidence pool.

Scientology may have cultish moments but they are not the same as more fringe-like cults. They all, however, have eluded sufficient scrutiny from established media, emphasizing why I relish the data I find in paranoid publishing. Only there do I find concerted effort to shine those spotlights on all the realities other people seek to obscure.

I hope this text serves you well. Documents like this should stay flexible, in a continual state of change. We should be able to continually add to them, subtract a sentence, add a phrase, and get its content continually recycled, and rebuilt time, and time again, so that each version seems custom made just for you. Alas, that is not how a finite published work exists, so this for now is our final product. I hope you got something out of it. My answers are not the only ones out there. I wish you luck on your quest.

A Few Additional Thoughts

A FEW YEARS ago I saw something that made me stare in amazement. I saw a large group of sex offenders from the other side of the Saint Peter facility gathered for a self-made rock concert. The Guns and Roses song, "Sweet Child of Mine," was being copied by that group of sex offenders. In that context the song sort of takes on a new meaning, as sex offenders are, quite commonly, people who rape children. They eschew society's name for them, pedophiles, instead calling themselves pedi-sexuals.

***

A couple of odd topics also ran through my mind in the course of pulling the final parts of this book together. I think they are at least tangentially relevant to elements of the discussion, so I'll lay them out and let you decide.

I'll label these tangents Operation Paperclip, MK Ultra, Peyote Indians, and Robert Anton Wilson/Illuminati.

Operation Paperclip was one of several codenames used by the U.S. during the last few months of World War II to hide their efforts to get German military scientists out of that country before Russia could get hold of them. Back in 1945, there were rules about people who could travel to the United States from the former Nazi Germany.

At that time, we had scientists by the dozens trying to come to America rather than starve in Germany or become slave labor in Russia. This included folks like rocket scientist Werner von Braun, who went on to found the American space effort. You could in a sense say that it was the Nazis who got America to the moon before Russia.

Von Braun was careful to only get captured by Americans, along with a convoy of his German rocketry. Von Braun's papers were changed, identifying him as being a reluctant Nazi instead of an ardent one. That was what Operation Paperclip did. American immigration workers were directed to ignore the fact that you only got to college or moved into the higher echelons of the Nazi hierarchy if you were loyal to the party.

Operation MK Ultra was the CIA's experimentation with using LSD and other drugs to try to create a truth serum. It was part of a larger project where they were trying to invent a new form of "no touch torture." The theory was that by scaring people on drugs, the CIA could get captured agents to crack under the pressure of experiencing the worst LSD trip possible.

MK Ultra got its name from a German war project. That is where the 'K' comes from. It is German for Kontrol, as in the phrase "mind control." The German program tried using drugs like marijuana and mescaline. That meant they used mescaline, experimenting with no touch torture even before LSD was created. Mescaline is a powerful natural hallucinogen used by the Mescalero, a Native American tribe. They consume it in spiritual rituals tied into being part of nature and letting nature be part of you.

In the 1970s, Robert Anton Wilson wrote a series of books on the "Illuminati," a secret society said to pull the strings of every major organization in the world. His books included riffs on hashish, on the Freemasons, and on the fate of Atlantis. He also wrote about marijuana and science fiction in his spin on Freemason-like ultra cabalistic secret societies. He said, amongst other things, that the red and white stripes of our flag and of George Washington's family crest were Freemason/Illuminati in origin.

How do all these "tangents" tie together? Wilson's secret societies were a welcome concept in an era when drug trafficking was forcing much of America into a speakeasy mentality. Illegal drugs have continued to be a silent service. Mescaline was used in the secret MK Ultra program. Operation Paperclip brought into the USA such projects as MK Ultra. I'll also throw into the pot a bit about opium. It was one of the first drugs I ever researched. It reached us because of a problem the British government had with China back in their colonial days. The Chinese, you see, were getting rich selling silk and tea to the British. The British needed a product to sell to the Chinese to offset that money flow. They came up with opium.

In 1773 the British took over the Bengal province of India from the Dutch. That, combined with their existing control of the Malwa province, meant they pretty well controlled opium production in the Far East. Then the British began selling the stuff into China. They were doing pretty good business until 1840, when the Chinese Emperor sent Commissioner Lin to Shanghai to destroy all of Britain's opium, about 15,000 chests. He also seized and destroyed about 5,000 chests of American opium.

This all became the opium wars and later on, the Boxer rebellion. Eventually, this led to the creation of a communist China, where Chairman Mao solved the Chinese peoples' addiction problems with bullets. Dead dealers and addicts became the cure. In modern times, President Rodrigo Roa Duterte of the Philippines has tried to copy that approach.

All this could be seen as leading up to one of today's big concerns: our once, and future, cocaine and crack drug use epidemic. Because the courts have said "yes" to peyote, then perhaps, someday our local Native American tribes may get the coca business given to them. Inca users, after all, are believed to be its original users.

And that's some of the historical background underpinning where America's narcotics addiction problems originated from, those same problems that exacerbate the thinking difficulties of the mentally ill in the U.S.

***

And so to sort of sum things up:

Number 1:

Mental health care is not designed to be fun or in any way appealing. It is designed to be cheap and as effective as a policeman's handgun. Just as how people in the U.S. do not want to surrender their firearms, bullied, depressed and/or mentally ill people rarely but all too often sadly seem to feel that shooting up a school or a darkened theater is more fun and productive than seeking psychological intervention and medication. That it's relatively rare doesn't offset the horror and tragedy of each instance.

In that intervention vein, when people get told they are going to be at a place like the Minnesota Security Hospital at Saint Peter for six months, their first choice is almost always to seek a legal remedy. They don't want to do six days or six weeks or six months, and when it gets up to six years, to them that's a life sentence.

People think that if they cooperate they will be essentially condoning the bullying ways of the state as it tries to convict them of possession of a dangerous mental illness. Such an event is often far worse than simply being found guilty of committing a crime, because a criminal sentence for many a similar activity might last six months or at worst a year, versus the indeterminate sentence of a mentally ill and dangerous commitment.

Number 2:

In mental health commitment you get no lawyers. The attorney, especially an overworked publicly appointed one, is really only there to make sure that when you get screwed it is in the legally prescribed fashion. They are not there to defend you.

Number 3:

As a mentally ill person, you are singled out as a member of a small group that gets no rights. You get no trial. No speedy trial. No public trial. No trial by peers. No protection of your First, Fifth, Sixth and Fourteenth Amendment constitutional rights. The mentally accused get no rights in court.

You cannot freely speak. You cannot avoid self-incrimination to get access to a trial. You cannot avoid huge fines to pay for your own incarceration, grossly disguised as the cost of your care, and I mean "care" in the loosest of terms.

Psychiatry, in this context, is not so much practiced as it is prosecuted.

Number 4:

What society has actually created in its mental health institutions is too often only a system of obedience schools for adult humans. The institutions more often value docility and control over returning people to health in order to ultimately return them to normal society.

Number 5:

Our mental health hospital system almost universally provides only preventative imprisonment for crimes not yet committed, and the preventative imprisonment is of indeterminate duration. You'll be there in the so-called hospital until the staff says unequivocally that you are cured! Given the current state of mental health therapy, for many people hospitalized at places like Saint Peter there is no way any unequivocal cure standard can ever be met. In fact, as of this writing, no one had *ever* been released as "cured" from the side of the Saint Peter facility that houses people committed for crimes of sexual deviancy, statutorily called criminal sexual conduct. In this instance, politics has stuck its massive paw into medicine, because no elected official has wanted to risk being labeled as the person who voted to let a "sexual pervert" out of "prison" — the prison that's called a hospital, not a prison — who then went and committed another such crime.

Number 6:

The mental health therapy process is an inexact one. There are cases where people declared "cured" later prove they were not, and far too many instances of people being kept in mental hospital prisons who need to no longer be there, who could function credibly well in community based facilities or supervision. The NIMBY, not in my back yard syndrome, however, dictates that getting halfway houses for people recovering from mental illness situated and licensed is extremely difficult in many communities and next to impossible for ones that might serve people with sexual deviancy diagnoses.

Number 7:

What I've called the "Proffitt Effect" in this volume absolutely needs to go national. After the one Saint Peter psychiatrist got fired for mistreatment of a patient, and his colleagues all subsequently quit in a show of "support," we saw nurse-practitioners, who in Minnesota can prescribe even controlled substances, replacing the absent MD psychiatrists.

The psychiatrists condoned and fostered conditions that made psychiatric care oxymoronic and burdensome, conditions that the current nursing staff does not condone. Bless those nurses.

And bless the fact that, when someone like Proffitt comes in and makes sweeping changes for the positive, very often the changes remain after that person moves on, especially when the changes involves replacement of significant personnel.

Number 8:

In mental health law, courts frequently tend to apply their energies as much toward creating expansive additions to their powers as they do to actually assuring that the accused get a fair and *impartial* evaluation.

The rights of the mentally accused tend to fall on deaf ears. When a mentally ill person asks for civil rights, the court often says it is not qualified to make a decision and defers to a medical doctor to answer the question. They thus duck out like Pilate dodged the Jesus question: "I wash my hands of this," et cetera.

Number 9:

There are a whole lot of places where Alcoholics Anonymous, Narcotics Anonymous, Scientology and a variety of religious traditions cross the needs of mentally ill people, because so many of the mentally ill are also impacted with substance abuse. AA and NA, and other twelve-step "for us, by us" programs help a whole heck of a lot of people maintain sobriety. Explicitly religious immersion experiences help many others. The need for medication to supplement such successful avenues is accepted by many. That contrasts with Scientology, which absolutely refuses to accept the use of any psychiatric medications.

In a book published early in 2013, Lawrence Wright delves deeply into the inner machine of Scientology. Whether it or similar exposés will affect the fortunes of that cult is still being played out. I have concerns because the fate of and funding for CCHR, the Citizens Commission on Human Rights, is closely tied to them. Since CCHR is one of the best funded groups out there in the business of criticizing psychiatry, I hope all comes to a productive ending.

Number 10:

There is the whole mental health parity funding issue. When genuinely mentally ill people are denied insurance and hospitalization coverage, there is truly a grand disconnect happening vis-à-vis getting them care they really need. Part of that has simply been economics. Until the adoption of the Affordable Care Act, only a few states mandated that mental illness be covered exactly like physical illness or injury. Insurance companies feared the added costs. Employers feared the increased premiums. Philosophically, some just fear we are opening the doors to Mary Copeland WRAP style hospitalizations, with no assurances that people won't use such hospitalizations as passports to malingering. There is also a fear amongst some that such funding will fill our psych wards to capacity with urban drug addicts and freeloaders instead of the truly mentally ill.

Contrast the questions about this kind of funding to that provided for the truly mentally ill and dangerous. There may never be enough money to care for the truly ill, but there rarely seem to be problems paying the bill when it comes to the captivity side of the house for criminals detained under mental health commitments.

Number 11:

The concept behind *Catch-22* becomes an important point of insight when looking for a diagnosis of "cured" that can get you out of a mental hospital puzzle palace. It almost becomes a chicken or egg scenario. If you have insight you will not petition for release. To petition for release you need a few doctors saying you should be released. If they look at the reasons for not releasing the patient then the question of insight becomes the central focus. When they closely inspect your insight, it becomes its own reason for not granting support. The accusation becomes the fact in evidence. And with the reverse, if you are *accused* of having no insight, that accusation alone is accepted as proof that you have no insight.

Furthermore, if you should decide to go over the heads of the doctors and address the question of your sanity or danger to society directly to the court, that becomes prima facie evidence that you are indeed dangerous, because the doctors would not be petitioning the court on your behalf if you no longer were. You're still ill just for the fact that you have petitioned the court for an answer. If you followed all this circular logic, welcome to *Catch-22*.

***

And one last final random note on an occurrence I mentioned briefly elsewhere in this text: There was a patient at Saint Peter for a portion of time while I've been there. His name was Jamal Rice, and he died at Saint Peter. The cause of his death may well go down in history as truly the only death of his kind. What happened was that some member of the staff called for an "emergency take down" of Rice.

About ten staff members piled on top of Rice. After they got up and sorted out the pile they realized that at its bottom was Rice, and that he was quite dead. He cannot complain, so I will dedicate this last paragraph as a commemoration to his share of our common complaints.

Afterword

If you have stayed with me to this point you have read through approximately 80,000 words to get to this *Afterword*. I hope you have found it worth your time and attention. I have come to realize that I have wasted years of time and a great deal of taxpayer money fruitlessly trying to defend my old, thoughtless high risk behaviors, none of which certainly benefited my underlining mental health issues. The result has been little but a tremendous amount of stress wrongfully delivered to my various case workers, to members of my family, to a number of true friends who have stayed with me through it all, and to an assortment of peers.

Until relatively recently there was little I could point to that could enable me to objectively lay claim to having achieved any major accomplishment, or realized any significant form of success in my life. I have, for instance, wasted years of my life repeating classes that I could have learned in one truly attentive semester. I treated most of my life before Saint Peter as one long party. I occupied the time of my life before Saint Peter with no real goals, with not even a nod to checking guideposts along the way.

With the mental clarity achieved with the help of my meds, I now understand that I have no valid excuses for my past behaviors. I now recognize that because I truly want to make a new start, keeping it all together and straightening up and flying right is a key to my recovery. Keeping it all together, I have tried to view the form of forced care I've experienced over the past nearly three decades as a blessing in disguise. I've been trying to view it as the cornerstone for a new mentally clear life, free of illicit mind altering substances that might impede maintaining this health.

I've been trying to view all my experiences over the past three decades as the route to becoming a productive member of society. I've been trying to view it as the way to achieve a respectful, more attentive life founded on concepts of fair play and honest work.

I continue working toward the goals of my treatment plan, working to become a repentant sinner who has been given the all too rare opportunity to be reborn as a healthy soul.

But at this point in time I also worry a bit as to how outside societal events might come to interfere with my progress. As I write this I wonder if the violent turbulence occupying many of our cities after acts of police violence against minorities, if the social divisiveness that was encouraged by soon to be former U.S. President Donald Trump, if our world virus pandemic might individually or collectively undermine or otherwise impede my mental health efforts?

Are things like racism, ultra-nationalism and classism going to be the new Vietnam or Afghanistan for this generation? Such mindsets are as poisonous to both individuals and the mainstream community as is the underground and criminal drug culture.

I'll reiterate that drugs are usually bad. The best recommendation will always be to just stay away from them if you can, because you really don't want to take the chance that they might trigger a previously controlled or unsurfaced mental health issue. Sadly, if that should occur, you'll encounter the reality that unless you can afford top of the line private psychological or psychiatric care, or can find successful control through twelve-step programs or deep religious connection, the alternative is something you really, really want to avoid. That alternative, a psychiatric help center affiliated with law enforcement, is usually a bad place you truly don't want to be.

If you need help I'll strongly suggest you try with all your physical strength and mental and emotional willpower to find it elsewhere than through law enforcement. Taking my own advice, whether I remain at Saint Peter or am released to live on the outside at a halfway house or on my own, I will continue to attend and participate at NA meetings. There I will be drinking nothing stronger than coffee. And across my living I'll be compromising my health with nothing worse than tobacco. And someday I hope to even get rid of that.

By the time this book goes to print it will be approaching my twenty-seventh year of abstinence from alcohol use and all drugs except those medically prescribed to help me control my schizophrenia. For me that status came with no choice, with incarceration, and looking forward if

I gain release I'll probably continue to be subject to regular toxicology screenings, maybe as frequently as weekly. Take my advice and try to avoid being where I've been. It's a best case for me, but it's not what you want to be looking forward to as your best case circumstance.

And I'll also look forward to a time when society will replace prison colonies like Saint Peter with real healing centers, and a universal health care system like what exists in Canada and much of Europe can eventually come in steps to the U.S. and provide the needed alternatives.

Thank you for reading this book.

About the Author

WILLIAM STRAWN DOUGLAS currently resides at the Minnesota Security Hospital, Saint Peter, Minnesota, where he was committed under a diagnosis of being Mentally Ill and Dangerous in 1993. That was the aftermath of an incident where he stabbed a young woman in the leg during a schizophrenic episode, thinking he could use the "incident" as a way to draw "the law's" attention to drug distribution activities he objected to.

Douglas, born in 1961, grew up immersed in the medical system. His father, William Wallace Douglas, was a physician at the world famous Mayo Clinic in Rochester, Minnesota. His mother, Nancy Georgetta Classon, was a nurse and nursing instructor.

Douglas has attended the University of Minnesota in Minneapolis. He is a Marine Corps veteran, has worked in the oilfields of Wyoming, and as a cook at the famed Seward Café on the West Bank area of Minneapolis. He admits to having been active for years as a user of what he calls short order soft drugs, and even participated in distributing some of them. He was never tempted, he says, to use the more serious addictive street drugs. He has also worked as a graphic artist.

In his life before Saint Peter, Douglas was an avid bicyclist. These days he spends his time reading science fiction, studying ideas about the shapes of future governments, and trying to combine the two in his fiction writing. Optimistic about how the treatment of his mental illness is progressing, he hopes to finally be released from Saint Peter in the not too distant future, and he hopes to return to school for a nursing degree to provide a professional credential to help his advocacy for change in forensic mental health.

About the Editor

LARRY ETKIN IS a veteran communications professional who has worked more than four decades as a writer, editor, publication designer, and public relations consultant and media planner. He has also served stints in the past as a radio and print journalist, and as the director of communications at two Minnesota state agencies, for a multistate rural environmental nonprofit, and for programs of the Minnesota Agricultural Experiment Station at the University of Minnesota. One of the agencies for which he headed up its office of public information was the Minnesota Department of Human Services. DHS is the agency responsible for state operated forensic services at the Minnesota State Security Hospital in Saint Peter.

Etkin has a master's degree from the University of Minnesota's Hubbard School of Journalism and Mass Communication, and a bachelor's degree awarded by the State University of New York-Fredonia. He currently works as an independent writer, editor, and communications consultant and practitioner in Minneapolis, Minnesota, doing business as "Etkin & Associates." He has designed and edited more than 100 books and scientific research monographs, including the cover graphic for this volume. He has received numerous industry and peer awards for his work and is also a published futurist.

MIX
Paper from
responsible sources
FSC® C100212

Printed in March 2021
by Gauvin Press,
Gatineau, Québec